Do We Have a S

MW00655483

Are we made entirely of matter, like sticks and stones? Or do we have a soul—a nonphysical entity—where our mental lives take place?

The authors Eric T. Olson and Aaron Segal begin this accessible and wide-ranging debate by looking at the often-overlooked question of whether we appear in ordinary experience to be material things. Olson then argues that the dependence of our mental lives on the condition of our brains—the fact that general anesthesia causes complete unconsciousness, for instance—is best explained by saying that our mental lives are physical activities in our brains rather than nonphysical activities in the soul. Segal objects that this view is incompatible with two obvious and important facts about ourselves: that there is only one of you rather than trillions of almost identical beings now thinking your thoughts, and that we exist and remain conscious for more than an instant. These facts, he claims, are presupposed in our practical and moral judgments—but they require us to be immaterial things. Olson is forced to concede that there is no easy and uncontroversial answer to these objections but doubts whether taking us to be immaterial would be any help. The debate takes in large philosophical questions extending well beyond dualism and materialism.

The book features clear statements of each argument, responses to counter-arguments, in-text definitions, a glossary of key terms, and section summaries. Scholars and students alike will find it easy to follow the debate and learn the key concepts from metaphysics, philosophy of mind, and other areas necessary to understand each position.

Key Features

- Is the only introductory book devoted to the debate between substance dualism and materialism

- Discusses both traditional and novel arguments for each position
- Debates important but infrequently discussed questions, including:
  - do we appear, in ordinary experience, to be material?
  - should materialism be the default view?
  - is there a good probabilistic argument for materialism?
- Written in a lively and accessible style
- Uses only a limited number of technical terms and defines all of them in the glossary

Eric T. Olson has a special interest in the metaphysical nature of human beings. He is the author of two other books: *The Human Animal: Personal Identity Without Psychology* (1997) and *What Are We? A Study in Personal Ontology* (2007).

Aaron Segal is the Michael and Bella Guggenheim Senior Lecturer in Philosophy at The Hebrew University of Jerusalem, and he has published widely in metaphysics, philosophy of religion, and analytic Jewish philosophy.

Little Debates About Big Questions

About the series:

Philosophy asks questions about the fundamental nature of reality, our place in the world, and what we should do. Some of these questions are perennial: for example, *Do we have free will? What is morality?* Some are much newer: for example, *How far should free speech on campus extend? Are race, sex and gender social constructs?* But all of these are among the big questions in philosophy and they remain controversial.

Each book in the *Little Debates About Big Questions* series features two professors on opposite sides of a big question. Each author presents their own side, and the authors then exchange objections and replies. Short, lively, and accessible, these debates showcase diverse and deep answers. Pedagogical features include standard form arguments, section summaries, bolded key terms and principles, glossaries, and annotated reading lists.

The debate format is an ideal way to learn about controversial topics. Whereas the usual essay or book risks overlooking objections against its own proposition or misrepresenting the opposite side, in a debate each side can make their case at equal length and then present objections the other side must consider. Debates have a more conversational and fun style too, and we selected particularly talented philosophers—in substance and style—for these kinds of encounters.

Debates can be combative—sometimes even descending into anger and animosity. But debates can also be cooperative. While our authors disagree strongly, they work together to help each other and the reader get clearer on the ideas, arguments, and objections. This is intellectual progress, and a much-needed model for civil and constructive disagreement.

The substance and style of the debates will captivate interested readers new to the questions. But there's enough to interest experts too. The debates will be especially useful for courses in philosophy and related subjects—whether as primary or secondary readings—and a few debates can be combined to make up the reading for an entire course.

We thank the authors for their help in constructing this series. We are honored to showcase their work. They are all preeminent scholars or rising-stars in their fields, and through these debates they share what's been discovered with a wider audience. This is a paradigm for public philosophy, and will impress upon students, scholars, and other interested readers the enduring importance of debating the big questions.

Tyron Goldschmidt, *Fellow of the Rutgers Center for Philosophy of Religion, USA*
Dustin Crummett, *Ludwig Maximilian University of Munich, Germany*

Published Titles:

Is There a God?: A Debate
by Kenneth L. Pearce and Graham Oppy

Is Political Authority an Illusion?: A Debate
By Michael Huemer and Daniel Layman

Selected Forthcoming Titles:

Should We Want to Live Forever?: A Debate
by Stephen Cave and John Martin Fischer

Do Numbers Exist?: A Debate
by William Lane Craig and Peter van Inwagen

What Do We Owe Other Animals?: A Debate
by Bob Fischer and Anja Jauernig

Consequentialism or Virtue Ethics?: A Debate
By Jorge L.A. Garcia and Alastair Norcross

For more information about this series, please visit:
https://www.routledge.com/Little-Debates-about-Big-Questions/
book-series/LDABQ

Do We Have a Soul?

A Debate

Eric T. Olson and Aaron Segal

Routledge
Taylor & Francis Group

NEW YORK AND LONDON

Designed cover image: Getty Images

First published 2024
by Routledge
605 Third Avenue, New York, NY 10158

and by Routledge
4 Park Square, Milton Park, Abingdon, Oxon, OX14 4RN

Routledge is an imprint of the Taylor & Francis Group, an informa business

© 2024 Taylor & Francis

The right of Eric T. Olson and Aaron Segal to be identified as
authors of this work has been asserted in accordance with
sections 77 and 78 of the Copyright, Designs and Patents
Act 1988.

All rights reserved. No part of this book may be reprinted
or reproduced or utilised in any form or by any electronic,
mechanical, or other means, now known or hereafter
invented, including photocopying and recording, or in any
information storage or retrieval system, without permission
in writing from the publishers.

Trademark notice: Product or corporate names may be
trademarks or registered trademarks, and are used only for
identification and explanation without intent to infringe.

ISBN: 9780367470265 (hbk)
ISBN: 9780367333645 (pbk)
ISBN: 9781003032908 (ebk)

DOI: 10.4324/9781003032908

Typeset in Sabon
by codeMantra

Dedicated to my parents, Susan and Robert Segal, of blessed memory. I owe to them my conviction that there is more to this life than we can see. May their souls be bound up in the bundle of life.

-A.S.

Contents

Acknowledgments

Eric T. Olson I am grateful to many people who commented on my portion of the book as it was taking shape: Laura-Jane Baxter, Richard Baxter, Stephen Cave, Miguel Garcia-Valdecasas, Jean-Baptiste Guillon, Christine Halsey, Isabel Jezierska, Edward Makin, Joseph Milburn, Aaron Segal, Jerry Viera, Karsten Witt, and an anonymous referee. Their thoughts resulted in numerous improvements.

Aaron Segal I am deeply appreciative of the extensive feedback I received from Eric Olson and Tyron Goldschmidt. They improved my contributions in countless ways, big and small. I also wish to thank those students at Yeshiva University and The Hebrew University of Jerusalem who took some version of my "Introduction to Metaphysics" and "Human Ontology" courses. They served to crystallize my thinking on both the big picture issues and many of the details of my arguments. I also want to thank Daniel Binenboym for his outstanding work in preparing the index. Finally, I want to thank an anonymous referee of this volume for their very thorough and insightful comments, and Dean Zimmerman for his wonderful foreword.

Foreword
Dualism and Materialism

Dean Zimmerman

A Conversation Still Worth Having

The words "dualism" and "materialism" are used in many different ways, to refer to an array of different distinctions. The meanings most relevant to the questions raised in this book are fairly simple. *Dualists*, like Aaron Segal, believe that human persons are not made of the same kind of stuff as rocks and plants and animal bodies. They are, instead, immaterial souls. *Materialists*, like Eric Olson, see no need for souls: at bottom, they think, we consist of nothing but ordinary matter — the same kinds of particles (or fields of force, or whatever) that can be found in non-living, non-conscious things.

A serious philosophical debate about the relative merits of dualism and materialism will seem anachronistic to some. But, really, it should need no defense. Dualism has arguably been the majority view for as long as we have records about such things; and perhaps, given the way our minds work, it is inevitable that we will continue to think of ourselves in dualistic ways.[1] As the default assumption of humankind, dualism surely deserves philosophical scrutiny.

Still, even highly commonsensical beliefs sometimes turn out to be false. Dualism faces serious head-on challenges. For example, it must answer the difficult questions raised by Olson's "Duplication Argument" and "Remote Control Argument." And there is little in the way of unambiguous empirical evidence for dualism—descriptions of hauntings and "near-death experiences" notwithstanding.

Refutation by Stipulation

Although the value of a book like this should, then, be obvious, it will not be obvious to those who believe that dualism was long ago shown to be incoherent. Critics sometimes stipulate meanings for "material" or "physical" that souls could hardly fail to satisfy. Then dualism is made easy to refute, by construing it as the view that souls are immaterial or nonphysical in the stipulated sense. Olson never attempts such sleight of hand. But these tricks are common enough to be worth mentioning in an introduction to the dualism-materialism debate. Explaining where they go wrong will help to reveal what is really at issue.

One line of stipulative criticism begins with the assertion that, if something is in space, it is automatically material, as a matter of definition.[2] Since souls are supposed to be immaterial, they must be outside of space altogether. But dualisms of this extreme sort face what Jaegwon Kim called "the pairing problem": How is it that my soul is reliably hooked up to just my brain and body, and no one else's, if not in virtue of coinciding (in space) with my body and not theirs?[3] Some materialists take this to be a knock-down refutation of dualism.[4]

An even simpler strategy for refuting dualism is to insist that, if something can causally affect a physical thing, it must itself—by definition—be physical. Thus, a *truly* nonphysical soul could make no changes in our brains or anywhere else in the physical world.[5] The human soul would at best be an epiphenomenal thing—causally affected by what goes on in our brains, but itself causally impotent. If dualism is—again, by definition—the view that souls are nonphysical, the view becomes patently absurd.

Real dualists—including the philosophers in the history books whom we all *call* dualists—will find such arguments bizarre and sophistical. Contemporary philosophers are free to lay it down that the word "immaterial," in their writings, is to be used in such a way that it does not apply to things in space. They are free to stipulate that the word "physical," as they use it, applies to anything that can affect the motion of matter. But if they then *also* stipulate that "dualism" is the view that souls are immaterial and nonphysical, dualists should be free to say: perhaps that is what *you* mean by these words, but it is not what *we* mean. Indeed, it is not what most medieval and Early Modern philosophers meant, when they distinguished souls from bodies.

Medieval dualists attributed locations to their souls. Since causation at a distance is impossible (they reasoned), souls must coincide, spatially, with the bodies with which they interact. They did, of course, believe that souls differed from ordinary material substances in systematic ways. According to a metaphysics inherited from Aristotle, ordinary bodies contain something called "prime matter"; and the medieval dualists denied that souls included any such material stuff. Bodies resist penetration by other bodies, but souls can coincide with anything. Bodies and souls have different *ubieties*—that is, different modes of location. In other words, although a soul occupies the same region as my body, it is present to that region in a different way than my body. Using what was once familiar scholastic jargon, they claimed that my soul is present "the whole in the whole and the whole in each part" of the region it occupies, while my body fills the region "the whole in the whole and a part in each part."

In the modern period, natural philosophers had little use for prime matter; so it no longer played a role in drawing the soul-body distinction. But views about the location and causal efficacy of the soul were otherwise not radically different. Take Descartes, for example—a paradigmatic dualist if ever there was one. Although he is often said to have posited souls that have no location whatsoever, this is arguably a misreading. Descartes often seems to agree with the medievals about the ubiety of souls: they are located within the bodies they affect, although they lack extension—that is, they are not extended in the same way as things made of matter.[6] And he certainly thought souls could move things around in space, at least things within the brain. Contemporary materialists can stipulate meanings for dualism that rule out Descartes as a dualist, but they will not thereby have refuted Descartes.

When critics of dualism make such stipulations, they fail to make contact with the actual views about persons and souls held by actual dualists, but they do succeed in drawing attention to facts that all plausible forms of dualism must countenance. If souls are capable of doing what we think persons can do, they must be deeply enmeshed in the physical world; and, in that case, calling them "nonphysical" is bound to be problematic. The nonphysicality of souls can only be understood as a matter of degree. Something that is in space, and that can move matter around, can hardly fail to interest the physicist. If there are laws governing soul-brain interactions, physics will want to know about them. It is not unreasonable, then, to look back at Descartes's doctrine of the soul and describe it as the view that, in addition to ordinary particulate matter, there are mental substances which are located in space and have physical powers. Traditional dualists of the medieval and Early Modern period might well have been willing to adopt a convention suggested by a fictional physicist in Terrel Miedaner's *The Soul of Anna Klane*: let us simply stipulate that "material" means "made from matter," and let "physical" apply to anything that can interact with things in space.[7] Then souls—according to Descartes and virtually every other philosopher who has been called a dualist—are *physical* but not *material*.[8]

But really, who cares how these words are used? That is not the important issue. Augustine, Descartes, Segal, and other dualists offer us reasons to reject the idea that a human person is made entirely of matter—that is, made of the kinds of stuff that can be found in ordinary, inanimate objects. What is important is whether the soul they posit is a better candidate for being me than any merely material body; not whether it satisfies some largely stipulative criterion for being "physical."

The Problems of Flux and Fuzziness

Although many historically influential arguments for dualism seem now merely quaint, the main arguments for dualism explored in these pages are still worthy of the attention that Segal and Olson give them; they have things to teach even those not convinced by them. What they show is that much remains mysterious about our nature.

How do I—a conscious human person—fit into a world full of objects made of matter? If dualism is false, and I am entirely material, I must be constituted by material particles (or by whatever physical reality underlies the quarks and electrons that make up the atoms in my body, whether or not that reality is ultimately particulate). However, when I look closely at the physical objects that are the best candidates for being me, they can all be made to seem unsuitable.

Segal offers two main arguments for dualism: one from "fuzziness", one from "flux". Both draw attention to the difficulty of locating ourselves in the material world.

First off, if I am a material object, there are disconcertingly many equally good candidates for being me. Focus in tightly upon the boundaries of my body, and you will find that I begin to look very "fuzzy" around the edges. Suppose that human persons are mere animals, and that animals are made entirely of the same stuff as rocks and stars. Then, wherever one finds an organism, there are ever so many hunks of matter that look like they "have what it takes" to be a thinking human person—for instance, one including a certain hair on my head, another excluding that hair. If one among this cloud of overlapping objects can think, what prevents all of them from thinking? And then, which one am I?

Perhaps that question could satisfactorily be answered by allowing that the vagueness of my boundaries is due to something like massive ambiguity. "I," in my mouth, might be a way of indeterminately referring to all the overlapping objects, just as "Everest" is indeterminate in reference among ever so many mountain-shaped hunks of rock. Each includes Everest's peak, but it differs slightly from the others in the distance it extends into the Himalayan foothills. "Mountain" is simply not precise enough to distinguish among them. But it is one thing to admit that each of countless overlapping hunks of rock has been climbed by every climber who summitted Everest; it is quite another to admit that each of countless overlapping animal-candidates located in the vicinity of my body is just as conscious as I am. Segal forcefully underscores the counter-intuitiveness of this result.

The response Olson favors is to deny that the many candidates are there, at least in the human case. With mountains, it is plausible to suppose that there are ever so many slightly different places at which we could draw sharp boundaries around different tracts of land; and we simply have not bothered to choose among them. There seems nothing wrong with stipulating that we mean something more precise by "Everest", if greater precision were required for legal purposes, say. Such stipulations could not fail because of some objective facts about the boundaries of hunks of rock. But if Olson is right, the case of organisms is not like that. As an atom is caught up into the life of a cell, it gradually becomes a part of the body. On Olson's picture of vagueness, as assimilation occurs, there are precise facts about the degree to which the body has the atom as a part; although the boundaries of organisms are a matter of degree, they are not a matter for stipulations. We could choose one of the many stages in the process and guess that it is *the* point at which an atom *definitely* becomes part of a cell. But we would almost certainly be wrong, and stipulation would not make it so.

The differences in degree of parthood do not, on Olson's account of material human bodies, correspond to different places at which a more precise boundary could have been drawn. The many different boundaries—corresponding to the different degrees of parthood—are out there in the world, objective "penumbral facts" (to misuse and repurpose a term) that do not depend upon the vagueness of our ways of carving things up.

Olson's account of the vagueness of living organisms is a respectable one.[9] It does, however, treat the vagueness of living things quite differently from the vagueness of non-living things such as mountains—or else it overturns the sensible "many candidates" account of the vagueness of physical objects, across the board. Olson posits an infinite number of degrees of parthood—relations that hold between particles and bodies, independently of our inclinations to treat some relationships as more significant than others. Many of us feel that the vagueness of ordinary objects simply *must* be a matter of our using rough-and-ready concepts that do not draw sharp enough lines. To us, Olson's approach will seem like the introduction of a new kind of hyper-fine precision in nature: objectively sharp lines, just infinitely many of them.

Segal's second argument against materialism is based upon the problem of flux. In the 17th century, Arnauld and Nicole drew very similar morals from this problem in their *Port-Royal Logic*:

> We consider the bodies of animals, and speak of them, as being always the same, though we are assured, that at the end of a few years there remains no part of the matter which at first composed them; and not only do we speak of them as the same body, without considering what we say, but we do so also when we reflect expressly on the subject. For common language allows us to say, —*The body of this animal was composed ten years ago of certain parts of matter, and now it is composed of parts altogether different.* There appears to be some contradiction in speaking thus; for if the parts were altogether different, then is it not the same body. This is true; but we speak of it, nevertheless, as the same body.[10]

Arnauld and Nicole agree with Segal that, strictly speaking, nothing can gain or lose parts. They would also have accepted his dualistic conclusion. If I were identical with the hunk of matter now constituting me, I would have to say that, quite recently, I was a widely scattered object and will soon be scattered once again. Rather than accept this bizarre conclusion, the dualist insists that I am not made of matter at all.

As Olson points out, a materialist could accept the conclusion and adopt what he calls "Heraclitean materialism": when we talk of our future and past, we are talking about our successors and predecessors—our "temporal counterparts." But there are other ways out of the flux argument, besides dualism, one of which Olson prefers over this quite radical Heraclitean response.

Crucial to the flux argument are Segal's reasons for thinking that things do not gain or lose parts. His argument depends upon the assumption that, for any bit of matter that a body might lose, there is a complementary part of the body that already existed, a remainder, consisting of all of the thing minus the bit. Call this remainder "body-minus." Recognition of things like body-minus leads to an ancient problem of decrease and increase. The thing that loses the part either comes to coincide with body-minus (but then there would be two exactly similar physical objects in the same place at the same time), or else body-minus has been annihilated (but simply by removing an external bit that was attached to it). Neither result is a happy one, and Segal concludes that the original body could not have lost the part after all. Similar reasoning prohibits the *gain* of parts. Together, problems of decrease and increase have led some philosophers to adopt a venerable doctrine known as "mereological essentialism": it is impossible for anything to gain or lose parts, and everything's actual parts are, in fact, essential to it—it could not possibly have had others.[11]

However, as Olson points out, one way out of the problem of decrease is to deny the existence of body-minus, before the bit is removed. More generally, one can deny that just any arbitrary collection of atoms constitutes a whole. Then the arguments for the impossibility of losing or gaining parts can be blocked at the first step. Olson prefers this sort of response to the flux argument over the Heraclitean one. Right where my body is, there is only one thing consisting of the matter caught up in my life, and it is a living thing, which can gain and lose parts. Collections of particles that do not now constitute the whole of this human organism, but that could come to in the future, or once did in the past, do not add up to anything at all—there is no such thing as body-minus, nor are other arbitrary subregions of my body occupied by material objects.

Arnauld and Nicole might ask: What about the matter, the hunk of stuff, now filling up a subregion like the one I said was occupied by body-minus? Surely there is such a thing as the matter in my hand, or in my kidneys; or the matter now making up my body, and the matter making up all of my body except for the tiny bit I will soon lose. If these exist, and are material objects, they are objects which are compact now but will soon be scattered. If Olson were to accept the existence of such things—mere hunks of matter, which cannot survive gain and loss of parts—in addition to human animals and the other organisms they sometimes constitute, he would have to countenance two material objects in the same place at the same time, yet completely indistinguishable: a human animal and the matter that temporarily makes it up. This is not a result with which he would be happy. If they are so similar, how could one be thinking and the other not?

Olson's response to Arnauld and Nicole is to ask: Why should we believe in these extra things, mere hunks of matter? Why not recognize only the collection of elementary material particles (which were and will be scattered), and the living body they briefly make up? These are tricky questions, but for now it suffices to say: it is far from obvious that Olson need countenance more than just the one whole, the organism.

The Doctrine of Temporal Parts

Neither Olson nor Segal considers a response to the problem of flux that is widely accepted by metaphysicians, and that would normally play a significant role in discussions of the persistence of persons through change: namely, a response that appeals to the doctrine of temporal parts. Although I am no more attracted to temporal parts than they are, the doctrine has really taken off since its introduction a little over a hundred years ago; and discussions of persons, and their persistence through time, are nowadays often conducted under the assumption of a temporal parts metaphysics.

Olson and Segal both accept what I'll call "Chisholm's Principle": Nothing distinct from me could be doing my thinking or feeling for me.[12] If everything persists by means of temporal parts, the problem of flux admits of an easy solution; but it leads to the violation of Chisholm's Principle, and it only makes the problem of fuzziness worse.

On a temporal parts picture of persisting objects, they are arbitrarily divisible into things of shorter duration. Early in the 20th century, Bertrand Russell used the "analogy of a cinematograph" to convey this idea.

> When, in a picture palace, we see a man rolling down hill, or running away from the police, or falling into a river, or doing any of those other things to which men in such places are addicted, we know that there is not really only one man moving, but a

succession of films, each with a different momentary man. ...
Now what I wish to suggest is that in this respect the cinema is
a better metaphysician than common sense, physics, or philosophy. The real man too, I believe, however the police may swear
to his identity, is really a series of momentary men, each different one from the other, and bound together, not by a numerical
identity, but by continuity and certain intrinsic causal laws. And
what applies to men applies equally to tables and chairs, the sun,
moon and stars. ... In saying this I am only urging the same kind
of division in time as we are accustomed to acknowledge in the
case of space. A body which fills a cubic foot will be admitted
to consist of many smaller bodies, each occupying only a very
tiny volume; similarly a thing which persists for an hour is to be
regarded as composed of many things of less duration.[13]

According to Russell, then, everything—including the bits of matter
I gain and lose—consists of temporal parts; and persisting things are
divisible into shorter and longer temporal parts, consisting of just
some of their instantaneous temporal parts. If an atom spends three
years as part of my body, that just means that a three-year-long temporal part of the atom is a small part of a three-year-long temporal
part of me.

The paradoxes about increase and decrease that led Segal to deny
the possibility of changes of parts are easily resolved within a temporal parts metaphysics. When body-minus comes to coincide with
body, that is just the brief sharing of temporal parts. The friends of
temporal parts are free to recognize the existence of the mere hunks
of matter Arnauld and Nicole posited. They are composed of temporal parts of particles that are almost always widely scattered, but
then briefly come together to form a temporal part that is compact
and constitutes the body of an animal—that is, the hunk of matter
and the animal share a common, brief, temporal part.

Although temporal parts may help make sense of change of parts,
and thereby enable one to dodge the problem of flux, they do have
their costs. My temporal parts are not supposed to be brief com-
panions, entities that happen to coincide with me. Rather, they constitute "all there is" of me, manifesting every feature I have during
the times they serve as my stand-ins. When I am conscious, they are
conscious—at least, the ones long-lived enough to have conscious
states. If my temporal parts are distinct from me, but doing my
thinking for me, Chisholm's Principle would seem to be violated.

A metaphysics of temporal parts also makes Segal's problem of fuzziness much worse than it already was. Segal argued that the vagueness of my spatial boundaries, right now, implies that there are hordes of conscious beings, as much like me as makes no difference, right where I am. The doctrine of temporal parts implies that there are now many, many more things coinciding with me, just as conscious as myself, in virtue of all the things that share my current temporal part. Whether these things have a moral status similar to myself, and what I owe them, are difficult questions.[14]

Many contemporary metaphysicians will be unmoved by the problem of flux, since the doctrine of temporal parts has become second nature to them. They should keep in mind, however, that adopting it only adds to the seriousness of the problem of fuzziness.

Enjoy!

Although a vague commitment to dualism may be implicit in the thinking of most people, the number of card-carrying dualist philosophers today is not large. My philosophical dualist club card was issued a long time ago; but if you apply for one now, the number on your card will not be much higher than mine. The view is still worthy of consideration, however, as Segal's contributions to this volume should make clear; not all of the arguments for dualism are silly or sophistical, and the materialist who takes them seriously will have to answer some difficult questions.

Olson is the very model of a modern-day materialist—by which I mean: he is the ideal sort of materialist to whom to pose these questions. Some materialists simply ignore dualism; others dismiss the view with mockery and miss out on the things they might learn by developing sober materialist responses to arguments like Segal's. Olson, by contrast, faces the problems Segal raises squarely. His goal is a metaphysics of the human person that remains faithful to a commonsensical, biological conception of ourselves as human animals, while not succumbing to the problems for materialism that motivate Segal's dualism. And Olson's criticisms of dualism are sharp, revealing the tensions that dualists like Segal must somehow manage. Iron sharpens iron, and the result is not so much a debate as a collaborative project—a book that represents the state-of-the-art concerning the metaphysics of persons.

Dean Zimmerman
Rutgers University
New Brunswick, New Jersey

Notes

1   Paul Bloom, no friend of dualism, attempts to explain the near inevitability of belief in immaterial souls in *Descartes' Baby: How the Science of Child Development Explains What Makes Us Human* (New York: Basic Books, 2004).

2   Julien Musolino, *The Soul Fallacy: What Science Shows We Gain from Letting Go of Our Soul Beliefs* (Amherst, New York: Prometheus, 2015), 134.

3   Jaegwon Kim, *Physicalism, or Something near Enough* (Princeton, N.J: Princeton University Press, 2005), 55–58.

4   Musolino, *The Soul Fallacy*, 132–136.

5   Daniel Dennett, *Consciousness Explained* (Boston: Little, Brown and Company, 1991), 35.

6   Robert Pasnau, *Metaphysical Themes 1274–1671* (Oxford: Oxford University Press, 2011), 328–339. My potted history of the dualism–materialism distinction, above, is much indebted to this book.

7   Terrel Miedaner, *The Soul of Anna Klane* (New York: Coward, McCann and Geoghegan, 1977), 168–169.

8   In Mark C. Baker and Stewart Goetz, eds., *The Soul Hypothesis: Investigations into the Existence of the Soul* (New York: Continuum, 2011), eight contemporary dualists discuss the locations of souls, the kinds of laws that might govern their interaction with the brain, the question whether souls would violate a law of energy conservation, and other issues. In order to find manageable laws connecting brain states with the conscious states of souls, Robin Collins posits nonconscious states that, in combination, give rise to "qualia"—the phenomenally felt characteristics of experience (see Collins's essay, "A Scientific Case for the Soul," in Baker and Goetz, 222–246). As Baker and Goetz point out, on Collins's view, the soul "has a rich set of physical properties as well as the mental/psychological properties that motivate asserting the existence [of] a soul in the first place"; his theory "counts as a type of substance dualism, because it is a novel kind of object (the soul) that has both sets of properties, and not just a familiar physical object like the body or the brain" (p. 218).

9   For a defense of this account of vagueness, see Peter van Inwagen, *Material Beings* (Ithaca, N.Y. ; Cornell University Press, 1990), 213–283.

10 Antoine Arnauld and Pierre Nicole, *The Port-Royal Logic*, translated by Thomas Spencer Baynes, 8th ed. (Edinburgh and London: William Blackwood and Sons, 1851), 147.

11 Roderick M. Chisholm, *On Metaphysics* (Minneapolis: University of Minnesota Press, 1985), 65–82.

12 Chisholm, 125.

13 Bertrand Russell, *Mysticism and Logic* (London: George Allen and Unwin, 1917), 128–129. (The passage was originally published in 1915.)

14 Olson has pointed out some of the moral difficulties to which the existence of these "subpeople" might lead; and Mark Johnston argues

that recognizing them leads to disaster. See Eric Olson, "Ethics and the Generous Ontology," *Theoretical Medicine and Bioethics* 31, no. 4 (2010): 259–270; Mark Johnston, "Personites, Maximality and Ontological Trash," *Philosophical Perspectives* 30, no. 1 (2016): 198–228.

Works Cited

Arnauld, Antoine, and Pierre Nicole. *The Port-Royal Logic.* Translated by Thomas Spencer Baynes. 8th ed. (Edinburgh and London: William Blackwood and Sons, 1851).

Baker, Mark C., and Stewart Goetz, eds. *The Soul Hypothesis: Investigations into the Existence of the Soul* (New York: Continuum, 2011).

Bloom, Paul. Descartes' Baby: How the Science of Child Development Explains What Makes Us Human (New York: Basic Books, 2004).

Chisholm, Roderick M. *On Metaphysics* (Minneapolis: University of Minnesota Press, 1985).

Dennett, Daniel. *Consciousness Explained* (Boston: Little, Brown and Company, 1991).

Johnston, Mark. "Personites, Maximality and Ontological Trash." *Philosophical Perspectives* 30, no. 1 (2016): 198–228.

Kim, Jaegwon. *Physicalism, or Something near Enough.* (Princeton, NJ: Princeton University Press, 2005).

Miedaner, Terrel. *The Soul of Anna Klane* (New York: Coward, McCann and Geoghegan, 1977).

Musolino, Julien. *The Soul Fallacy: What Science Shows We Gain from Letting Go of Our Soul Beliefs* (Amherst, New York: Prometheus, 2015).

Olson, Eric. "Ethics and the Generous Ontology." *Theoretical Medicine and Bioethics* 31, no. 4 (2010): 259–270.

Pasnau, Robert. *Metaphysical Themes 1274–1671* (Oxford: Oxford University Press, 2011).

Russell, Bertrand. *Mysticism and Logic* (London: George Allen and Unwin, 1917).

van Inwagen, Peter. *Material Beings* (Ithaca, NY: Cornell University Press, 1990).

Opening Statements

Chapter 1

Why I Don't Believe in Souls

Eric T. Olson

Contents

DOI: 10.4324/9781003032908-2

It's raining pigs and noodles,
It's pouring frogs and hats,
Chrysanthemums and poodles,
Bananas, brooms, and cats.

Jack Prelutsky

1.1   The Question

The world is full of material things: pigs, noodles, frogs, hats, and lots more. Pigs and frogs are made of bone and muscle and organs. Noodles are made of starch and protein, and hats can be made of nearly anything. But they're all made of matter. Matter itself is made of atoms, and atoms are made of even smaller particles. Arranging these particles in the right way gives you a pig or a noodle. They have no further ingredient: take away the particles and there's nothing left.

We know that there are material things. One of the biggest questions in philosophy is whether there are *only* material things, or whether there's something else as well. Does the world contain both physical things made of matter and also nonphysical things not made of matter?

There are no uncontroversial examples of immaterial things, but opinion surveys show that most people believe in them. A god of the sort worshiped by Muslims, Jews, and Christians, for example, would not be a physical thing made of matter. It may sometimes be depicted as a material thing—as a bearded man in Michelangelo's picture of the creation of Adam, for example—but that's not meant to be taken literally. Few people think that gods really have shape or size or color (except in special cases where they temporarily assume these features, as with Krishna or Christ). They're depicted in that way because an immaterial thing would have no visual appearance that an image could show. A picture of a god can't help but show it as a physical object—but that has to do with the nature of pictures, not the nature of gods. If there were a god, the world would contain both material things and at least one immaterial thing. Angels and ghosts, if they exist, would also be immaterial. And so would the number 42, if *it* exists. It would have no physical size or shape or location. (Imagine trying to visit the number 42, or any other number, and take a selfie with it.)

This book is not about gods or angels or pigs or numbers, fascinating though they are, but about ourselves. It's about whether *we* are material or immaterial. Pigs and frogs are made entirely of atoms—atoms of the same kinds, in fact: carbon, oxygen, nitrogen, and so on. Their difference lies entirely in the way those atoms are arranged. They're made from the same ingredients but using a different recipe. Our question is whether the difference between you and a frog is also just a difference in the recipe—a matter of how atoms are arranged—or whether it goes deeper. Are we so different from frogs that we're *not* made entirely of atoms?

This being a yes-or-no question, there are just two possible answers. One is that we *are* made of matter and nothing else. The atoms making up a frog (a large one) could be rearranged to make up you or me. By a cosmic coincidence, your current atoms might have made up a frog a million years ago. Arranging atoms in the right way produces an intelligent human person. We have no further ingredient. As it says in the book of Genesis, "Dust you are and to dust you will return." We differ from other material things in many ways—frogs can't write doggerel and we can't lay eggs—but that's only because our atoms are arranged differently.

This view is called **materialism**. In common parlance, "materialism" usually means an attitude that assigns a high value to money and material possessions. A materialist in this sense is the sort of person who cares more about the quality of his car than about the quality of his marriage. But that's a completely different sense of the word: our being made of matter has no implications about the value of material possessions. (Nor do materialists in the philosophical sense value material possessions more than non-materialists do.)

The other answer is that we're *not* made entirely of matter. We may perhaps have atoms as parts, but we have another part (at least one) that's not physical—that is, without mass, temperature, chemical makeup, or other physical properties. This part is commonly called a **soul**—though this is a dangerous term, which I'll say more about in §1.2. Call the view that we're not made entirely of matter **immaterialism**.

The big names in the history of philosophy are divided on this question. Aristotle, Aquinas, Hobbes, and Spinoza, for example, were materialists; Plato, Descartes, Leibniz, and Berkeley were immaterialists. And although the vast majority of contemporary philosophers take us to be material things, I wouldn't be writing this if I considered the matter settled.[1]

> There are material things, such as pigs and noodles. There may also be immaterial things, such as gods or angels. This book is about whether we ourselves are material things—materialism— or at least partly immaterial things—immaterialism.

1.2   Sharpening the Question

If you ask a philosopher a question, you're more likely to get a request for clarification than a straight answer. That's not because philosophers are obsessively pedantic, but because they've learned to distinguish different questions where the untrained eye sees only one. This isn't special to philosophers: if you ask a historian about the fall of the Roman empire, she's likely to ask for more detail about which event you were thinking of. But it's especially common in philosophy because philosophical questions are by their nature hard to state clearly.

Suppose you asked me whether each of us has an *essence*. There are many different questions that this might express, and I'd have no idea what answer to give until I knew more about what you meant by "essence." If you were unsure and couldn't make your question any clearer, I'd try to help by offering a more precise formulation and asking whether that's what you had in mind. But there's no point in having a debate before we know what the question at stake is.

The clearer we can make a question, the easier it will be to find the answer. This is not just a tiresome chore that we need to get out of the way before the fun starts, like tidying the house before a party. Stating a question clearly and precisely is just as much a philosophical task as answering it, and can be just as challenging. So it's worth lingering a little over our question.

I've put it by asking whether we're made entirely of matter (as materialism says), or at least partly of something immaterial (as immaterialism says). But although this is a good approximation, it's not quite right. Immaterialists don't think we just happen to have an immaterial part, in the way that we happen to have a gallbladder. They think this part is in some way *vital* to us. Though a gallbladder is useful, you can get by without one; but no immaterialist thinks you could get by without a soul. Plato and Descartes didn't think you could have your immaterial part removed (whatever that might amount to) and carry on more or less as before. What's special about it is not just that it's immaterial.

Imagine an exact duplicate of you but without an immaterial part. She'd be made up of precisely the same kinds of atoms as yours, in the same numbers and arrangement. She'd have the same shape, size, mass, temperature, anatomy, and physiology, and no x-ray, CT scan, or exploratory surgery could ever distinguish her from you. Would there be *any* noticeable difference? If we sent her home in your place, would your friends and family have any reason to suspect that she wasn't you? Would she herself think she was you until the facts of the situation were explained to her?

Immaterialists say that there would be a very obvious difference: the duplicate would be completely unconscious. Her brain would be just like yours and would pass all neurological tests, but without an immaterial part she would have no mental life. Making a thinking, conscious being out of atoms, the immaterialist says, is an impossible task. It would be like trying to make a habitable building out of jam and whipped cream. Atoms, no matter how you arrange them, can no more produce thinking than jam and whipped cream can produce a warm, dry place to live in. Just as you need strong and durable materials to make a house, you need an immaterial thing to make a thinker. (I'll follow tradition in using the word *thinking* to include all mental properties and activities: conscious awareness, belief, emotion, perception, and so on. In this sense of the word, having a headache is a sort of thinking. A thinking thing is simply a thing with a mental life.)

So this immaterial part is not special only by being immaterial. It has a power that no material thing can have: to produce thinking. Someone could ask whether each of us has an immaterial part that makes no difference to anything else, but that question would have no philosophical interest. In fact, all immaterialists that I know of say not just that our immaterial part enables us to think, but that the part itself thinks. It's not merely the "seat" or "arena" of thinking (whatever exactly that might mean), but a thinking thing. So what we call a human being is really two things: a material thing that can't think and an immaterial thing that can.

This immaterial thinking thing is, again, what immaterialists call a soul. Our question is whether we have souls in that sense of the word. But note that this is a very narrow and specialized sense. When Jimi Hendrix complained that manic depression had captured his soul, he meant that this condition dominated his mental life. That has nothing to do with an immaterial thinking part, and is compatible with materialism. To "look deep into your soul" is to try to discover, by introspection, the beliefs, desires, and emotions that drive your actions. It doesn't require those things to reside in anything immaterial. To "sell your soul" is not literally to sell anything, but simply to act against your strongest moral principles for personal gain. Ordinary talk of souls is not intended to be philosophically rigorous.

To make matters worse, the word "soul" is not used consistently even in philosophy. Aristotle and his followers—most notably St. Thomas Aquinas—thought that all living things, including worms

and trees, have something called a soul.[2] This "soul" is not an individual thing, however, but rather a sort of capacity or power of the
organism. Although *your* soul consists partly in your ability to think,
a tree's soul has nothing to do with thinking or awareness. (Aristotle
didn't take trees to have mental lives.) A human soul in this sense of
the word is not a thinking thing. It's not the sort of soul that immaterialists are talking about; our having souls in the Aristotelian sense is in
fact a version of materialism. In this book the word "soul" will mean
nothing more and nothing less than an immaterial thinking thing.

You might be tempted to say that your soul is your *consciousness*.
This is a different sense of the word "soul." Consciousness is a property: one that we share with pigs and poodles but not with brooms
and hats. It's the property of being conscious, as opposed to being
unconscious. Another name for it is *sentience*. Both materialists and
immaterialists agree that this property exists; what they disagree
about is what sort of things have it: whether material or immaterial
things. The souls that feature in this book are the things that immaterialists think have the property of consciousness.

Most immaterialists think that a soul in our sense can continue
existing after death, making it possible for us to have an afterlife. But
that's a further claim: immaterialism itself is not committed to this
possibility. (Nor does materialism by itself rule out our having life
after death: see van Inwagen 1978.)

Again, the term "soul" as Aaron and I use it is simply an abbre-
viation for "immaterial thinking thing." Reading into it other ideas
associated with the word is likely to cause confusion.

Immaterialism is often said to be a familiar view, held by billions
of people. I don't think this is true. It *is* true that billions of people
believe in something they *call* a "soul": some sort of spiritual aspect
that makes us different from pigs and noodles, perhaps, and which
departs from the body at death. Beliefs of this sort appear to come
naturally even to small children (Bloom 2004). But they have little
clear content, and it's hard to say what follows from them. They fall
far short of saying that each of us has an immaterial thinking part.
That's a very specific thought that you're unlikely to have unless
you've been exposed to academic philosophy.

> Immaterialism says that we're immaterial or have an immaterial
> part: a "soul." But what's special about a soul is not just that it's
> immaterial, but that we could have no mental life without one.
> In fact the soul itself, if it exists, is the thing that thinks. This

is a narrow and specialized sense of the word, different from nonphilosophical and even some philosophical uses. A soul in our sense is simply an immaterial thinking thing.

1.3   Animals

Immaterialism says that our mental lives take place in an immaterial soul. Does it follow that animals too have souls? They certainly have mental lives. No owner of a dog or cat can doubt that it's sometimes curious, frightened, bored, or hungry. Poking a dog with a sharp stick is cruel—not just to the people who love it, but to the animal itself. You can't be cruel to a hat or a broom, no matter how much it's loved. Hats can't suffer, but dogs clearly can. That's why we have laws protecting the welfare of animals but not the welfare of hats.

But if our mental lives take place in a soul, it's because they can't take place anywhere else. We can think only because we have a soul. Wholly material things can't think: that's why a physical duplicate of you without a soul would have no mental life. In that case the mental lives of animals must also take place in a soul.[3] And if electronic computers could literally be conscious or have beliefs and preferences—as opposed to merely simulating them—then they too would require immaterial souls.

Could it be that *our* thinking takes place in the soul but animal thinking goes on in the brain? Though that may seem a natural view, it's very hard to defend. It raises awkward questions: if animal brains can produce thinking, why can't human brains? And if human brains *can* produce thinking, why suppose that our thinking takes place in a soul?

You might reply that animal brains simply can't produce the special sort of thinking that we do. The "lower" mental powers of pigs and poodles—sensation, desire, and memory, for example—can reside in wholly material things, but "higher" mental powers require a soul. And as only human beings have these higher powers, only we have souls.

There certainly are mental powers that only human beings have: the ability to count to 100, for example, or to plan for the day after tomorrow. And maybe these powers are in some sense "higher" than a poodle's capacity to feel the warmth of the sun on its back. But the proposal relies on two claims. The first is that the higher powers require a soul and the lower ones don't: the physical world can achieve a certain level of mental sophistication but no more. The second is that this distinction marks off human beings from all other animals. Both these claims are doubtful.

The only reason I know of to suppose that material things can never have higher mental powers is the thought that they can't have mental powers at all. There is reason to suspect that thinking is something that a physical object could never do (a point we'll return to in §1.9), but the proposal that material things can have *some* mental powers goes against this idea. If a material thing can enjoy the warmth of the sun, why should it be impossible for one to plan for the day after tomorrow? And even if we could answer this question, how do we know that apes, elephants, and whales have only "lower" mental powers—that they lack any of the mental abilities that require a soul? It's hard to see any good answers to these questions.

Nearly all immaterialists say that it's absolutely impossible for a material thing to think: being material is incompatible with thinking, just as being round is incompatible with being square. If any material thing *could* think, a human animal could, and in that case our bodies would think and we'd have no need of a soul.

So if we have souls, it appears that pigs and poodles must have them too. A porcine soul would be an immaterial thing just as a human soul is, only with different mental abilities. This is not an objection to immaterialism, but it does have interesting theological implications. It may be that when we die, our souls continue existing and pass to the next world. (Again, this doesn't follow from our having souls, but it's widely held.) That would suggest that the souls of pigs and poodles survive death too.

I won't speculate about how porcine souls might spend their time in the afterlife. But these considerations about animal souls create a complication for us. In setting out the question for debate in §1.1, I gave pigs and poodles as examples of material things—things made entirely of atoms. Yet they have mental lives. And if their mental lives don't require *them* to have an immaterial soul as a part, ours presumably don't either. Taking pigs and poodles to be material things might seem to presuppose, without any argument, that we don't have a soul—the very point at issue in the debate.

Now I didn't have to use pigs and poodles as examples of material things, and I could have avoided the problem by sticking with hats and brooms. But my assumption that animals are material things was not meant to be controversial. I was using the word "animal" to refer to things made entirely of atoms: call them **physical organisms**. If animals have souls, there is perhaps also a thing composed of an animal's atoms together with its soul: call it an **ensouled organism**. An ensouled organism would be a compound of a physical organism and its soul. (In the next section I'll explain what it is for a soul to "belong to" an organism: what makes it the soul of that particular organism rather than another.) Physical organisms are entirely material things; ensouled organisms are not.

When I described pigs and poodles as material things, I was speaking of physical organisms. The pigs and poodles to which immaterialists attribute mental lives, by contrast, would be ensouled organisms, as they deny that physical organisms can think. Materialists, of course, deny that there *are* any ensouled organisms. We could put our question—whether we have a soul—by asking whether pigs, poodles, and human beings are physical organisms or ensouled organisms.

> Immaterialism says that our mental lives require an immaterial soul. In that case the mental lives of animals require one too. If a poodle's brain could produce its thinking, it's hard to see why a human brain could not produce ours. So if we have souls, both human beings and conscious animals are made up of a physical organism and a soul.

1.4 Materialism, Immaterialism, and Dualism

I've called the view that we're made entirely of matter *materialism* and the view that we're not—that we have an immaterial part enabling us to think—*immaterialism*. I need to say a little more about these terms.

Materialism as I've stated it is a claim only about human beings. It differs from the more comprehensive claim that *everything* is made of matter—that there are no immaterial things—which, unsurprisingly, is also called "materialism." (As we saw earlier, "materialism" can also mean a lust for material possessions. This shows the danger of relying on technical terms. Every "-ism" word, without exception, has different senses, and you can't expect people to know which one you mean unless you tell them.) We might call this more comprehensive claim **global materialism**. It could be that *we*'re made of matter, but certain other things are not: gods or angels, say. That would be consistent with materialism as I've defined it, but not with global materialism. Global materialism entails materialism but not vice versa. (One claim **entails** another if it's impossible for the first to be true and the second false.) The two claims are commonly held together: most believers in an immaterial god are inclined to think that we too are at least partly immaterial, and likewise most immaterialists believe in a god. But belief in a god is logically compatible with materialism about human beings, and immaterialism is compatible with atheism. A number of important philosophers are both theists and materialists.[4]

Immaterialism is not quite the same as **dualism**. As the name suggests, dualism says that there are two basic kinds of things: thinking things or things with mental lives, and material things or physical objects. What's more—this is the controversial bit—nothing belongs to both kinds. So dualism consists of these principles:

1. There are thinking things.
2. There are material things (wholly material).
3. Nothing is both a thinking thing and a material thing.

The world is divided into two realms, the mental and the physical. (Though dualism as defined here doesn't rule out the existence of a third realm that is neither mental nor physical. It says that the mental and the physical are exclusive, not that they're exhaustive.) For the reasons I gave in §1.3, nearly all dualists make the stronger claim that nothing could possibly both think and be material.

This view is often called "Cartesian" dualism, after its 17th-century advocate René Descartes.[5] It's also known as **substance** dualism. That's because it's not a claim about mental states or activities or properties, but about the things that are *in* these states, *engage in* the activities, and *have* the properties: about thinking beings. And the metaphysicians' term for a thing that is not a state or an activity or a property of something else is "substance." A cat, for example, is a substance, but its grin is a state or activity of the cat. The qualification is important because there's another view called **property dualism**, which will come up later. I'll use the word "dualism" by itself to mean substance dualism.

The difference between dualism and immaterialism is this: while both say that all thinking things are immaterial, dualism makes the further claim that there are material things. Immaterialism is neutral on this point: it neither affirms nor denies the existence of material things. Dualism is a version of immaterialism, but not the only version. It could be that we're immaterial because *everything* is immaterial: there is no such thing as matter and the physical world of pigs and noodles is unreal. The apparent existence of material things would then be nothing more than the occurrence of certain nonphysical sensations in souls, so that the information our senses provide is like an animated film rather than live-action footage. The sensations involved in perceiving a tree would be all there is to a tree, just as the painted images shown on the TV screen are all there is to Bugs Bunny: they're not made by filming an actor in a rabbit suit. The world would consist entirely of immaterial beings and their mental activities. This view is called **idealism**. Idealists are immaterialists but not dualists. In their view, the world is not divided into two realms, the mental and the physical: there's only the mental. They're not dualists, but **monists**.

I'm going to assume the reality of material things. That's not because this is obvious or uncontroversial (though few philosophers deny it), but simply because it makes things easier. Idealism is a topic for another book.

Nearly all dualists say not only that that there are material things, but that our souls interact causally with them. Changes in your sense organs cause sensations in you: light from this page affects your eyes, which send signals to your brain, which processes them in a way that enables you to see the page by producing visual sensations in your soul. That's how you get knowledge of the physical world. And when you stand up, that physical action is caused by a decision or other mental act taking place in your soul. (We'll return to this point in §1.10.) Without this interaction, you'd be unable either to perceive physical things or to affect them. When a soul relates in this way to a physical organism, we call it the soul *of* that organism, and we call the organism the soul's *body*.

Now I've stated immaterialism as the view that we're not made *entirely* of matter, but are either partly or wholly immaterial. This means that the view comes in two versions. One is that we're partly immaterial and partly material: we have both an immaterial part and a material one (Swinburne 1997: 145). Each of us is a compound of a soul and a physical organism or body: we are, in other words, "ensouled organisms." Call this **compound immaterialism**.

The other version of immaterialism is that we're wholly immaterial: each of us simply *is* a soul. You have a body in the sense of interacting with a physical organism in a special way, but that thing is not a part of you. Nor are your hands and feet parts of you: they're yours only in that you can move and feel them. You are entirely invisible and intangible, and we "see" you only in the loose sense of

Compound immaterialism doesn't say that each of us *is* both a soul and a body. That, understood literally, is not a coherent position. If I were a soul, I'd be entirely immaterial, as souls have no material parts. If I were a body, I'd be entirely material. So if I were a soul and I were a body too, I'd be entirely immaterial and also entirely material, which is of course impossible. The view is rather that I'm *made up* or **composed** of my soul and my body, just as a table is composed of a flat top and four legs. My soul and my body are parts of me, and I have no parts outside of them.

seeing something else that stands in for you, namely your body. Call this **pure immaterialism**.

So compound immaterialism says that our bodies are parts of us and pure immaterialism denies this. Compound immaterialism says that we relate to our bodies as the New World relates to South America; pure immaterialism says we relate to our bodies as North America relates to South America.

I think immaterialists ought to be pure immaterialists. Compound immaterialism says that I'm composed of a thinking soul and an unthinking body. But am *I* not a thinking thing? The compound of my soul and my body "thinks" only in the loose sense of having a part—the soul—that does its thinking for it. It thinks in the same sense that it's foot-shaped. If one thing thinks my thoughts only by somehow relating to something else that *really* thinks them, isn't it clear that I'm the second thing?[6] I must then be my soul, as pure immaterialism says.

The difference between these two views will have little bearing on my arguments, but it will be vital to Aaron's case for immaterialism.

All immaterialists that I know of say not only that we human beings have an immaterial soul, but that all thinkers have one. Substance dualism adds the further claim that there are material things. Idealists deny that there are material things; they're immaterialists but not dualists. Nearly all immaterialists say that we have material bodies that interact with our souls. "Pure immaterialists" say that we *are* souls, "compound immaterialists" that we're made up of both a soul and a body.

1.5 "The Mind"

One final point of clarification. Our question is whether we're made entirely of matter or whether we have an immaterial part—a soul—that enables us to think. You may be tempted to put this by asking whether *the mind* is made of matter. (My students, and many professionals too, find this temptation irresistible.) It's clear enough that we have minds, right? Aren't we asking whether these minds are material or immaterial, physical or nonphysical?

I would much rather not put things like this. "Mind" is a dangerous word, especially in possessive constructions like "my mind." It invites us to see minds as *things* that we in some sense *have*. Having a mind would be like having a mother, even if it's not quite the same sort of having. And it suggests that the expression "my mind," like "my mother," is the name of a certain entity. This raises what sounds like a completely new question: what sort of things are these minds of ours? This is not the same as our original question, which was about our own nature. There would be no point in trying to answer it until we have a clear definition of phrases like "Eric's mind." Why introduce this mysterious new question when we already have a perfectly good one?

Speaking in this way of people's minds is in fact worse than obscure: it can lend illegitimate support to immaterialism. Consider Socrates. If minds are things that we have, he certainly had one. What sort of thing was it? How could it be described? Well, we say that Socrates had a cunning and inquisitive mind. On the face of it, that sentence suggests that his mind was cunning and inquisitive. But we can't say that Socrates' mind had a beard, or a snub nose, or that it stood five feet, eight inches tall in its socks. It's not that this would conflict with what we know about Socrates' biography, but that it's incompatible with the meaning of the word "mind": the statements are patently absurd. If the term "Socrates' mind" is the name of a thing, it looks as if it must be a thing that did *not* have a beard or a snub nose. It must be a thing having mental properties like being inquisitive but not physical properties like being snub-nosed: an immaterial thinking thing.

This gives us a quick and dirty argument for immaterialism. Socrates' mind could hardly be a different thinking thing from Socrates himself, with its own thoughts: it couldn't be, for example, that Socrates had an inquisitive mind but was himself completely incurious. If his mind thinks, its thinking must be *his* thinking. But if it's immaterial (because it can't have physical properties), then for Socrates to think is for him to relate in some way to an immaterial thinking thing. On the natural assumption that this immaterial thinker would have to be Socrates himself or a part of him, it would follow that he thinks by having an immaterial thinking part. And the same would go for the rest of us. We appear to have derived immaterialism from the very meaning of the word "mind."

The *"mind" argument*, as we might call this, is not serious, and I've given it only to show how the careless use of a word can lead us astray. Where does it go wrong? Consider an analogous argument. Socrates had a kind heart. The term "heart" here is of course metaphorical, but what sort of thing could this metaphorical heart of his be? How could we describe it, beyond its being kind? We certainly can't say that it had a beard or a snub nose. Reasoning analogous to the "mind" argument thus leads to the conclusion that Socrates' heart is something that did *not* have a beard. Since Socrates himself had one, his heart must be a second kind thing in addition to him: an absurd conclusion.

It's evident that the term "Socrates' heart" here is not the name of a thing that Socrates in some sense *has*. Having a kind heart is not like having a kind mother. To say that Socrates had a kind heart is to say no more than that Socrates himself was kind. Putting it in terms of his heart simply indicates that we're speaking of his character or emotions. That's why we can't say that his heart had a beard: having a beard is not a matter of character or emotions.

The "mind" argument appears to commit the same fallacy. The term "Socrates' mind" (in ordinary language, anyway) is not the name of a thing that Socrates in some sense has: having an inquisitive mind is not like having an inquisitive mother. To say that Socrates had an inquisitive mind is just to say that Socrates himself was inquisitive. Putting it in terms of his mind simply emphasizes that we're speaking of his cognitive properties—of his knowledge and reasoning. That's why we can't say that his mind had a beard: having a beard is not a cognitive property.[7] So although it may be correct to say that Socrates' mind was inquisitive and wrong to say it had a beard, this does nothing to suggest that his mind was a thing having mental but not physical properties.

The source of the trouble is the word "mind," used in the possessive sense. This is essential to the quick-and-dirty argument: we can't restate it in any other way. If we replace "Socrates' mind" with "the thinker of Socrates' thoughts," for example, it breaks down: to say that the thinker of Socrates' thoughts had a beard would be rather stilted—it's the sort of thing that only a philosopher would say—but it doesn't sound *wrong*, in the way that "Socrates' mind had a beard" sounds wrong.

The word "mind" is often used in less troubling ways. Sometimes it's a synonym for "soul": materialism denies that there are any minds in this sense. More often it's used not to speak of any particular thing, but as a way of referring to the mental in general. Consciousness, memory, belief, perception, emotions, and dreams, for example, are mental phenomena, and we refer to them collectively as "the mind," just as we refer to metabolism, photosynthesis, reproduction, and other biological phenomena as "life." If you take a course in the philosophy of mind, you study "theories of mind" such as **behaviorism** and **functionalism**: accounts of the basic nature of mental phenomena. But none of this requires us to think of a mind as a sort of entity that each of us has one of. We may say that frogs have minds and hats don't, but this is just to say that frogs but not hats have mental properties.

When philosophers ask whether the mind is physical, they're not asking whether a certain thing that each of us has is physical, but simply whether mental phenomena are physical. Many things happen in the brain: fluids circulate, hormones are secreted and absorbed, electric currents flow, complex organic molecules are constructed and broken down. The question is whether some of these physical activities are dreams, thought processes, and sensations, in the way that some human movements are dances. Are mental activities physical activities? Or are they entirely nonphysical activities distinct from anything going on in the brain? This question is often called the *mind-body problem* (though that term is not used consistently). Important though it is, however, it's not the main topic of this book. Our question is not about mental activities, but about the beings engaged in them—not about belief, perception, or dreaming, but about the things that believe, perceive, and dream.

The two questions are of course connected. If mental activities are physical, then they don't go on in an immaterial soul, in which case there *is* no soul. The arguments of §1.11 and §1.13 will exploit this fact. But our task is not to give an account of the nature of belief, perception, and other mental phenomena. It's not even to explain how mental activities relate to physical activities in the brain. It's to say whether we ourselves are material or immaterial.

So take care with the word "mind". No philosophical question or claim was ever made clearer by being put in terms of this word. Whenever you come across it, it's worth trying to rephrase the point without using it. You'll understand the question or claim better for attempting this. If you find that you can't do it, that may not be your fault: it may be the author who's confused. In §1.7 we'll see a real example of a great philosopher being led into a muddle by the word "mind."

> It's best not to put our question by asking whether *the mind* is material or immaterial. The term "mind" can sound like a name for a thinking thing that each of us in some sense *has*, and that thought will only lead to confusion. Asking whether the mind is material or physical is legitimate if it means whether mental activities are physical. But that's not our question: this debate is not about mental activities, but about the things that engage in mental activities.

1.6   Do We *Seem* to Have a Soul?

Are we made entirely of matter, then, or do we have an immaterial soul? Before tackling this big question, let's try a smaller one. Never mind which view is true. Which one *seems* true on the face of it— before we consider scientific evidence or philosophical arguments? If the infallible Oracle were to announce that we're made entirely of matter, would you be surprised? Or would you be more surprised if she said the opposite?

Some philosophical claims are much more surprising than others. Some look immediately plausible or even obvious; others have the opposite appearance. And some fall somewhere in between. Most people find idealism surprising: we don't expect everything to be ultimately mental. No one uncorrupted by philosophy will be surprised to hear that there are material things independent of our experience. Neither materialism nor immaterialism is as startling as idealism. They're perhaps more like theism and atheism: neither strikes us immediately as true and we can see why people disagree. Both materialism and immaterialism have an intuitive appeal. But their appeal is different: materialism fits better with ordinary experience, whereas immaterialism is motivated by considerations about what we can imagine. Let's consider first the intuitive appeal of materialism.

Our sense experience presents us as material things within the physical world, not as immaterial things in a special sort of two-way communication with it. We seem to have a shape, a size, and a spatial location. The appearance is not that I somehow relate to something *else* that has a human shape, but that *I* have it. Or consider that bodily sensations like pain have a felt location. You always feel them somewhere, even if they're hard to localize precisely. And this location seems to be within you. You seem to be located wherever you can feel sensations: to extend more or less out to the skin.

I say "more or less" because there are exceptions. Amputees often have sensations that seem to be located where their missing part used to be: in a "phantom limb". It can feel just like a sensation in their left foot, even though they no longer have a left foot. And since the sensation seems to be located within *them*, this gives them the appearance—the false appearance—of extending beyond their skin.[8] Contrariwise, if a limb is numb and paralyzed for a long period, it can feel alien, like a foreign body attached to you rather than a part.[9] In that case it may seem as if you extend less far than your skin. But if the feeling we have of our spatial extent is not always accurate, this only reinforces the fact that we appear to be spatially extended, and therefore material.

Some resist this last step and claim that immaterial souls are extended in space (Hasker 1999: 192). Maybe a soul could have the size, shape, and location of a physical organism: it could literally be five feet, eight inches tall and have a volume of 69 liters. Our being extended would not then imply that we're material. But even if that's right, we appear to have other properties that an immaterial soul could not have. For example, our feet don't feel like tools that we manipulate or foreign bodies that sometimes cause us pain. They feel like parts of us. Or again, we're visible and tangible. When you look in the mirror, you see yourself, not merely some other object. If you shake my hand, you're not just touching an object that I relate to in a special way: you're touching *me*. So it appears, anyway. Our senses seem to tell us that we have physical properties beyond just shape and size: we reflect light and have a solid surface; we have weight, temperature, and anatomical structure; we exclude other material things. If we were wholly immaterial, all these appearances would be misleading.

We appear, then, to have material parts. But do we appear to have *only* material parts? Or is the appearance just that at least some of our parts are material, leaving it open whether we have immaterial parts as well? That's less clear. When you see yourself, you see a physical organism. You don't see an immaterial soul. The senses present us as having material parts and not as having an immaterial part. But it doesn't follow that they present us as *not* having an immaterial part. The senses can't detect things that are invisible and intangible. They're completely blind to the existence of anything immaterial: they tell us nothing either for or against. A partly material thing would look and feel the same as a wholly material one. So although sense perception doesn't give the appearance that we have a soul, it doesn't give the appearance that we don't have one either. If we did have a soul, it would make no difference to our sensory experience. Our senses tell us that we have material parts, contrary to pure immaterialism (the view that each of us *is* a soul), but they don't seem to tell us that we're *entirely* material. Our ordinary experience seems consistent with our being composed of a soul and a body.

As we saw in §1.4, though, this view—compound immaterialism—has the awkward consequence that we have our thinking done for us by some other thing. The view that we *are* the immaterial things that do our thinking—the sensible version of immaterialism, it seems to me—goes against the appearance given by the senses.

Now the fact that the senses present us as at least partly material things doesn't mean that we really are even partly material. We know that things aren't always as they seem. The earth appears to be stationary and the heavenly bodies appear to move around it once a day. Yet we know that this is an illusion: what looks like the sun's moving across the sky is really the earth's spinning on its axis like a carousel. The appearance that we're made of matter could also be an illusion. If we were souls intimately related to physical organisms as pure immaterialism says, the appearance would be just the same. The point is only that we *seem* to be at least partly material things.

> To the senses we appear to be material things in the physical world, not immaterial things interacting with it from outside. We seem to see and touch each other, and to have hands and feet as parts. But the senses don't seem to tell us that we're *entirely* material. They tell us that we have material parts, but not that we have no immaterial parts. The senses tell against pure immaterialism, but not, it seems, against compound immaterialism.

1.7   The Argument from Introspection

Even if our senses tell us that we're made at least partly of matter, other aspects of our experience might tell us the opposite. Close your eyes, block up your ears, and ignore all bodily sensations. What do you now appear to be? Not a material thing. Without sensory information, there is no appearance that there even *are* any material things. Do you appear *not* to be a material thing, then—that is, to be wholly immaterial?

Descartes seems to have thought so. Here's a passage from the Sixth Meditation:

> There is a great difference between the mind and the body, inasmuch as the body is by its very nature always divisible, while the mind is utterly indivisible. For when I consider the mind, or myself in so far as I am merely a thinking thing, I am unable to distinguish any parts within myself; I understand myself to be something quite single and complete. Although the whole mind seems to be united to the whole body, I recognize that if a foot or arm or any other part of the body is cut off, nothing has thereby been taken away from the mind ... By contrast, there is no corporeal or extended thing that I can think of which in my thought I cannot easily divide into parts; and this very fact makes me understand that it is divisible. This one argument [is] enough to show that the mind is completely different from the body.
> (Descartes 1984 (1641): 59/ AT VII 85f.)

When we look within, Descartes says—when we consider ourselves merely as thinking things—we see ourselves as incorporeal, unextended, and indivisible. Introspection presents us as entirely immaterial.

The passage is not easy to interepret. It never explicitly says that we're immaterial, though it's clear from the *Meditations* as a whole that this is what Descartes means. His official conclusion is rather that "the mind is completely different from the body." His argument for this is that the body is divisible into parts but the mind isn't—and if x but not y is divisible into parts, then x and y must be different things. The mind really would have to be different from the body. But what these claims amount to depends on the meaning of the terms "the mind" and "the body."

I said earlier that "the mind" often refers simply to mental phenomena like beliefs, preferences, and sensations, much as the word "life" refers to biological phenomena such as nutrition and photosynthesis. That's not what Descartes means by it here. He's not saying that mental phenomena are indivisible into parts. It's not clear what that would mean, nor would it have any bearing on whether we ourselves are indivisible.

By *mind*, Descartes seems to mean *thinking thing*: something with a mental life. He speaks of "the mind, or myself in so far as I am merely a thinking thing," taking these terms to mean the same. You and I are minds. That's how he most commonly uses the word—though he's not entirely consistent about it, as we'll see. To say that we're minds in this sense is not controversial: it just means that we think, which both materialists and immaterialists accept. The important claim is that the mind is not divisible into parts—implying, as we now see, that you and I are not divisible into parts. I'll return to this claim in a moment.

What does Descartes mean by "the body"? Not the human body, or *his* body. His being different from his body would be compatible with his being divisible into parts and wholly material: he might, for example, be his brain. When he speaks of "the body," he means material things generally—as he indicates when he says, "there is no corporeal or extended thing that I can think of which in my thought I cannot easily divide into parts." In saying that he's different from the body, he's denying not just that he's *his* body, but that he's a body or material thing at all.

So we can summarize the argument like this (reverting to Descartes' first-person formulation):

1.   All material things are divisible into parts.
2.   I am not divisible into parts. So
3.   I am not a material thing.

It has the form "All Fs are G; x is not G; so x is not F." And if its two premises are true, the conclusion must also be true.

Are the premises true? Well, it's doubtful whether absolutely all material things are divisible into parts. Trees are; molecules are; even atoms are. But as far as we know, it's physically impossible to split the quarks and electrons that make up atoms. This was discovered three centuries after Descartes' death, and we can forgive him for not knowing it. But the point doesn't matter, because it's clear that none of *us* is a quark or an electron. If I'm any material thing, I'm one that's divisible into parts. Replacing 1 with this claim would give the same result.

The crux of the argument is its second premise, that I'm not divisible into parts. My hands and feet are not parts of me, nor are any atoms or quarks: otherwise you could divide me into parts by separating them. Why suppose that?

Descartes answers: "When I consider myself in so far as I am merely a thinking thing, I am unable to distinguish any parts within myself." This again is confusing. To be *merely* a thinking thing is to do nothing but think—to engage only in mental activities. If that were my condition, then in playing tennis my own activity would consist only of perceiving various physical movements and giving the appropriate commands to my body. It would be my body that actually hit or missed the ball. If I were a material thing, by contrast, I'd be engaged in many entirely nonmental activities: running, breathing, digesting food, and so on. I wouldn't be *merely* a thinking thing. If I *were* merely a thinking thing, it would follow straightaway, without any premises about divisibility into parts, that I was not a material thing, making Descartes' entire argument redundant.

But suppose we ignore the word "merely" and take Descartes to be saying simply, "When I consider myself in so far as I am a thinking thing, I am unable to distinguish any parts within myself." He seems to be confident that I'm not divisible into parts because I can't detect any parts by introspection—that is, when I consider myself as a thinking thing. When I close my eyes and look within, so to speak, I might detect certain feelings, thoughts, or sensations—mental activities—but I'm not divisible into such activities in the way that a house is divisible into bricks or boards. (Descartes says this explicitly in a section that I omitted from the quotation.) In any event, the important question is whether I have any *material* parts—parts that are material things, like hands or atoms. If I have no material parts, I can't be a material thing. That enables us to rewrite the argument once more:

1*. If I am a material thing, I am divisible into material parts.
2*. I am not divisible into material parts. So
3. I am not a material thing.

I'm sure Descartes would be happy with this restatement. But the new version of the second premise remains questionable. As we've seen, Descartes argues for it by saying that when I ignore the evidence of the senses and look within, I don't detect any material parts, which seem true. But does this show that I *have* no material parts? Might I have parts that I can't detect by introspection?

Suppose there were a thinking being that really was made of matter: a physical organism, say. This is a possibility that Descartes hasn't yet ruled out. Such a thing would have plenty of material parts. But would it be able to detect them by looking within? It seems not. Introspection can reveal only its psychological nature (and not even all of that). It may reveal certain mental activities, but it will never reveal any material parts, even if such parts are responsible for its mental life. No being could ever tell by introspection whether it had material parts. Not seeing any parts in introspection is like not seeing any ravens in the dark: it's no reason to suppose that there aren't any. For all Descartes' intended audience knows at the beginning of the argument, it may be possible for a material thing to think, in which case our inability to detect any material parts by introspection would be compatible with our having vast numbers of them.

But there's more: Descartes says that if a part of the body is cut off, "nothing has thereby been taken away from the mind." Doesn't this show that the parts of the body are not parts of the mind, and thus that the body and the mind are distinct?

But remember my warning about the word "mind." What does it mean to say that nothing is taken away from the mind? In the rest of the argument, "mind" means "thinking thing." The mind—*my* mind—is just me: otherwise showing that the mind is immaterial would not show that *I'm* immaterial. But that's not what the word means here: we can hardly say that cutting off an arm would take nothing away from *me*. It's true that if I were a soul, cutting off an arm would not take away any of my parts, and you might put this by saying that it would take nothing away from me. But to suppose that I'm a soul would assume the conclusion that Descartes is trying to argue for.

When he says that cutting off my arm would take nothing away from the mind, he seems to mean that it would not diminish my mental abilities: I could still reason and plan and remember just as well as before. (This is an example of the exercise I recommended earlier: to rewrite any piece of philosophy containing the word "mind" in other terms.) This is of course not true for all body parts: cutting away my brain would certainly diminish my mental abilities. But apart from that, the fact that cutting off an arm would not diminish my mental abilities doesn't look like a reason to deny that my arm is a part of me.

Now Descartes never actually says that the amputation would leave my mental abilities intact, which I'm sure he too would take to be irrelevant to the argument. Nor does he say that it would take nothing away from me, which looks false. He says, rather, that it would take nothing way from *the mind*. The argument can't be stated without using that term. It has to be put like this:

A. Cutting off my arm would take nothing away from the mind (*my* mind). So,
B. My arm is not a part of my mind.
C. I am my mind. So,

D. My arm is not a part of me.

And the same would go for other putative parts of me. But we can see that this reasoning involves an equivocation: it uses the word "mind" in two different senses. In the claim that cutting off an arm would not diminish my mind (A), "my mind" means something like my mental abilities. That would make B true: my arm is not one of my mental abilities. But in the claim that I *am* my mind (C), the term has to mean something else: not my mental abilities, but the thing that *has* them. The argument commits the same fallacy as this one:

E. The Eiffel Tower is in Paris.
F. Paris is in Texas. So,
G. The Eiffel Tower is in Texas.

G is false: there is a Paris, Texas, but it's not the one with the tower. The "Texas" argument relies on understanding the term "Paris" in one sense in E and in another sense in F and G. Likewise, Descartes' argument relies on understanding the term "my mind" in one sense in A and B and in another sense in C and D. If we restate it in a way that avoids this equivocation, it collapses. This is another incautious use of the word "mind."

> If I were literally made up of mental abilities—the ability to perceive, to reason, to remember, and so on—in the way that a house is made up of bricks and boards, the term "my mind" might mean the same in C as it does in A and B. But this would be no help to Descartes. It would contradict his claim that I can detect no parts within myself, as well as his assumption, which he makes explicit elsewhere, that I'm a substance. What's more, a thing composed of mental abilities is not a material thing: it's not made of atoms. To claim that I am such a thing would presuppose the argument's conclusion, namely that I'm immaterial.

So Descartes' reasoning fails to show that we have no material parts. Still, it may show that this is how we appear in introspection. That would mean that the appearances are equivocal: to the senses we may seem at least partly material, but introspection presents us as entirely immaterial.

Descartes argued that when we look within ourselves we detect no material parts. He inferred from this that we don't have any, and thus that we're entirely immaterial. But introspection could not detect any material parts even if we had them: it reveals only our mental properties. The argument shows at most that we appear, in introspection, to be immaterial.

1.8   Immaterialism and the Imagination

Turn now to the main question: do we have a soul, or are we made entirely of matter? Immaterialism gets much of its appeal from our ability to imagine undergoing things that no material thing could undergo.

I sometimes imagine myself in my brother's body: being suddenly able to move it at will and to perceive the world through its sense organs. (There are lots of comic stories and films with this sort of premise.) It's not part of my fantasy that I *am* my brother. I only feel compelled to pretend to be, because I can't explain how I got to be in his body. Nor is it part of the story that any matter has moved from my body to his—that my brain was transplanted into his head, say. Yet somehow *I've* moved. And it seems impossible for a wholly material thing to move from one place to another without any matter moving. At best an *im*material thing could do that. So if I could move to my brother's body in this way, I couldn't be a wholly material thing. My daydream is incompatible with materialism.

Or we might imagine having life after death. Nearly all organized religions, and many versions of new-age spiritualism too, hold it as an article of faith that we have life after death—but no one would take this doctrine seriously if they couldn't already imagine it. We picture ourselves dying and being cremated, yet in our mind's eye we continue existing in an immaterial state, perhaps observing it all from above. But no wholly material thing could become wholly immaterial. Only a thing that was already at least partly immaterial could do it. The fantasy seems to presuppose that we're already immaterial.[10]

Now the mere fact that we can imagine something doesn't mean that it actually happens. But we needn't claim that we really do change bodies or have life after death. It would suffice if we *could*—if it were not absolutely impossible. Given that it *is* impossible for any wholly material thing, it would follow that we're not wholly material:

1.   Each of us could continue existing in a conscious state after our matter is completely dispersed.

2. No material thing could continue existing in a conscious state after its matter is completely dispersed. So,
3. We are not material things.

(Or replace "continue existing in a conscious state after its matter is completely dispersed" with "move to another body without any matter moving.") Call this the "survival argument."

It's logically **valid**: whatever has a property that no material thing has—even a modal property (one that concerns what's possible)—cannot be a material thing. The reasoning is analogous to this: the mineral sample can be scratched by a knife, but quartz can't be, so the sample is not quartz. The conclusion follows even if the sample is never actually scratched. (How could we know that it can be scratched if we never scratch it? Well, how do we know that a wine glass is fragile if we never break it? The answer, roughly, is that it resembles others that have broken or been scratched.)

Most philosophers are happy to accept the argument's second premise.[11] The difficult thing is to establish the first. Our ability to imagine something, no matter how vividly, is no guarantee that it's in any sense possible. If I can imagine having life after death, I can also imagine finding an enormous prime number, failing to find a larger one, being told by astonished colleagues in the mathematics department that there *is* none larger, and winning a Fields medal for my achievement. Yet it was proved more than 2000 years ago that there can be no largest prime number. Not even God could discover it.

And for all I've said, our surviving the dispersal of our matter may be equally impossible. It *would* be impossible if we had no soul. If there were wholly material beings with our mental powers, they would imagine having life after death or waking up in someone else's body just as we do. Yet (given the argument's second premise) they'd be mistaken in believing that these things are possible for them. And for all we know, that may be our own situation: it could be that we ourselves are wholly material, in which case it's no more possible for us to survive the dispersal of our matter than to discover the largest prime, despite our ability to imagine it.

So although considerations about what we can imagine may lead us to believe that we have a soul, they offer little actual evidence for it. What we can imagine is not a reliable guide to what's possible. And unless we can argue that something really is possible for us but not for any material thing, reflections on body-swapping or life after death will offer no support for immaterialism.

We can imagine undergoing things that no material thing could undergo: surviving the sudden and complete dispersal of our matter, for example. If such a thing were even possible, it would rule out our being material things. But our ability to imagine something is no good reason to suppose that it's possible: we can imagine many absolutely impossible things.

1.9   Could a Material Thing Think?

I said that immaterialism gets much of its attraction from the appearance that we have properties that no material thing could have. One property that we certainly have is *thinking*. We have mental lives. Yet it's hard to imagine how any wholly material thing could have a mental life. This thought was expressed vividly by the German philosopher Gottfried Wilhelm Leibniz in 1714 (where "perception" means any mental activity):

> Perception … cannot be explained on mechanical principles, i.e. by shapes and movements. If we pretend that there is a machine whose structure makes it think, sense and have perception, then we can conceive it enlarged, but keeping to the same proportions, so that we might go inside it as into a mill. Suppose that we do: then if we inspect the interior we shall find there nothing but parts which push one another, and never anything which could explain a perception. Thus, perception must be sought in simple substance, not in what is composite or in machines.[12]

Consider again what goes on in the brain. Fluids circulate; organic molecules are constructed and broken down; electric currents flow. If we were to examine this activity in detail—if the brain were enlarged or we ourselves shrunk down so that we could walk around and inspect it—we'd see that it's all just machinery. It would be like a mill or an engine, with solid parts moving and pushing and pulling. And it would be evident, Leibniz says, that none of that activity would be anything mental: we wouldn't see any sensations or emotions or dreams.

Nowadays we know that electrical and chemical events don't consist of solid parts pushing and pulling like wheels and belts in a mill. But that's not important: if the movement of wheels and belts could not be mental activity, the movement of electrons, which is what electric currents and chemical reactions consist in, could not be mental either. No physical mechanism of any sort could ever amount to thought or awareness. There's nothing mental about anything we could see going on in a physical object.

Imagine that you're enjoying the aroma of buttered toast. If this experience were a physical activity, we could literally see it by examining your brain closely enough. It might not be easy to see: it might consist of many different and widely scattered activities, like a national election in a large country. But none of it would be hidden. What would it look like? We know how an experience appears "from the inside": what it's like to *have* one. But how would an experience appear "from the outside"? What would *someone else's* sensation of smelling buttered toast look like to you? Or if you could see a sufficiently detailed image of your own brain in real time while smelling the toast, what would your olfactory sensation look like on the screen?

If mental activities are physical, this question must have an answer: there must be something that a sensation would look like to an outside observer. Yet there seems to be nothing that it could possibly look like. Mental activities, it appears, are simply not the sorts of things that can be seen. But everything that happens in the brain can be seen. It follows that mental activity cannot take place in the brain, or in any other physical mechanism. It can only take place in something nonphysical.

This argument has an important advantage over other arguments for immaterialism. If it succeeds, it not only shows that we must be immaterial, but also explains why no *material* thing could think. Without such an explanation, no argument for our being immaterial will be satisfying. I said in §1.8 that the survival argument would be just as convincing for material thinkers as it is for immaterial ones: they'd have the same reason to suppose that they could survive the dispersal process as we have to suppose that we could. Yet they'd be wrong to infer from this that they have a soul. That leaves us wondering what reason we have to suppose that we ourselves aren't making that mistake. Leibniz's argument would address this worry by ruling out the possibility of material thinkers. Immaterialists are confident that material things don't think, but none of the arguments for immaterialism, apart from this one, purport to tell us why they don't.

What should we make of this argument? It's true, I think, that no one knows what a thought or sensation or emotion would look like from the outside. We have only the faintest understanding of how physical activities of any sort could be mental activities. Perhaps we can't even conceive of a material thing's thinking by virtue of its physical workings. It's this mystery that Leibniz is trying to articulate.

But is it anything more than a limitation on our part? Perhaps a close examination of your brain really would reveal your thoughts and sensations. We wouldn't recognize them, of course. There's no reason why we should: things don't always look like what they are. That the relation between the mental and the physical should be so opaque to us may be challenging for materialists: they'll want to say something about why the physical basis of the mental is so much harder to understand than the physical basis of life, and why mental activity looks so utterly *unmental* from the outside. But this hardly shows that mental activity could not be physical. For all we know, scientifically more advanced beings could understand exactly how certain physical activities in the brain are thoughts, sensations, and emotions. *They*'d know what your sensations would look like. It may only be a mystery to *us*.

Suppose you're editing photos on your phone or computer. If the device were enlarged so that you could examine it in all its detail, you'd see only electrons in motion. Nothing would look like your photos, or like the process of adjusting their contrast. Yet no one infers from this that the editing process could not *be* the movement of electrons, and must go on in an immaterial part of the computer that we can't see. That's not a serious alternative explanation. That editing photos can be an electrical process may be mysterious—most of us have no conception of how it could be—but we accept it because there's no serious alternative.

The reason we're reluctant to accept that mental activity is physical is that there *is* a serious alternative: mental activity might be nonphysical activity in the soul. That would explain why nothing in the brain looks like it: no physical activity could possibly look like nonphysical activity. It seems less mysterious to suppose that our mental lives consist of nonphysical activities in an immaterial soul than that they consist of physical activities in the brain.

But is it really less mysterious? Do we understand any better how an *im*material thing could think than how a material thing could? It may be true that picturing a physical organism in our mind's eye can never tell us how it could think, no matter how much detail we add. But suppose we try to picture an immaterial thing in our mind's eye. Can we see how *it* could think? Of course, we can't imagine it enlarged so that we can see its working parts, because it hasn't got any parts. There's nothing to imagine. No mental picture could show

how an immaterial thing thinks in the way that a mental picture of a mill can show how it grinds wheat into flour. It looks as if we couldn't possibly understand how an immaterial thing thinks. We can only accept that somehow or other it does. And that's not due to any limitation on our part: it would be the same no matter how knowledgeable or imaginative we were.

But then we may as well suppose that, somehow or other, certain *material* things think. Our inability to see how a material thing could think can't be a reason to suppose that thinking must be done instead by an immaterial thing, because we can no more see how an immaterial thing could think.

If a material thinker seems more mysterious than an immaterial one, it's because we can form a detailed mental image of a material thing and see that it's no help in understanding how it could think. But because we can't form a mental image of an immaterial thing, we don't ask how *it* could think. That an immaterial thing might think doesn't seem puzzling because we can't imagine examining one in detail and then trying, without success, to see any thinking. But the fact remains that we have no more idea how an immaterial thing could think than how a material thing could. Our inability to form a visual image of an immaterial thing might make the mystery of its thinking less evident, but it does nothing to dispel that mystery. Detail always invites questions and doubts. It's easier to see the shortcomings of a detailed proposal than those of one with no detail. Vague proposals always sound better: that's why politicians favor them. Oftentimes the more we know about something, the less happy we feel about it. But we don't want to take comfort in ignorance.

So if there's a problem here for materialism, accepting immaterialism won't solve it. This is not an objection to immaterialism itself. Though the claim that thinking takes place in an immaterial soul lacks detail, that's not by itself a reason to reject it. The objection is only to the thought that this lack of detail makes it less mysterious, giving us a reason to prefer it to materialism.[13]

> It's hard to understand how a material thing could have a mental life, because we can see no connection between any physical activities and anything mental. And if no material thing could have a mental life, we can't be material things. But it may be that material things can think even though we have no idea how they do it. And we have no more understanding of how an *im*material

thing could think. Our inability to see how a material thing can think provides no reason to suppose that we're immaterial.

1.10   The Interaction Problem

I don't claim to have shown that there's no evidence for immaterialism. I've only tried to say something about why people are drawn to it and why this intuitive appeal is not a good reason to accept it—just as the intuitive appeal of materialism is no good reason to accept it either. Aaron will give serious arguments for immaterialism later in the book.

I turn now to the case for materialism. I'll discuss three arguments. As materialism is true just if immaterialism is false, they take the form of objections to immaterialism.

The most common and historically influential objection is that immaterial things could not interact causally with material ones.[14] Lift your right index finger. Have you done it? Immaterialists say that your finger rose as a result of a mental act occurring in your soul: a decision or act of will. Without it your finger would not have risen. Your decisions make a difference to your actions: if you had decided not to raise your finger or made no decision at all, the movement would not have occurred. Almost no one supposes that you would act exactly as you do no matter what you decided or if you had no mental life at all: materialists only deny that these decisions take place in the soul.

So immaterialism implies that there is a physical event—the movement of an electric current, a change in the velocity of a particle, or the like—that was not caused, or at least not entirely caused, by other physical events, but rather by something nonphysical. That physical event led, by a complex chain of physiological mechanisms, to the rising of your finger. That's how the soul acts on the body. And when the body acts on the soul—when your sense organs enable you to perceive something—the same thing happens in reverse. Yet the soul cannot be detected in a brain scan or have an effect on any physical instrument. How, then, can it make a difference to what happens in the brain? As Daniel Dennett asks (1991: 35), how can the soul "both elude all physical measurement and control the body?"

This objection comes in many different versions. One common starting point is that there's no way of saying *how* nonphysical events could bring about physical ones or vice versa, as we can when a physical event causes another physical event. How does smoking cause cancer? Well, tobacco smoke suppresses the immune system, reducing its ability to stop the growth of tumors. How does the smoke suppress the immune system? That has to do with chemical reactions between molecules in the smoke and in the smoker's immune cells. How do these chemical reactions take place? They depend on the chemical properties of atoms, which are determined by the number and arrangement of their electrons. And so on. There is a mechanism that explains how one event causes the other, even if we don't always know what it is. But there can be no mechanism explaining how an event in the soul causes an event in the body. You can't break it down into smaller steps.

Now although this looks true, there isn't *always* a mechanism that explains how physical causation happens. Perhaps the account of how smoking causes cancer will eventually arrive at the level of elementary particles. Maybe all physiological processes consist ultimately in interactions among such particles, because living things are entirely composed of them. But suppose we ask why the particles interact in those ways and not otherwise. Why, for example, do electrons repel each other with such-and-such a force? This question has no answer: they just do. We describe this behavior by formulating **laws of nature**: the particles do this and not that, depending on the circumstances. But if we ask why the laws themselves are this way and not that, there's no answer, or at least none that science has discovered. Sometimes we can explain why one law holds by appealing to other laws: the laws about the temperature, volume, and pressure of gases, for example, can be derived from laws governing molecular movements. But some laws of nature are *basic*, in that they don't hold by virtue of other laws.

And the interaction between souls and physical objects might also be governed by basic laws. Why do they interact in these ways and not others? Perhaps this question has no answer: they just do. We can describe these interactions by formulating laws of nature: particles do such-and-such when they relate in a certain way to a soul having a certain combination of sensations, beliefs, preferences, and emotions, and they do something else otherwise. But if we ask why the psycho-physical laws are this way—why particles behave as they do in the presence of a soul—there's no answer, or at least none that science has discovered.

Would basic psycho-physical laws be more troubling than basic physical laws? They'd certainly be very different from those known to science. There only a few basic physical laws. They have to do with a small number of measurable properties—mass, velocity, force, charge, and so on—which enables them to be expressed in the form of mathematical equations. (You'll remember these equations from science class: that force is equal to mass times acceleration, for example.) If there were basic psycho-physical laws, by contrast, there would be many of them: there are a vast number of ways in which our mental activities cause actions, and in which our sense organs cause experiences, and they can't be derived from a small number of principles. What's more, they would deal with phenomena that are not quantitatively measurable—belief, emotion, sensation, and so on—and would not be expressible in mathematical equations.

The existence of such laws, completely independent of the laws of physics, would be very surprising. We'd need a good reason to believe in them. There is currently no scientific evidence for their existence: no one has observed particles behaving in ways that can be explained only by appeal to nonphysical causes in a soul. That said, science has not established that there are no such laws either—that all movements of particles can be explained in terms of physical causes.

A different objection to soul-body interaction is that it would violate the laws of physics: the laws to do with force, velocity, mass, and other physical quantities that it's the business of physics to discover. It would be literally miraculous. Again, when you raise your finger, immaterialism suggests that a decision in your soul causes a "triggering event" in the brain, which in turn causes your finger to move. Without that nonphysical act, the triggering event would not occur. The physical events leading up to this triggering event are not enough to bring it about—otherwise your finger would rise whether you decided to raise it or not and your decisions would make no difference to your actions. Given those previous physical events, the laws of physics tell us that the triggering event *won't* occur. Yet it does.

The laws of physics may sometimes leave it open whether the triggering event occurs, given the previous physical events. They may tell us only that it has a certain chance of occurring—much as if you're dealt a random card from a standard deck, there is no law saying whether it will be an ace, but only a law saying that this event has a one in 13 chance. But even in that case, an event in your soul could not make a difference to whether your finger rises unless it gave the triggering event a *different* chance of occurring.

The claim, then, is that your soul could cause physical events to happen only by overruling the laws of physics. Those laws may govern the behavior of physical things not directly affected by a soul, but if immaterialism is true they don't govern the behavior of all physical things. Some physical events are instead governed by non-physical laws: by basic psycho-physical laws. It's not just that the scientists are mistaken about what the physical laws are. They're also mistaken in supposing that physical objects are governed by physical laws at all: instead they're governed by an amalgam of physical and psycho-physical laws. But science tells us that physical objects *are* governed by physical laws: that's well confirmed by experiment. So science tells us that we haven't got souls.

But this objection is not quite right. If science appears to rule out soul-body interaction, it's because it presupposes that the physical world is *causally closed*: it's not affected by anything outside it. Whenever we try to explain an event by appealing to laws of nature, we presuppose that the event and its physical causes are not affected by anything else. Your physics teacher will tell you that an iron bar gets longer when you heat it, owing to the laws of thermal expansion. But those laws allow that you *could* heat the bar as much as you like without making it any longer, if someone kept cutting off the end of it. That wouldn't violate the laws of thermal expansion because they presuppose that there is no such interference—that the apparatus in the experiment is a closed system.

Soul-body interaction implies that the physical world—the totality of physical events—is not causally closed. It's affected by things outside it: by events in the soul. This happens every time you act deliberately. Does science tell us that the physical world *is* causally closed—that physical events have only physical causes? The "causal closure of the physical," as this principle is called, would rule out dualistic interaction. But it has not been established by scientific experiment or observation. It's true that physicists assume, in their scientific practice, that the causes of physical events are always themselves physical: if they can't discover a physical cause of something, they never infer that it must have a nonphysical cause. But this doesn't mean that physical events can never *have* nonphysical causes.

Consider, by analogy, the hypothesis that there is a god who sometimes intervenes in the physical world by preventing things that would otherwise happen or by causing things that would otherwise not happen: healing someone from an otherwise-fatal illness, say. This would imply that the physical world is not a closed system. Certain physical things would behave otherwise than the established laws of physics say they must. Physics may be right about the behavior of physical things not directly affected by divine interventions, but it wouldn't be right about the behavior of all physical things.

Does science tell us that there is no such god? No: again, it hasn't established that the physical world is a closed system. There are many well-known objections to theism, but this isn't one of them. The fact that we never *observe* any divine interventions may be evidence against theism, just as the fact that we never observe brain events that are known to have no physical cause would be evidence against immaterialism (a point I'll return to in §1.11). But that's another matter. The interaction problem says not that we never observe soul-body interaction, but that it couldn't happen.

It would of course be more satisfying if we could account for the known facts in terms of physical phenomena—we know that the physical world exists—rather than by appealing to something nonphysical. We ought to explain things in terms of divine intervention only if we absolutely have to: only if they must have *some* explanation but there's no good physical account. Supernatural explanation should be a last resort. And the same goes for explanations that appeal to immaterial souls. But although this is a fair point, it's not about soul-body interaction in particular, but about the superiority of simple explanations over complex ones. It would be better not to appeal to nonphysical entities even if such things were not thought to interact with physical ones.

The thought that materialism is preferable to immaterialism because it's a better explanation of what we observe will take up the remainder of this opening statement.

> Immaterialism implies that if our decisions have any effect on our actions, non-physical events in the soul must bring about physical events in the body. This means that some physical events do not occur as the laws of physics lead us to expect. Yet this doesn't mean that such events would violate physical laws, but only that physical events sometimes have nonphysical causes. And science has not established that this never occurs.

1.11   The Duplication Argument

Here's the second argument for materialism. Saying that human beings can't have a mental life without an immaterial soul is analogous to saying that cars can't run without a radiator. Claims like this can be tested by experiment. We could test the second claim by comparing cars with radiators and cars without, leaving everything else the same. We might test-drive 100 normal cars (cars with an internal-combustion engine) and 100 cars just the same only without a radiator. Presumably we'd find that most or all of those with radiators perform well and all those without overheat and break down, supporting the conjecture that cars need a radiator.

Likewise, we could test the immaterialist's claim by comparing the mental properties of 100 healthy, adult human beings with souls and 100 without souls but otherwise the same. Immaterialism would lead us to expect those with souls to have mental lives and those without to have none. Of course, we don't know whether there *are* any souls: that's what we're trying to find out. But we could get around this difficulty by creating human beings without souls but otherwise just like the rest of us and seeing whether *they* have mental lives. If they do, it would show that human mental lives don't require a soul; if not, it would suggest the opposite.

How could we do the experiment? Earlier I imagined a machine that can make a perfect physical duplicate of any object (van Inwagen 2014: 262–265). It first scans the object, recording the precise nature and arrangement of its atoms. This takes only a moment and is harmless. It then uses the information gathered in the scan to arrange new atoms of the same numbers and types in exactly the same way, resulting in a perfect duplicate of the original, right down to the last atom. And since the physical properties of a thing are determined by the nature and arrangement of its atoms, the new object will be physically identical to the original. Put a toaster into the duplicator, and it will produce an identical toaster with the same appearance, toasting powers, electricity consumption, and so on. Put in a cup of tea and the result will be another cup of tea with the same volume, temperature, mineral content, aroma, and flavor. If the tea was swirling clockwise when the scan was made, the new tea will be too. The duplicate won't remain just like the original for long—owing to differences in its surroundings or random changes, it will soon begin to diverge—but when it's freshly made, it will be exactly as the original was when it was scanned.

Now suppose we put you and 99 of your friends through the machine. It will produce 100 beings physically identical to the originals in every way: the same size, weight, eye color, and number of hairs—even the same stomach contents. But as the machine only arranges atoms, we wouldn't expect it create any souls. We'd no more expect the duplicates to have an immaterial part than we'd expect cars built without a radiator to leave the factory with radiators. The thought is that we can find out what a human being would be like without a soul by observing these duplicates.

We know that the duplicates would be biologically alive. Biochemistry has established that life is an entirely physical phenomenon. It's vastly complex, but there's nothing nonphysical in it. To make a living thing, you need only arrange the right sorts of atoms in the right way. A nonliving thing physically identical to a living thing would be like a square thing physically identical to a round thing.[15]

But would the duplicates have a mental life? Materialism implies that they would. In fact your duplicate would have the same mental life as you. (Or at least *intrinsically* the same. She may not have any beliefs about your Aunt Agatha, because she'd never have met or heard of her. But she'd have beliefs with content indistinguishable from yours. Let's set this point aside.) Materialism at least strongly suggests that the mental arises from the physical: things are conscious or intelligent because of their physical nature. So a physical duplicate of you with no mental life, or one radically different from yours, would be no more possible than a physical duplicate of you that was a lifeless corpse. The duplicate wouldn't remain mentally identical to you for long, just as she wouldn't remain physically identical; but when she was freshly made, she'd be mentally just like you were when you were scanned.

If mentality requires an immaterial soul, however, the duplicates would have no mental life. Unless they were somehow provided with a soul, they'd be alive but unconscious and unresponsive. Immaterialism implies that a physical organism is like a radio. A radio can't produce sound by itself; it can only receive signals from a transmitter and convert them into talk or music. When it receives no signals, it's silent. Just so, immaterialism implies that a physical organism can't by itself produce thought, but can only receive signals from a thinking soul. When it receives no such signals, it's comatose.

So if physical duplicates of us without a soul would be conscious and intelligent just as we are, their mental lives would be entirely caused by physical activity—and so presumably would ours. That would strongly support materialism. If they'd be unconscious, it would be because mental life requires a soul.

What if the duplicates had some of our mental powers but not others—if they had the mentality of toddlers, say? That's what would happen if only the "higher" mental powers mentioned in §1.3 required a soul while more primitive mentality resided in the brain. This too would support immaterialism, though a complicated and messy variety of it.

Now we haven't got the technology to actually do the experiment. And that may be just as well: it probably wouldn't be a good thing for there to be someone else just like you. She'd want to spend your money, have your dinner, and sleep in your bed. She'd expect exclusive rights to your partner and children. There would be all sorts of conflict. Worse, the machine could malfunction and produce a conscious being with some dreadful defect. The university ethics committee would never allow it.

So we can only make an educated guess about the outcome. I said the duplicates would be alive. How do we know that? Well, science has established that biological life consists entirely of physical activities; and if the experiment is done properly, the same physical activities will go on in both the duplicates and the originals. What's more, we never find nonliving objects physically indistinguishable from living ones—corpses that pass all physiological tests for life, with normal vital signs and so on. We always find great physical differences between living and nonliving things. This would lead us to expect a physical duplicate of you to be alive even if we knew nothing about the physical basis of life. Any other result would go against everything we know about biology.

What about the duplicates' mental properties? We know far less about the physical basis of the mental than about the physical basis of life, but we'd still expect the duplicates to *have* mental lives. Just as we never find nonliving objects physically indistinguishable from living ones, we never find unconscious beings physically indistinguishable from conscious ones.

It's true that when someone is delivered unconscious to the accident-and-emergency department, the physical cause of her condition is not always apparent—just as it's not always apparent why a car doesn't run. But in the case of recalcitrant machines, there's always some physical defect that more thorough investigation can reveal. If a mechanic told you that there was no physical cause of your car's overheating, you'd look for another mechanic. And when someone is unconscious long enough for the neurologists to look thoroughly, they generally find a physical defect that accounts for her unconsciousness. In fact we're just as confident that it must have a physical cause as we are in the case of misbehaving cars. If a neurologist assured you that there was nothing physically wrong with your comatose loved one, you'd look for another neurologist.

We don't find cases where one person has a normal mental life and another has severe dementia, to the point where she can't recognize her closest relatives or remember what happened yesterday, without any neural difference. People with dementia are never physically just like the rest of us. The difference is only too evident in CT scans: their brains have wasted away. And adult human beings with no mental life at all invariably show cerebral damage and little or no brain activity. Medical science has found that severe mental defects are always correlated with physical abnormalities. A being physically just like you but no more conscious than a stone would go against everything we know about neurology.

But if mental activity required a soul, that's precisely what we'd expect to find: comatose people with completely normal brains, whose lack of any mental life is due to the absence of a soul, like intact radios that produce no talk or music because they're too far from a transmitter to receive signals.

So even though we'll never have a duplicating machine, the fact that we don't find physically normal human beings with severe mental disabilities strongly suggests that mental activity is a sort of physical activity and does not take place in the soul. In that case we don't have souls. Call this the *duplication argument*.

> Immaterialism implies that a physical duplicate of you without a soul would have no mental life. Yet we'd expect such a duplicate to have a mental life like yours. That's because we never find human beings who are physically normal but have severe mental defects or lack any mental life at all. This finding suggests that mental life is a physical activity in the brain rather than a nonphysical activity in the soul.

1.12   Emergent Dualism

I concede that the argument is not conclusive. Suppose we actually had a duplicating machine and the ethics committee allowed us to use it on human beings. Imagine finding, after hundreds of tests, that the duplicates always had precisely the same mental properties as the originals. It wouldn't follow that material things can think. An immaterial soul might still be needed.

How? Well, duplicating the body might duplicate the soul as well. It could be that whenever a human being is created, whether by duplication or in the usual way, the gods create a soul and attach it (that is, establish a causal connection enabling the soul to move the body at will and to perceive by means of its sense organs). That would prevent us from creating a physical duplicate of you without a soul. Having a soul would be a variable we couldn't control for. In that case no amount of physical duplication would produce any result that bears on whether thinking requires a soul. Although physical duplicates of thinking beings would always think in the same way, this would not be because thinking is in any way physical, but because the gods always attach the same sort of soul to both. And the reason why human beings who are comatose for long periods are always observed to have badly damaged brains would not be that mental life takes place in the brain, but that the gods never attach a soul to an organism unless its brain is intact.

But although this may be possible, it's not the most likely explanation of what we observe, either in the duplication story or in real life. What makes something a good explanation is a large topic in the philosophy of science, but everyone agrees that, other things being equal, simple explanations are better than elaborate ones, and natural is better than supernatural. If there's a natural explanation for something—one that appeals only to things of the sort investigated by the natural sciences that would be a good explanation if it were true—it would be unreasonable to reject it in favor of an explanation involving divine intervention. Or at least this is so unless there are compelling grounds for rejecting the natural explanation. This is not to say that divine interventions cannot occur or that supernatural explanations can never be true. The point is only that it's wrong to reject a good natural explanation in favor of a supernatural one without an extraordinary reason.

Recall our finding that cars with radiators usually run well and cars without one overheat. The obvious explanation of this is that cars can't run without a radiator. But it's not the only possible explanation, and it doesn't strictly follow from what we observe. For all the experiment tells us, it could be that cars don't need radiators at all. What prevents them from overheating is instead a nonphysical *wotsit*—a part not made of steel or any other material and entirely exempt from the laws of physics. Wotsits can't be installed by factory workers, but only by the gods—who, for reasons known only to themselves, choose to supply one to all and only cars with radiators.

This too is a possible explanation of what happens in the automotive experiment. But it's obviously not a very good explanation. It would be far better to suppose that the radiator keeps the engine cool. For the same reason, the fact that human beings have similar mental powers when they're neurologically similar and only then is better explained by the hypothesis that mental powers are caused by the nervous system than by the hypothesis about the gods attaching a soul.

Now my story about the gods is crude and unimaginative, and I told it only by way of illustration. There may be a better account of the observed correlation between mental properties and brain physiology that immaterialists could give. Some propose that brain activities themselves create an immaterial soul and cause it to think, by a natural process requiring no divine intervention.[16] The same sort of brain activity always creates the same sort of soul. In that case the brain activity of your physical duplicate, being just like yours, would create a perfect duplicate of you soul, giving her a personality, beliefs, memories, and other mental features identical to yours, just as we'd expect to find if we did the experiment. This view is sometimes called **emergent dualism**, as it says that the soul "emerges" naturally from brain activity.

Is it a good alternative to materialism? It says that physical organisms have the power to bring new objects into existence ex nihilo. They don't just produce thinking: they produce thinking beings. Creating a soul is not like creating a dance by moving in certain ways, but like creating a dancer—and not out of preexisting material, in the way that you might make a puppet out of wood, but out of nothing. Such a power is usually attributed only to supernatural beings. It's what happened when, according to the first verse of Genesis, God created the heavens and the earth: he made something where previously there was nothing apart from himself. We'd need a very good reason to accept that the ordinary neural activity of pigs and poodles does this. (Remember that what goes for human beings goes for all sentient animals.)

And while the proposal attributes to physical organisms the godlike power of creating thinkers out of nothing, it denies them the more ordinary power of *thinking*. It says that an organism's neural activity is sufficient to cause thinking, but only in something else: it can cause thinking only by creating a new being and causing *it* to think. That's like saying that radiators can't cool engines, but they can create, out of nothing, an immaterial wotsit that does so. Wouldn't it be better to say simply that organisms think?

You might answer (as Leibniz did—recall §1.9) that the very idea of a material thinker is inconceivable: no matter how carefully we examined its physical workings, we'd never see how they could amount to anything mental, disqualifying the materialist's account of what would happen in the duplication experiment. But whatever merit this reasoning may have, it's no use here. If it's inconceivable that a material thing might think, it's equally inconceivable that it might produce an immaterial thinking thing out of nothing: no examination of its physical workings would ever make it intelligible.

The observed correlation between mental and physical defects need not be explained by saying that we're material things and our mental life is physical. The explanation could instead be that some process attaches a soul to all and only animals with intact brains. It could be a deliberate act on the part of the gods or even a natural phenomenon. But this would be extravagant and mysterious compared with the materialist's explanation.

1.13   The Remote-Control Argument

My final argument for materialism doesn't turn on specialist knowledge or imaginary experiments, but on familiar facts.

We know that small changes in the brain—general anesthesia or a blow to the head, for instance—can cause unconsciousness. They shut down all mental activity. That's what we'd expect if mental activity takes place in the brain: mechanical or chemical changes in the brain affect its functioning, and as one of its functions is to produce thinking, they could bring it to a stop. But what if mental activity takes place in the soul? It's got no parts to be displaced or chemistry to be altered. How could changes in the *brain* stop the *soul* from functioning? The mystery is not how events in the brain could cause changes in the soul: that would be a version of the interaction problem of §1.10. Even if physical events could affect the soul, as they would in ordinary perception, it would still be a mystery how they could stop its activity altogether.

What changes in the brain *could* do is disrupt the soul's communication with it. Immaterialism suggests that the brain is where the soul interacts with the physical world: it's the interface between the immaterial realm and the material one. The information from your sense organs is passed to the brain, processed, and then transmitted to the soul, where it causes sensory experience. And when you raise your finger, a mental act in the soul sends information to the brain, which converts it into nerve signals that cause muscles to contract or relax and produce the intended movement. A knock on the head could prevent the brain from sending sensory information to the soul, leaving you unable to see, hear, or feel: everything would go dark and silent and numb. And it could prevent the brain from receiving commands from the soul, leaving you unable to move. It would cut off your access to the physical world. But because the soul shares no parts with the brain, we'd expect the rest of its functioning to continue unhindered, so that you remained fully conscious and clear-headed. Yet you can't remain conscious unless your brain is working properly.

Likewise, immaterialism would lead us to expect alcohol in the bloodstream to interfere with the brain's functioning, hampering bodily movements and perhaps distorting the sensory information it passes to the soul. But mental activity not involving bodily movements or sense perception—remembering where you left the keys or making plans for next week, say—should continue unhindered. Yet it doesn't.

Immaterialism suggests that the relation between the body and the soul is like that between a remote-control drone and its human operator. The soul affects the body's movements much as you might affect a drone's, and the soul perceives the physical world by means of the body's sense organs much as you might "see" through the drone's camera. Head injuries could disrupt the soul's communication with the brain, just as damaging the drone can disrupt your communication with it: the screen and controls would go dead. But that wouldn't prevent you from remaining conscious. We'd expect the functioning of the body and the soul to be as independent as the functioning of a drone and its operator, contrary to our experience with head injuries. If we have a soul, what we actually observe is like a human being whose mental life can't continue even for a moment unless she's in communication with an intact drone. Damaging the drone knocks her out cold, and we can revive her only by repairing it.

The fact that small changes in the brain stop all mental activity suggests that it doesn't take place in an immaterial soul, but in the brain. This has been called the *remote-control argument*.[17]

> Immaterialism suggests that the body stands to its soul as a remote-control drone stands to its operator. Changes in the body may affect its ability to communicate with the soul, but not the soul's ability to function. The fact that small changes in the brain cause complete unconsciousness suggests that mental activity takes place in the brain.

1.14   Electric Dualism

Most immaterialists accept that the soul can't function independently of the brain. Although the soul and the body are in one way like a human being and a remote-control drone, in another way they're like a light bulb and its power source (Swinburne 1997: 310, Hasker 2011: 216). The bulb can do nothing in isolation, but plugged into a source of electricity it lights up. The soul, likewise, can do nothing unless it's "plugged in" to an intact body. General anesthesia and head injuries stop mental functioning by cutting the soul's power, as it were: they switch it off like a light. Call this proposal **electric dualism**. (This doesn't imply that neural activity *creates* the soul as emergent dualism says, though the two views are often combined.)

I said that the interaction between the soul and the body would consist in an exchange of information: the soul gets sensory information from the body and sends commands that cause the body to move in the intended way. That's how it is with drones and their operators: what passes between them is information. Electric dualism says that there's an additional causal connection: the body gives the soul something it needs in order to function.

This gift can't be just information. Temporarily cutting off someone's supply of sensory information doesn't immediately stop all mental activity: instead it causes the experience of sensory deprivation. This is not to say that a soul could function if it *never* received any sensory information. Complete sensory deprivation over a long period would almost certainly impair your mental functioning. Try to imagine being completely unable to see, hear, feel, taste, or smell anything for a week. It would probably cause severe mental breakdown. But a sudden lack of sensory information would not stop your mental functioning instantly, like switching off a light. Yet that's precisely what head injuries and general anesthesia do. The soul needs more from the brain than just sensory information: it needs something analogous to energy.

But it can't literally be energy. Energy is a physical quantity—measured, you may recall from science class, in joules or calories—and an immaterial soul can no more have it than it can have mass or temperature. Whatever the soul gets from the brain, it can't be anything physical. What could it be, then? Why does the soul need it? And how could the brain produce it and transmit it to the soul? No answer to these questions has ever been proposed. No one knows how electric dualism could be true.

But there's a deeper mystery. The proposal says that the soul can think only when it's "plugged in" to the right sort of organism. Mental life requires both physical activity in the body and nonphysical activity in the soul. The soul's activity is thinking, even though it can't occur without the body—yet nothing the body does is thinking, even when accompanied by a functioning soul. The soul can't think on its own, but the body can't think at all. What accounts for this asymmetry? Why is it the soul that thinks with the help of the body, and not the body that thinks with the help of the soul? If thinking requires those activities, what makes only one of them thinking? And why is it the soul's activity and not the body's? If electric dualism is true, these questions must have answers. But it's hard to see what the answers could be.

Of course, in our analogy we can see that only the bulb lights up. And we can see why: only the bulb has a mechanism—an incandescent filament, say—for converting electric current into light. But this feature doesn't carry over to the case at hand. We know that the soul and the body are different: one is immaterial and one is material. And their activities are different: the soul's activity is nonphysical and body's is physical. But this tells us nothing about what makes one of these activities mental and the other nonmental.

Imagine a pair of conjoined twins, Lefta and Rita. Despite having just one arm each, they learn to play the guitar: Lefta presses the strings and Rita strums. Suppose their music teacher described this by saying that Lefta plays the guitar with Rita's assistance. He accepts that Lefta can't play alone, but insists that Rita can't play at all: she only helps Lefta. That would be baffling. How could Lefta be playing the guitar if Rita isn't? We can see how they differ: Lefta has only a left arm and Rita only a right one. And we can see how their activities differ. But these differences tell us nothing about why only what Lefta does counts as playing the guitar. The teacher's description looks completely arbitrary and unwarranted: there's no more reason to say that Lefta plays with Rita's help than that Rita plays with Lefta's help. The electric dualist likewise says that although the soul and the body each do something necessary for thinking, only the soul thinks. But until we're told what makes the soul's activity mental and the body's nonmental, this looks just as arbitrary as the claim that only Lefta plays the guitar.

You may reply: What the body does can't be thinking because it's inconceivable that a material thing might think (§1.9); it must be the soul that thinks. But we can no more see how a material thing could enable an immaterial soul to think than we can see how it could think itself. So this is no reason to suppose that it's the soul and not the body that thinks.

We can see that thinking (in human beings at least) requires physical activity in the body. The most obvious explanation of this fact is that our bodies think. If it's instead our souls that think, they must somehow be unable to function without the body's help: thinking must require contributions from both the soul and the body. That leaves no reason to suppose that souls think rather than the bodies.

> Most immaterialists accept that the soul can't function without an intact body. They say that what passes between them is not just information, but also some sort of "energy," so that the soul is like a light bulb and the body like its power supply. But this leaves a mystery: if thinking requires both the soul's contribution and the body's, why does the soul think with the body's help, rather than the body thinking with the help of the soul?

1.15 Cooperative Dualism

The sensible thing to say about Lefta and Rita is that they play the guitar *together*. Guitar-playing consists of two separate tasks: pressing the strings with the left hand and strumming with the right. Each twin performs one of these tasks, and their activities add up to playing the guitar. They each do something necessary for playing, but neither contribution is itself playing. They play the guitar in the way that you and I might sing a duet.

We could avoid the problems facing electric dualism by saying likewise that the soul and the body think together. They each do something necessary for thinking, but neither contribution is itself thinking. Thinking consists of two separate tasks, each performed by a different entity. It's a cooperative undertaking: a sort of duet sung by a soul and a body together.

So the body doesn't think, and the soul doesn't either. The thinker is composed of both. The body has no mental life, but it does something that enables something else to have one. And it's the same with the soul. Each of us is a compound of an unthinking body and an unthinking soul. We have two parts, one material and one immaterial, that each produce something nonmental, and these ingredients combine to produce our mental activity. We might call this **cooperative dualism**. (The "compound immaterialism" that I described in

§1.4 also says that each of us is composed of a soul and a body, but it says that the soul thinks, which cooperative dualism denies: a subtle but important difference.)

Cooperative dualism has several advantages over electric dualism. Most obviously, it avoids the hard question of what makes the soul's activity, but not the body's, thinking. It says that neither is: thinking is what you get when they're combined. What's more, it says that the soul can function without any help from the body, just as we would expect a wholly immaterial thing to do. The soul has no need of any mysterious nonphysical "energy" from the body. Consider the remote-control argument again. That small changes to the brain can stop all mental activity would be puzzling if mental activity took place in the soul, which would remain undamaged. But if mental activity had both a physical component in the brain and a nonphysical one in the soul, changes in the brain could stop it by removing the physical component, even if the soul continues to function. If you and I are singing a duet and I suddenly lose my voice, the duet will stop, even if you continue to sing. Likewise, stopping your brain activity would stop your mental activity, even if your soul, so to speak, keeps on singing.

And cooperative dualism fits better than other versions of immaterialism with what we know about cognitive defects. Damage to the visual cortex at the back of the brain can prevent people from recognizing faces and other ordinary objects, even though their vision is normal and they can accurately describe the shape of what they see. Damage to other brain areas can prevent the formation of new memories: people with this condition often have a good memory of events from long ago, yet can't recall anything that happened three minutes before (Sacks 1987: ch. 2, Ramachandran 1999: 15–17). We know that memories are stored in the brain, because a cerebral hemorrhage or blood clot can destroy them. There are countless examples like these. Electric dualists say that remembering and recognizing take place entirely within the soul, yet somehow require the brain's help. We've seen the drawbacks of that view. It would be far less mysterious if these activities took place in the brain. That could be because they take place *entirely* in the brain, as materialists say. Or they could consist of both a physical component in the brain and a nonphysical one in the soul, as cooperative dualism says. Either view would explain why brain damage can affect these abilities.

But for all that, I don't know of anyone who has ever advocated cooperative dualism. It has a number of troubling implications. Most obviously, it goes against the scientific evidence. If our imaginary machine were to create a physical duplicate of you without a soul, cooperative dualism suggests that it would be completely unconscious, as the soul's essential contribution would be missing. That fits badly with the fact that we never observe beings physically just like healthy people but with no mental life. Cooperative dualism would make it possible for someone to have a healthy body but a defective soul, because the soul's functioning would not depend on the body. So we'd expect to find mental disabilities due entirely to such a defect—people who can't recognize faces or form new memories, or are even completely unconscious, despite having perfectly normal brains. Yet such cases are unknown.

And cooperative dualism is not actually a version of Cartesian dualism. It doesn't divide the world into unthinking bodies and thinking souls. It says that there are both material and immaterial things, but neither is able to think. The soul (if we can call an unthinking part by that name) is no more a thinking thing than the body is. It must instead have some nonmental character. It has to *do* something—to engage in some sort of activity that combines with brain activity to produce thinking. Call this activity "X." Cooperative dualism may be a sort of substance dualism, in that it divides objects into two separate and exclusive realms. But these realms are not the physical and the mental, but the physical and X.

This is not merely inconvenient for those who like philosophical views to fall into neat categories. It downgrades the status of the mental. Traditional dualism says that the physical and the mental are *fundamental*, in that they don't consist in anything else. Material things don't have their physical properties by virtue of having nonphysical properties at some deeper level; nor do souls have mental properties by virtue of having certain nonmental properties. Both the physical and the mental are, so to speak, bedrock foundations of the world. Cooperative dualism denies this: it allows that the *physical* is basic, but not the mental. Mental activity consists in something nonmental, namely the body's physical activity together with X, the activity of the soul. The mental is derivative and second rate. That goes against every immaterialist instinct.

Finally, it makes the soul entirely unknowable. No one knows what X might be, or even how to find out. We can investigate the nature of material things by doing physics or biology, but there's no science of X. Psychology is no help: it can investigate the mental nature of soul-body compounds, but there's nothing psychological about X. All we can know about the soul is that whatever it does somehow combines with neural activity to produce thinking.

This would undermine most of the arguments for immaterialism. The "mill" argument of §1.9, for example, tries to show that we must be immaterial because only a soul could think. But cooperative dualism denies that a soul can think: it says that thinking is something the soul and the body do together. Any reason to think that mental activity could not possibly arise out of physical activity in the body will be a reason to think that it couldn't arise out of physical activity together with nonphysical activity either. Descartes' argument from introspection (§1.7) tries to show that we perceive no material parts when we look within, and must therefore be wholly immaterial. Again, cooperative dualism denies this and says that we have all the material parts of our bodies. It's incompatible with Aaron's arguments for immaterialism too, as we'll see. Cooperative dualism would imply that for thousands of years immaterialists have been fundamentally mistaken about the nature of the soul.

> Electric dualism is mysterious by saying that although body and soul are both necessary for thinking, only the soul thinks. We could avoid this mystery by saying that the soul doesn't think: the body and the soul each do something nonmental, and these activities combine to produce thinking in a thing composed of the two entities. Brain damage could then stop mental activity by stopping its physical component. But this proposal would make the soul unknowable and undermine most arguments for immaterialism.

1.16   Mysteries

Cooperative dualism is unattractive: no one will suppose that we have an immaterial part that doesn't think. All immaterialists will say that the soul thinks. Yet the fact that head injuries cause unconsciousness shows that it can't do so without some sort of "energy" from the body.

This leaves a number of mysteries. What is this "energy"? How does the body create it or transfer it to the soul? Why does the soul need it? (Why should a wholly immaterial thing be unable to function without help from material things?) And why, given that the activities of both the soul and the body are required to produce thought, is it only the soul that thinks?

These are mysteries about electric dualism in particular. Further puzzles arise on any version of immaterialism. Its greatest mystery is often said to be how the soul could interact with the body: how your nonphysical intention to raise your finger could make it rise (§1.10). To my mind, a far greater mystery is why it should be *im*possible for a *material* thing to think. (Or if a material thing *could* think, why don't our bodies actually do so?)

The arguments for immaterialism do nothing to answer this question. Even if we could establish that we thinkers are immaterial, that would do nothing to explain why physical organisms *don't* think. Or at least this is so unless we argue (as Leibniz did) that we must be immaterial precisely *because* no material thing could think. But any reason to doubt whether a material thing could think looks like an equally strong reason to doubt whether a material thing could help to produce thinking in the soul—yet head injuries show that material things do help to produce thinking. So arguing that we're immaterial is only the beginning of the immaterialist's work. We'll still want to know why material things can't think.

You might suppose that materialists are no better off in this respect. It's not enough for them to argue for their view: they also need to explain how it's possible for a material thing to think. (They needn't deny that an immaterial thing could think: they might believe in gods or angels. They only deny the existence of human souls.)

I just said that *im*materialists face a hard question:

Question 1 (for immaterialists): Why is it impossible for a material thing to think?

But materialism raises a hard question of its own:

Question 2 (for materialists): How is it possible for a material thing to think?

If immaterialists have no good answer to their question, you might think, that's no grounds for complaint, as materialists haven't answered theirs either.

Now theories of mind such as behaviorism and functionalism purport to tell us how a material thing can think. But even if those theories are completely wrong, the two questions are disanalogous. The immaterialistic analog of the materialist's question is not why a material thing could never think, but how an *im*material thing could think. If materialism demands an answer to question 2, immaterialism demands an answer to a third question:

Question 3 (for immaterialists): How is it possible for an immaterial thing to think?

(Cooperative dualists need to say instead how a thing composed of a soul and a body could think, as well as why a soul could not.) As we saw in §1.9, no one has any answer to this question.

And given the causal dependence of the mental on the physical, immaterialism raises the further question of how the body's activity enables the soul to think. In other words,

Question 4: How is it possible for a material thing to *produce* thinking?

Of course, materialists too face this question. But by their lights it's the same as question 2: knowing how a material thing can produce thinking will tell us how it can think.

Both materialism and immaterialism raise hard questions, and neither will be satisfying until they're answered. Both require an account of how a material thing can produce thinking (question 4). Materialists have had much to say about this—it's what philosophy of mind textbooks are mostly about—but immaterialists have said almost nothing. And immaterialism raises two further questions: how a soul could think and why a physical organism can't (questions 3 and 1). However the arguments for the two views stack up, immaterialists have a lot more to explain.[18]

> Immaterialists need to show not only that we're immaterial, but also that material things can't think. Materialism requires an account of how a material thing *can* think, but immaterialism needs an account of how an *im*material thing can do so. And given the causal dependence of the mental on the physical, immaterialists face the question of how a material thing can *produce* thinking. That leaves immaterialism with more to explain than materialism.

Notes

1 Eminent recent immaterialists include Robert Adams (2007), Colin McGinn (1997: ch. 9), Alvin Plantinga (2006), Karl Popper (1977), Richard Swinburne (1984, 1997, 2019), Peter Unger (2006: see esp. §7.3, 376–381), and Dean Zimmerman (2011).
2 Barnes (1982: 65–68) is an accessible summary of Aristotle's view. There are many interpretations of the Thomistic view, none of which I entirely understand. Enthusiasts might have a go at Shields and Pasnau (2016: ch. 6).

3 No immaterialist that I know of believes that animals think without having a soul (Swinburne 1997: 182 is a typical discussion). Descartes notoriously denied that animals have mental lives at all (Descartes 1985: 139–141/AT VI 56–59).
4 Baker (1995, 2005); Hudson (2007); Merricks (1999, 2001); van Inwagen (1995, 2007).
5 Descartes was a great mathematician as well as a philosopher. You may have encountered the Cartesian coordinate system named after him.
6 Chisholm (1976: 104). For more on compound immaterialism, see Olson (2007: 168–171).
7 The matter is actually more complicated (Olson 2017), but the complications don't affect the current point.
8 Sacks (1987: ch. 6). Ramachandran and Blakeslee (1999: 59f.) explain how you can produce this experience in yourself without amputating a limb.
9 When the neurologist Oliver Sacks was suffering from this condition he described himself as an "internal amputee" (Sacks 1984: 75).
10 Swinburne (1984: 22–30, 2019: 68–80), Hart (1988), and Plantinga (2006: 4–11) give arguments of this sort.
11 Merricks (2007) proposes that when Christ became human, a wholly immaterial thing became wholly material—which, if possible, would cast doubt on 2. But as this presupposes materialism, it's no help in the present context.
12 Monadology §17. The translation is quoted in van Inwagen (2014: 174) and originally appeared in Leibniz (1981: lv). Bennett (2001: 286–293) is a good discussion. Foster (2001: 25–28) and Plantinga (2006: 11–22) defend the argument.
13 This section borrows extensively from van Inwagen (2014, ch. 10), which I enthusiastically recommend.
14 It was made immediately upon publication of Descartes' *Meditations* in the 17th century, most ably by Elizabeth of Bohemia: see Hatfield (2003: 266–269).
15 You can find a detailed account of the physical basis of life in the opening chapters of any biology textbook. Pross (2012) is an accessible account of what we know and don't know in this area.
16 E.g. Hasker (1999: 190, 2011: 213–216); Unger (2006: 336–340); Zimmerman (2011: 174–176); Swinburne (2019: 9).
17 Van Inwagen (2014: 260). See also Churchland (1988: 20), Hasker (1999: 153f).
18 These final two sections are based on Olson (2021).

Chapter 2

Why I Believe I Am a Soul

Aaron Segal

Contents

2.1 Chili Peppers, Chinchillas, and Chileans

Chairs, chili peppers, and Cheerios are very different from one another. But science has taught us that despite these differences they're all ultimately made from the same *kinds of stuff*: the same basic elements, all of them catalogued in the periodic table, just arranged and stuck together in different ways.

DOI: 10.4324/9781003032908-3

I'm not like that. Obviously, I'm very different from chairs, chili peppers, and Cheerios, just as each one of those things is different from the others. But on top of that, I'm not even made from the same kinds of stuff that they are. Indeed, I'm not made of stuff at all. As we might put it, *I'm not made of matter*. Or so I say. But please don't accuse me of some sort of self-centered superciliousness. I think the same is true of you. I think the same is true of Chicagoans and Chileans. I think the same is true of *all of us* human beings. As a matter of fact, I think the same is true of some other non-human creatures as well—things like chinchillas and chihuahuas, who can think and feel. But since this debate is about us, about what we human beings are like, I will set aside the question of whether such non-human sentient creatures are made of matter. As it is I have my work cut out for me.

"Are you seriously suggesting that chinchillas and chili peppers are not ultimately made from the same kinds of stuff? Have you not studied middle school biology?" The answer (to the first question) is: Yes and No—it depends on what you mean by "chinchillas." If you're referring to the furry little animals that some people breed for their fur, then the answer is No, I'm not suggesting that they and chili peppers are ultimately made from different kinds of stuff; or, worse still, that they are not made of stuff at all. Of course, they're made of stuff—they've got fur, after all! But if you're referring to whatever it is that gets irritated when a breeder pokes and prods a furry little chinchilla animal, then the answer is Yes, I am suggesting that *that* thing, the thing that gets irritated, isn't made of the same kinds of stuff as a chili pepper or even a little furry chinchilla animal, and that it isn't made of stuff at all.

I maintain that we are not made of matter. I mean this in an unqualified and straightforward way. Other philosophers say that we aren't made of matter, but then they go on to say that although we aren't *entirely* made of matter, we are at least *partly* made of matter. In their view, you might have a whole human organism as a part, along with all of *its* parts (your eyes, ears, limbs, organs, etc.); or maybe all of your material parts are inside your cranium (cerebrum in, legs out). Whatever the case may be, they think you have quite a few parts that are or are made of atoms of the kinds listed in the periodic table. The reason they nonetheless say "you aren't made of matter" is because they think you *also* have some part that *isn't* like that. They think you have an immaterial part, or a soul, as people often put it. I don't qualify or moderate my view in that way. In my view, you have no material parts at all. If someone wants to build one of us from scratch, the periodic table is just the wrong place to look for raw ingredients. Speaking strictly, you don't *have* a soul; you *are* a soul.

It'll keep things shorter and clearer in the long run if we introduce some technical terms.

> An object is **wholly material** when all of its parts are material objects.
> An object is **wholly immaterial** when none of its parts is a material object.

At least in principle, there might be objects that are neither wholly material nor wholly immaterial: such objects would be amalgams, having both material and immaterial parts.

Eric and I use

> "**materialism**" to name the view that you're wholly material.

And we use

> "**immaterialism**" to name the denial of that view—i.e., to name the view that you have at least *some* part or parts that are not material, that you are either an amalgam or wholly immaterial.

And finally, we use

> "**compound immaterialism**" to name the version of immaterialism that says you're an amalgam, and
> "**pure immaterialism**" to name the version of immaterialism that says you're wholly immaterial.

In these terms: I endorse not just immaterialism, but pure immaterialism.

Dualism

Many people use the word "**dualism**" or "**substance dualism**," to express the view we call immaterialism. It's true that "dualism" is a prettier word. But the word "dualism" has two disadvantages.

First, it suggests that we have a genuinely dual nature, that we are in fact amalgams made up of *both* material parts and an immaterial soul and *that* view is incompatible with the view I actually hold, i.e. pure immaterialism. According to the view I hold, we have no material parts at all.

Second, if the term "dualism" is to have anything to do with the duality of matter and mind, then the view it expresses must imply that *there are* both material objects and immaterial ones and maybe even that they're equally real (whatever else it suggests about whether we are amalgams or wholly immaterial). But immaterialism is neutral on the question of whether there *are* any material objects, let alone whether they're as real as the immaterial ones.

So I beg your indulgence in using a slightly uglier but less misleading word. Of course, nothing of substance hangs on the choice of technical terms, as long as we're all clear on what they mean. As long as you can keep all the distinctions straight, feel free to mentally substitute the word "dualism" wherever I write "immaterialism."

You may have noticed that pure immaterialism (and a fortiori, immaterialism) is a "negative" claim, not in the sense that it's *bad* if true, but in the sense that it says what you *aren't*, i.e. that you're not at all material. From this negative claim, we can derive very many more substantive claims about you. For example, it follows from pure immaterialism that you don't walk, talk, or chew gum, at least not speaking strictly. After all, no purely immaterial thing (a thing that has no material parts) can *itself* walk, talk, or chew gum—the best it can do is somehow or other move something *else* around, something *material*, in such a way that the material thing walks, talks, and chews gum. But these further substantive claims derived from pure immaterialism are themselves negative; they say that you don't do this and you don't do that. Do I have anything positive to say, you might ask, about what you are like and what you can do?

Well, yes, I do have positive things to say about you. But don't expect much by way of flattery or even provocation: the positive things are boring, uncontroversial, and pretty much uncontested. They include the following: you think and feel, you desire things and believe other things, you weigh considerations, come to decisions, and intend to do certain things. All this can be put by saying,

(1) You have a mental life

You, *your very own self*, are (often) consciously aware of your environment and yourself and come to believe certain things and form certain plans. And all of that, I say, is strictly true.

Moreover, you don't just form plans, you very often act on them. Your beliefs and desires, your decisions and intentions, have real-world consequences: they bring about movements and other changes to your body and to other material objects besides. Thus, your decision to go make yourself a cup of coffee causes your body to start making its way over to the coffee machine. And vice versa. Certain things that happen to your body cause you to think and feel a certain way. Thus, when your toe inadvertently bangs into the side of the chair you will (typically) feel pain as a result. We ordinarily describe that sequence of events by saying, "you stubbed your toe." All this can be put by saying that

(2) You causally interact with material objects

You, *your very own self*, very often bring about change in the "material world" and are changed in turn by what goes on there. And all of that is strictly true.

These are banalities and points of agreement between me and the materialist. (At least between me and the garden-variety materialist. Some materialists deny that we have any mental life, because they deny that anything has any mental life. See Churchland (2006). Although these philosophers might be better understood as holding that *we* don't exist at all. In that case, they wouldn't be materialists in our sense of the term, since materialism is a view about what we are, and so it presupposes that we exist. In any case, I will henceforth ignore the view that we have no mental life.) These banalities wouldn't be worth stating but for the fact, which I've already highlighted, that in my view it's *not* strictly true that you have a "material life." You don't yourself move around or touch the coffeemaker; but you do cause your body to do so. Lest you think my view is even more austere than it is, or further from the materialist's than it is, I have gone ahead and made the banal explicit.

> Materialists hold that you are made entirely of material things. I disagree. Indeed, I hold that you aren't made of material things at all. But there are some important points of agreement between the materialist and me: we both agree that we really do have mental lives, and that we interact with things in the material world.

2.2   Is Materialism the Default?

My view is now on the table. I will soon turn to arguments for it. More exactly, I will turn to arguments for immaterialism, in general, and pure immaterialism, in particular. I will take the banalities, (1) and (2), for granted. But I want to address a preliminary issue. Suppose it turns out that (as you see it) neither side has any good arguments, or that both sides have equally good arguments, so that the balance of arguments favors neither side. What should you believe *then*?

Some people seem to think that if you find yourself in such a situation you should believe that you're a material being, that materialism is the default, that the burden of proof lies on *me*, the defender of immaterialism—as if materialism is innocent until proven guilty, and immaterialism is guilty until proven innocent [see Lycan (2009, §I) on mid-20th-century materialists].

If that were right, then immaterialism would be relevantly like the thesis that there are *exactly* one billion trillion stars in the observable universe. I doubt there are any good *arguments* for or against such a thesis, but it is surely guilty until proven innocent. After all, what's the likelihood that it's precisely *that* number? [One billion trillion is the number that results from a back of the envelope calculation, based on a rough estimate of the number of galaxies in the observable universe (ten billion) and an estimate of the average number of stars per galaxy (100 billion). But if the rough estimate of the number of galaxies in the observable universe is off by just 1—and the average number of stars per galaxy is exactly what we think it is—then our back of the envelope calculation will be off by 100 billion. The margin of error, in absolute terms, is pretty gigantic.]

Presumably, if immaterialism is guilty until proven innocent, it's not for *that* kind of reason; it's not as though immaterialism involves an arbitrary choice of exactly one of vastly many hypotheses that are evidentially on par with one another. So what *are* the reasons that one might treat immaterialism as guilty until proven innocent? I can think of several. At least one of them has to do with the appearances regarding us human persons in particular. This reason suggests that as regards us specifically, we *seem* to be material things, and so barring any conclusive or compelling argument to deny the appearances, we should stick with them. I will not at this stage address that argument; I will merely register my dissent. (I will discuss this reason in much greater detail in §4.2.)

But there are other putative reasons to grant a presumption to materialism, having very little to do with *us* and a lot to do with being material. These are reasons of a quite general sort, which would in principle apply to *anything* whose existence we have good reason to believe in but with regard to which we don't have a conclusive argument whether it is material or immaterial. I want, already at this stage, to explain why I am not moved by reasons of this kind to think that immaterialism bears some special burden of proof.

> What should be our starting point regarding the question of whether we are material? Some people think that materialism is innocent until proven guilty. Why would anyone think that? We'll look now at two answers to that question that exploit alleged differences between the category of material things and the category of immaterial things.

2.3   Matter Is Well Understood (Or Is It?)

Allow me to present the first putative reason in the form of a speech, a speech that someone who does grant a presumption to materialism might give:

> Saying that a thing is immaterial is not to characterize how it *is*, it's to characterize how it *isn't*. It's to say that it *isn't* material (it's right there in the prefix, "im.") What's worse, saying that a thing is immaterial rules out saying much of anything at all about how the thing is (as opposed to how it isn't). If this weren't already evident, if should be evident from what you, Aaron, have

managed to say about me. Since you take me to be an immaterial thing, the only positive things you could muster were that
I have a mental life and that I causally interact with material
objects. As to the latter: it doesn't seem to be about how I am *in
and of myself*, it's about how I'm related to other things. As to
the former: you have done next to nothing to explain what it *is*
about me that gives me the capacity to have such a mental life.
Saying that I'm immaterial hardly goes any way at all toward
explaining my having that capacity! (It might turn out that being
immaterial is *required* in order to have the capacity for a mental
life—more on that later—but it is at most a necessary condition,
not a sufficient one.) And so saying that I am immaterial ren-
ders me a *je ne sais quoi*, a something-we-know-not-what, that
is somehow capable of thinking and feeling.

Saying that a thing is material, by contrast, *is* to characterize
how the thing is in itself. It's to say that it's material (notice the
lack of any prefix.) What's more, saying that a thing is material
makes room for saying *quite a bit more* about how the thing is in
itself. You can (usually) say how much it weighs and what color
it is and how it tastes, and many other things besides; indeed
there are whole branches of science devoted to all the things one
can go on to say.

So, if we have no decisive arguments either way, then we
should believe that I am material, rather than immaterial. And
that's what we should believe because it's an instance of a more
general principle that says something like this: for any entity A
and any two exclusive and exhaustive categories, KnowNot and
WellUnderstood (categories so-called because entities belonging to the first category are we-know-not-whats and entities
belonging to the second category are well understood), in the
absence of any decisive argument as to whether A belongs to
KnowNot or WellUnderstood, we should believe that A belongs
to WellUnderstood.

So goes the first putative reason. Set aside the question of why we
should believe the general principle just stated. (But I can't help
but ask: why should we push things into the well-understood column rather than the know-not-what column, other than to satisfy
a groundless wish that the world is predominantly amenable to our
understanding?) Set aside the contention of many immaterialists that
just as no immaterial object can have physical properties like size and

shape, no material object can have mental properties like thought and feeling. (That contention would do something to restore parity between the categories of the material and the immaterial. But it has no place in a discussion of what to believe in the *absence* of any decisive arguments, since it would itself *constitute* a decisive argument in favor of immaterialism. After all, if anything is certain in this area, it's that we do have thoughts and feelings. So we'd *have* to be immaterial, if no material object could have thoughts and feelings.)

Instead, focus on the question of whether material things really are better understood than immaterial things. Are they really? Start with the feature, being material (or materiality). It's admittedly natural to think that something's having that feature is a matter of how that thing is (as opposed to how it isn't) and indeed how it is in itself (as opposed to how it relates to other things). But it's far from obviously the case that that's right, a point that emerges once we ask what it *means* to say something is material. What *is* it to be made of matter, anyhow? Can we correctly and informatively provide a definition of "matter" or "material," and if so, how?

I wish I didn't have to discuss these questions, because they're very knotty, I don't have the space to do them justice, and frankly, I don't know the answers. But I guess I have no choice. I'll put my discussion of various extant alternatives in a text box. Feel free to skip the box and go directly to my own suggestion if knotty definitional questions don't excite you.

Defining "Material"

It pretty clearly won't do to say that a thing is by definition material just in case it's **made of the elementary particles we know of**: quarks, leptons, and bosons. For that would misclassify the elementary particles we don't know of as immaterial. It would mean that most dark matter isn't matter. And even if it turns out to be true that there are no other kinds of elementary particles, and no dark matter, those aren't the kinds of things that should be true *by definition*.

Some suggest that a thing is by definition material just in case it's **in space**. But that doesn't seem right. As far as I can tell, there's nothing incoherent about the idea of an immaterial thing located in space (see Lycan 2009: 558). Think of angels and demons. Likewise, some suggest that a thing is by definition material just in case it's **extended in space**. But that doesn't seem right to me either. For one thing, as far as I can tell there's nothing incoherent about the idea of an immaterial thing being *extended* in space. Think again of angels and demons. For another thing, the idea of a *material* thing having *no* extension—being in space but having a size of 0 cubic meters—isn't obviously incoherent, either. Think of the *tip*—the point all the way at the top—of a perfectly conical birthday hat (Zimmerman 1991, citing Suarez). (Or, if that idea is incoherent, it's because the idea of *anything* being in space but having a size of 0 cubic meters is incoherent; but then this definition comes to the same thing as the first one.)

Others suggest (Swinburne 2019, Bailey 2020a) that we start with the idea of a material *feature*—or, as it's more commonly put, a physical feature—and then define what it is to be a material *thing* in terms of that. So we might say that a thing is by definition material just in case it has *some* physical feature; or that *all* of its features are physical features; or that *all* of its essential features are physical features (a feature is essential to a thing if it can't exist without it); or that *all* of its intrinsic features are physical features (a feature is intrinsic if it says something about how its bearer is in itself). But none of the proposals in this family will do. Some of them face specific problems. For instance, being such that all of its features are physical features is unnecessary for being material: there could be a material object that has some features, some mental features, maybe, that are not themselves physical (or at least that shouldn't be ruled out by definition!); likewise for being such that all of its essential/intrinsic features are physical features. There are some fancy ways to deal with some of the specific problems (see Bailey 2020a).

But there's a more general problem, which is that we'd need to explain what is meant by "physical feature." It plainly won't do in our context to say that a feature is by definition physical just in case it can only be had by a material thing (or only by something that's at least partly material). That may well be true—and I think it is true—but then we can't go on to define "material thing" in terms of "physical feature"; that would make for too little a definitional circle. And every other attempted definition of "physical feature" of which I am aware is subject to counterexample—and in conjunction with any definition of "material object" in terms of "physical feature" would misclassify clearly immaterial things as material.[1]

These difficulties might suggest that we jettison in the definition any mention of "physical feature" in general and instead just provide some finite list of (physical) features (like mass, charge, …), such that a thing is by definition material just in case **it has one (all, some-specified-number, …) of the features on that list.** But the idea of there being such a finite list is utterly implausible. Think of the infinitely many mass-like features there could have been that "behave" just a tad bit different from how mass "behaves." ("Schmassive" things, for example, attract each other with a force inversely proportional to the cube of the distance between them, and so on.) More generally, it just seems obvious that there could have been physical features that we don't know about.

The best *I* can do is to say that a thing is by definition material just in case **its movements are subject to some completely general law.** More exactly, a thing is by definition material when there is some completely general law that relates its states to its own movements or the movements of other things. A law is completely general when it makes no mention of any *particular thing*. The law of universal gravitation, which says that *any* two things attract each other with a force proportional to their mass and inversely proportional to the square of the distance between them, is a completely general law. And so are all the laws that physics deals in. None makes any mention of any special, particular thing. They tell you how *anything* with such and such shareable features is liable to move, or make other things move, in these-and-those circumstances. On the other hand, a law (if such there be) that says that when *Aaron Segal* decides to lift a hand then *this* hand (the one currently typing) will move, is *not* a completely general law. So, the idea is, a material thing is subject to some law of the kind that physics deals in. A material thing's movements can be lawfully predicted in virtue of the *sort* of thing it is—whether that's having a certain mass, or electric charge, or schmass—not (just) in virtue of the *particular* thing it is. Not so for immaterial things. Even if there were angels and demons located in space, there'd be no such shareable features in virtue of which one could reliably predict how they'll move or make other things move.

Now, I have some misgivings about my proposed definition of "material," which I won't rehearse here. What I wish to impress upon you is that it's not clear what being material comes to, and on what seems to me the most promising understanding of what it comes to, it's far from obvious that it says something about how its bearer is in itself; indeed, it's far from obvious that it says something about how its bearer *is*, at all (as opposed to how it isn't). For notice that according to my proposed definition, being material seems very much like being the Queen's subject—attributing either of these features to a thing is a matter of saying how that thing must behave in virtue of something or someone *else* (a law of nature or the Queen). Saying of someone that she's the Queen's subject is certainly not a way to characterize how that person is "in herself." It's not even clear that it's a way to *positively* characterize the person, whether in herself or in relation to something else: saying what the person *must* do can equally well be thought of as saying what she *can't* do—she must pay taxes just in case she can't engage in any sort of tax evasion—as specifying the ways in which she's *not free* to behave as she wishes. (Rene Descartes made a similar point about finitude and infinitude; despite the "in-" prefix, he thought of infinitude as *positive* and finitude as saying that the thing *fails* in one or more ways to be infinite.)

So much for the generic feature, being material. How about more specific features, like weight, taste, and smell, that only material things can have? Won't those give us insight into material things, insight that we don't have regarding immaterial things? Well, no, none of those features really tells us what the thing is like in itself. Take a red hot chili pepper. How much do you really understand about what the chili pepper is like *in itself*? You know, for example, that the chili pepper is red and very "hot." But we scientifically literate folks now believe that the redness and the "heat" have at least as much to do with *us* as they do with the chili pepper. Redness, for example, is a matter of being disposed to cause a typical human observer to have a reddish visual experience when observing the object in typical conditions. Or, if we're even more scientifically literate, we might think that redness is a matter of being disposed to reflect light with such-and-such a mix of wavelengths. Either way, it's a matter of how the red thing tends to *behave*, or *interact* with other things, not about how it is in itself.

Or so I say. Some philosophers think that the color (taste, smell, etc.) of an object isn't a **disposition** in the way I have suggested. Redness, they would say, is whatever *underlying* feature a thing has *in virtue of which* it has the dispositions mentioned above. Color science has taught us that the underlying feature is the thing's atomic composition and structure: it's *because* of a thing's atomic composition and structure that it has the reflectance dispositions that it does.

But, even if they're right, that'll just move the KnowNot bulge in the carpet of reality down a level. What's meant, I ask, by a thing's "atomic composition"? Presumably, what's meant is a specification of the *types* of atoms, i.e. the *elements*, that it's made of; which is in turn a specification of its atoms' fundamental physical features, features like mass, charge, and spin. But those features are *themselves* dispositions. Having a positive charge of 1 coulomb, for example, is a matter of being disposed to repel and attract other charged items with such-and-such a force (given by Coulomb's Law). No further progress toward understanding what the building blocks are like *in themselves*.

Or so I say. Some philosophers think that the charge (mass, spin, etc.) of an object isn't itself a disposition. Having a positive charge of 1 coulomb, they would say, is whichever intrinsic feature a thing has that Coulomb's Law happens to *connect* to the disposition to repel and attract other charged items with such-and-such a force.

But, even if *they're* right, that'll just keep the KnowNot bulge in the carpet of reality exactly where it was. What *else* do we know about the feature, having a positive charge of 1 coulomb? Nothing. Could we tell if God or some other miracle-worker changed a thing's charge but kept its dispositions the same? No. (See Shoemaker 1980, Lewis 2009.) A thing's charge is indeed (on this view) a matter of how the charged thing is in itself, but we have absolutely no understanding of *it*, of charge itself. All we understand about a charged object in light of its being charged is that it has *some* intrinsic feature—some *je ne sais quoi*—that we call "charge" and as a matter of fact is hooked up by the laws with certain behaviors. So much can be understood about a thinking immaterial thing as well!

> At bottom, all we *really* know about material things is how much they push and pull each other and how their position in space changes over time (Russell 1927, ch. 14): hardly illuminating about what they're like *in themselves*. The material world is at the end of the day at least as hidden and ill-understood as the immaterial world. So even if there were some good reasons to suppose that we are more likely to belong to a better-understood category than to a less-understood category, that would give us no reason to think we're material.

2.4   Matter Uncontroversially Exists (Or Does It?)

So much for the first general reason one might treat materialism as the default. Here's a second one, again in the form of a speech:

> Uncontroversial examples of material things are easy to come by. That is, there are plenty of things that both uncontroversially exist and are uncontroversially material. Uncontroversial examples of immaterial things, on the other hand, are hard to come by. That is, there are few if any things that both uncontroversially exist and are uncontroversially immaterial. Numbers? Controversial whether they exist. God? Controversial whether He exists *and* controversial whether He's immaterial. Satan? Same. Indeed, it's not as though these candidates are individually controversial, but that it's still uncontroversial that there *are* immaterial things. No, it's a matter of controversy *whether there are any immaterial things at all.*
>
> So, if we have no decisive arguments either way, then we should believe that I am material, rather than immaterial. And that's what we should believe because it's an instance of a more general principle that says something like this: for any entity A and any two exclusive and exhaustive categories, Controversial and Uncontroversial (categories so-called because it is a matter of controversy whether anything at all belongs to the first category, while not a matter of controversy that something or other belongs to the second category), in the absence of any decisive argument as to whether A belongs to Controversial or Uncontroversial, we should believe that A belongs to Uncontroversial.

So goes the second putative reason. Set aside the question of why we should believe the general principle just stated. (But I can't help but ask: why should we push things into the Uncontroversial column rather than the Controversial column, other than to satisfy a groundless preference for barren landscapes over lush ones? Note that the question the principle is meant to settle is not whether entity A *exists*—its existence is being taken for granted—but rather whether it's of a kind with other things we take to exist, as opposed to being something novel. The answer the principle advances seems to assume that the world tends to be simpler and more monolithic, rather than richer and more variegated. But what reason do we have to think the world tends to be simple and monolithic rather than rich and variegated? Consider the following case: the SETI Institute finally detects an intelligent radio communication from a nearby galaxy, which when interpreted correctly says as follows: "We are alive and intelligent. We are made from …" Unfortunately, just at that moment their communication cuts out. Suppose that what else we know about the galaxy is so meager that it gives us no indication of whether these intelligent lifeforms are carbon based, or silicon based, or something else entirely. What shall we then believe, if anything, about what these things are made of? Supposing we're materialists, we should presumably think that *we're* made of carbon. Shall we believe, therefore, that *they too* are made of carbon, just because it's uncontroversial that there are carbon-based intelligent life forms? That seems misguided. It seems to me we should suspend judgment on the matter, taking no position one way or the other.) Instead, focus on the question of whether it really is uncontroversial that there are material things. Perhaps if we pay attention only to contemporary Western sophisticates, the view that there are material things will end up being uncontested. If we widen our view to consider the whole of mankind, in all ages and places, matters look different. Many Buddhists, and some others, believe that there isn't *anything* at all; that at least as far as *things* go, there aren't any. A fortiori for *material* things. But even granting that there are things, a venerable philosophical tradition, called **idealism**, has it that the material world is at best second class: it's a mere shadow of the *real* world, an idea in a mind or minds.

Idealism

That's a rough and ready characterization of idealism. A more precise characterization will come later (§4.8), but it's good enough for now. Whether idealism entails the *denial* of material objects is a subtle question, one that turns in part on the knotty question we discussed of what it means to be "material." I take it, though, that for the purposes of challenging the alleged advantage of the category of material objects, it doesn't much matter whether the tradition takes material objects to be second-class denizens of this world or to be entirely nonexistent. Either way, the category of material objects can hardly be thought to enjoy any advantage over the category of the immaterial.

Idealism can be supported in many ways (see Berkeley 1734a/b, Foster 1982, Robinson 1982, Adams 2007, Goldschmidt and Pearce 2017). One way (Adams 2007) appeals to the *hiddenness* of the material world—to the fact that we don't know anything about what it's like in itself—which I've already discussed. Here I want to mention another way, which appeals to the *evanescence* of the material world—to the fact that it seems to "evaporate," not when we get our hands on it, but when we try to wrap our minds around it. Take something rock-solid. Like a rock. It might be difficult to actually break it in two, but presumably it *has* a right half and a left half: the two halves are right there, and you can point at them. Indeed, everything that's extended in space at all—even if it occupies just a trillionth of a cubic foot—would seem to *have* a right half and a left half, even if you can't point at them because your finger is too big.

But that suggests that our rock-solid rock is on much less solid footing than we thought. For if that's right, then there seem to be just two options: either our rock is ultimately made of parts that are not extended at all, that are literally *point-sized*, or this division can go on indefinitely, that our rock has no parts that themselves have no further parts, it's just parts all the way down, ad infinitum. Neither of these options seems reasonable. How could some things, even infinitely many things, that aren't extended at all come together to make up something that *is* extended (Bayle 1710: 3077, Segal 2016)? And could there even *be* things in space that have no extension at all? On the other hand, how could a thing with parts have no *ultimate* parts: at each level of decomposition, our rock would derive its being from the level below, but then where did its being come from in the first place (Leibniz 1686, Adams 1994: 335–336)? Either way, the material world looks like nothing but a mirage that disappears upon careful examination.

Although I think these and other reasons should in fact lead us to accept idealism, I am not asking you to accept idealism, or Buddhism, or any other view according to which there are no material objects. That would make my job far too easy. If there are no material objects, then, of course, we're not material objects. My point is just that the existence of material objects is far from uncontroversial, and with good reason. And so even if the general principle about controversial and uncontroversial categories is right, it gives us no reason to grant a presumption to materialism.

Reasonable people can deny the existence of immaterial objects. But reasonable people can also deny the existence of material objects. Neither the immaterial nor the material is an uncontroversially populated category. So even if there were some good reason to suppose that we are more likely to belong to an uncontroversial category than to a controversial one, that would give us no reason to all to think we're material.

The upshot of this and the previous section: before the arguments come in, the matter is wide open—the material world, if it exists, is far too hidden and evanescent for materialism about human beings to carry any general presumption in its favor. Let's now examine the arguments with an open mind, free of any prejudice in favor of the material.

2.5 The Arguments

There are many arguments for immaterialism, in general, and a bunch for pure immaterialism, in particular.

Some arguments for immaterialism appeal to *empirical claims or discoveries*, whether in the form of:

* Reported observations, such as near-death experiences (cf. Fischer and Mitchell-Yellin 2016) or out-of-body experiences (Taliaferro 1994, ch. 3), or
* Scientific theories, such as quantum mechanics (Halvorson 2011)

Others appeal to certain putative *moral facts about ourselves* and in particular to moral features that we ostensibly couldn't have if we were material. Philosophers variously claim that if we were material, we:

* Couldn't have free will (Cover and O'Leary-Hawthorne 1996) and hence plausibly couldn't be morally responsible for anything we do, or
* Couldn't have inherent moral worth (Harrison 2016, cf. Bailey and Rasmussen 2016)

No *possible* material configuration, they say, could have free will or have inherent moral worth. Materiality, they allege, is simply incompatible with these important moral features.

A good number rely on certain putative *mental facts about ourselves* and in particular to mental features that we ostensibly couldn't have if we were material. Philosophers variously claim that if we were material, we:

- Couldn't be conscious (Leibniz 1991, sec. 17)
- Couldn't have a unified point of view (Hasker 1999, ch. 5)
- Couldn't have states (such as thoughts, beliefs, desires) with propositional *content*, like the belief *that Michael Jordan is the best basketball player ever* (Plantinga 2006)

No *possible* material configuration, they say, could be conscious or have a unified point of view or think about things. Materiality, they allege, is simply incompatible with these important mental features.

Still other arguments are based on *religious considerations*. Philosophers variously suggest that immaterialism is:

- Made plausible or probable by the view that there is a God (Taliaferro 1994, Plantinga 2007; but see Bailey 2020b and Bailey 2021)
- Suggested by certain religious scriptures (Cooper 1989, Steiner 2015)
- Required by more specific religious views, such as resurrection of the dead (Plantinga 2007, but see *inter alia* van Inwagen 1978, Zimmerman 1999, Hudson 2001, and Baker 2007)

And perhaps the largest group of arguments are based on *metaphysical considerations*. They point to very general aspects of the world: either to how it actually is (such as what things have which parts) or to how it could have been different (such as what things can survive which sorts of mishaps).

My brief summary hopefully gives a sense of the number and range of arguments for immaterialism that philosophers have put forward. I think it's fair to say that there are many more arguments for immaterialism than there are for materialism (see Lycan 2009). But, of course, quality matters much more than quantity. The real question is not how many arguments there are on each side, but which arguments are *good* and *how* good.

Some of the arguments for immaterialism that I've outlined aren't very good at all. But some of them are, at least in the sense that they deserve careful consideration. Indeed, there are more good ones than I have space here to carefully consider. So I will concentrate on just three, all of the metaphysical variety.[2] Two of these three are not only good but also *successful*; that is, I think they succeed in showing what they aim to show. But I will start with one good argument that I think nevertheless fails. I start with it because it is the most influential and well known—if you've read anything philosophical about the soul, you've probably encountered this argument—and because I think it is still instructive.

> The arguments for immaterialism are many and varied. Some of them are worthy of serious consideration, and I will seriously consider three. I'll begin with one that is famous, although unsuccessful in my view. We'll then give two less famous arguments, which do succeed.

2.6   You and Your Body Can Go Their Separate Ways

The 17th-century philosopher, Rene Descartes, is perhaps best known for having begun his *Meditations on First Philosophy* with radical doubts. He points out that he often misperceives things, and sometimes, such as when he's sleeping, his experiences are completely wide of the mark; he might dream that he's delivering a lecture, while he's in fact lying in his bed in his pajamas. But then, the specter of radical error looms: if our senses can mislead us some of the time to some degree, how do we know they're not misleading us all the time to an even greater degree? After all, Descartes notes, it's **conceivable** that there aren't really any trees or houses, tables or candles, chili peppers or chinchillas: he can easily imagine it being the case that he's simply deluded in thinking these things exist. Indeed, it's conceivable that he doesn't really have any arms or legs, or even a torso or a head. It's conceivable that he's just a disembodied spirit, being deceived by some other evil spirit into thinking that he has a body. He can't rule out any of these possibilities, and so it doesn't seem like he can know the simplest of things, like that he has two arms and two legs, or that he's sitting at a table in his living room.

But as he finds himself mired in these doubts, he comes to the realization that there is something that he *can* rule out: he can rule out the possibility that he doesn't *exist*. After all, even if he is in fact deceived in thinking that there is an "external world," he still is *thinking* that there is an "external world," and he can't well be thinking anything at all if he doesn't exist! So he can know with certainty that he thinks, and that he exists. And from there, it's but a hop, skip, and a jump to God's existence, and from God's existence, it's but another hop, skip, and jump to the "external world," and so Descartes can know after all that he has arms and legs and that he's sitting at a table in his living room. Or so Descartes argues. We can ignore those "hops, skips, and jumps," since they're rather dubious, and in any case, our aim here is not to defeat skepticism.

But neither is it to support skepticism, whether about our having a body or about anything else. After all, I'm not trying to argue that we don't *know* that we're material; I'm trying to argue that we're *not* material. Which brings us to the question: what is the relevance of any of this? In general, one can't infer that *p* is *true* from the fact that *p* is *conceivable*. Perhaps I can't rule out the possibility that I just inherited a billion dollars. It's *conceivable* that I'm so misguided about my financial and familial situation that I did in fact just inherit a billion dollars. Alas, it hardly follows that I did in fact inherit a billion dollars.

Enter Descartes' very clever move. In its essentials, the move is this: it's true that *in general* it doesn't follow that *p* is true from the fact that *p* is conceivable, but for *some* instances of *p*, it does. In particular, if *p* says of some *X* and *Y* that they're distinct/identical, then from the fact that what *p* says is conceivable it *does* follow that what *p* says is true. In order to explain the move in more detail, two points of introduction are in order.

First, I have studiously avoided using the language of "identity" to *characterize* materialism and immaterialism. One *could* use such language to characterize the views: the former as the view that I am identical with some wholly material object, and the latter as the view that I am not identical with any wholly material object. But usually there's no *need* for such highfalutin language. We can just say, as we have done, that materialism is the view that I *am* a wholly material object, and immaterialism is the view that I'm not. No explicit talk of "identity" there. But in order to appreciate Descartes' clever move, we'll need to think explicitly about the relation of identity, and its negation, distinctness. Two things are distinct when they're indeed two things; otherwise, i.e. if there's just one thing there, then "they" are identical. They're not identical in the way that identical twins are identical—identical twins are two things, not one, even if they are qualitatively indistinguishable. No, they're identical in the way that Muhammad Ali and Cassius Clay Jr. were identical; there was just one person there, with two ways of referring to him.

Second, I'm now going to shift from speaking of what's conceivable to speaking of what's possible. A situation is possible, in the intended sense, if it *could have* come off, if it's a way things *could have* gone. In addition to all the different situations that actually came off—which are evidently possible, since the world actually went that way—there are very many situations that didn't actually come off but presumably could have. Situations like the Red Sox beating the Mets in the 1986 World Series, or there being one more star in the Milky Way than there actually are, are presumably possible, even if they're not actual. The relationship between possibility and conceivability is a delicate one: the former is a matter of what reality is like (what are the possibilities for it), the latter is a matter of how we can *think about* what reality is like (what are the ways we can imagine it to be). Now, it could be that our best, or only, *evidence* for the possibility of some situation is that it's conceivable—a point to which I'll soon return—but they are still different features of a situation. And the one directly relevant to Descartes' clever move is possibility, not conceivability. (At least if his move is to have a good chance of success.)

With that background in place, we can now state the claim that's at the heart of Descartes' clever move. The claim is this:

> **Necessity of Identity:** For any things x and y, if x is in fact identical with y, then necessarily, so long as x exists or y exists, x is identical with y

Suppose Muhammad Ali and Cassius Clay Jr. are identical (as "they" in fact are). Then, there's no possible situation in which, say, Ali exists, but he's not the very same thing as Clay. Of course, Ali could have existed but not have been *called* "Cassius Clay Jr." He could have existed but not have been called "Cassius Clay Jr." *or* "Muhammad Ali"—he could have been called "Yoel Teitelbaum" instead. But he still would have *been* Muhammad Ali and would have *been* Cassius Clay Jr. Cassius Clay and Muhammad Ali couldn't have been two people: they couldn't have been like Cassius Clay and George Foreman. There's just one person there, after all.

If this isn't obvious enough on its own, we can give an argument, based on what's known as Leibniz's Law (named for another 17th-century philosopher, Gottfried Leibniz):

> **Leibniz's Law:** For any things x and y, if x is identical with y, then for any feature F, x has F if and only if y has F.

Everything has exactly the same features as itself. What could be more obvious? So now consider this feature: being essentially identical with Cassius Clay Jr.

> A thing is **essentially** F when it's not possible that the thing exists and isn't F, or equivalently, when it's necessary that if the thing exists then it's F.

Clearly enough, Clay has not only the feature of being identical with Clay but also the feature of being essentially identical with Clay. There's no possible situation in which Clay exists but where he is someone other than Clay. So given Leibniz's Law, and the fact that Ali is in fact identical with Clay, we can conclude that Ali *also* has the feature, being essentially identical with Clay. By exactly parallel reasoning, we can show that Clay has this feature: being essentially identical with Muhammad Ali. From which it follows that there's no possible situation in which either Ali or Clay exists, but they're not identical with each other.

All of this should seem rather trivial. But its significance is apparently far-reaching. Suppose someone proposes that I *am* the human animal lying in my bed. That is, that I'm *identical with* the human animal lying in my bed. Given the Necessity of Identity, such a proposal would be refuted by the mere *possibility* of my existing without being identical to *that very animal*. For if I am in fact identical with the human animal lying in my bed, then according to the Necessity of Identity, there'd be no possibility of my not being so identical. And, so the argument goes, it sure seems to me like I could exist without being identical to that very animal; it seems like I could exist without that very animal existing *at all*. For as Descartes led me to see, I can easily understand and imagine in great detail a situation in which I have been dreaming or deceived for quite some time, and the human animal and the bed in which it's supposedly in don't really exist at all. If I've been dreaming or deceived, then I am *there*. But if the human animal in my bed doesn't exist, then *it's* not there for me to be identical with it. Conclusion: I can imagine that I exist without being identical with the human animal in my bed. But if it's imaginable, that's very good evidence that it's possible. So it's possible that I exist without being identical with the human animal in my bed. And the same goes, for the same reason, for *any* wholly material object one might propose to be me. That is, for any wholly material object whatsoever, it's possible for me to exist but not to be identical with that object. But then, given the Necessity of Identity, we're in fact not identical with any wholly material object; in other words, we're not wholly material.

That was the argument. It might have been easy to miss or hard to follow. So let's put it step by step. Put on your materialist cap and pick your favorite wholly material candidate for being me. Since you can't tell me your favorite candidate, I'll just assume it's the human animal sitting in my chair. (That's what Eric thinks I am, and in any case it won't matter.) Call that human animal, "Goofy." (That's how you say "my body" in Hebrew, and I'm kind of goofy.) Then, I can convince myself that I'm not in fact identical with Goofy with the following argument:

(1) If I am identical with Goofy, then necessarily, so long as I exist, I am identical with Goofy (instance of Necessity of Identity)
(2) Possibly, I exist but I am not identical with Goofy (e.g. because Goofy does not exist)

Therefore,

(3) I am not identical with Goofy

I could even use **Leibniz's Law** directly and bypass the appeal to the **Necessity of Identity**:

(1) If I am identical with Goofy, then:
    I have the feature, being essentially identical with Goofy, if and only if Goofy has the feature, being essentially identical with Goofy (instance of Leibniz's Law)
(2) I do not have the feature: being essentially identical with Goofy
(3) Goofy has the feature: being essentially identical with Goofy

Therefore,

(4) I am not identical with Goofy

Each of these two arguments is **valid**. That is, there's no way for its premises to be true but its conclusion false.

Indeed, each is **formally valid**: that is, it's valid because it has a certain logical form, and any argument of that logical form is valid.

The form of the first argument is:

(1) If p, then necessarily q
(2) Possibly, it's not the case that q

Therefore,

(3) It's not the case that p

Take any two declarative sentences, plug one of them in for "p," the other one in for "q." The conclusion of the resulting argument will follow ineluctably from the premises.

The form of the second argument is:

(1) If p, then:
           q if and only if r
(2) It's not the case that q
(3) r

Therefore,

(4) It's not the case that p

Take any three declarative sentences, plug one of them in for "p," another one in for "q," and the last one in for "r." The conclusion of the resulting argument will follow ineluctably from the premises.

Premise (1) of each is pretty clearly true: I'm not going to entertain challenges to Leibniz's Law or the Necessity of Identity. There are quibbles about whether premise (1) of each argument really is an instance of the relevant principle, but I will set aside these niceties. And premise (3) of the second argument is evidently true. The only real question is regarding premise (2) of each argument. How do I know that it's possible for me to exist without being identical with Goofy?

Well, how do we know, regarding any state of affairs about which we don't (yet) know that it's the way the world is, that it's at least a way a world could be? A plausible answer, one which brings us back to Descartes' own formulation of the argument, is that if we can *conceive of*, or *imagine*, a certain situation, then that's at least very good evidence that the situation is possible, i.e. a way a world could be. There might be other ways to know that a situation is possible—without knowing that it's actual—but all our argument requires is that imagining it is *one* way.

Then, we're reminded of Descartes imagining himself thinking, and so existing, without his body existing. So I go ahead and imagine myself thinking, and so existing, without Goofy. And my thus imagining is very good evidence that it's possible for me to exist without Goofy.

There are numerous refinements of this basic idea, which differ regarding the exact details of the imagined scenario. In one version, I follow Descartes and simply imagine being disembodied, having long been deceived by some evil spirit. That might be difficult for some to imagine: can I really imagine, they wonder, being *completely* disembodied? So in another version, I imagine waking up one day with an entirely different kind of body (like a giant insect), my old body having been vaporized at the very instant that I get a new one. (If you haven't already done so, read Kafka's *The Metamorphosis* to get a vivid sense of what this would be like.) That too might be difficult for some to imagine: can I really imagine, they wonder, persisting through an *instantaneous* vaporization of my body? So in another version, I imagine sitting at the breakfast table reading the morning paper, and my cells being very rapidly and entirely replaced; so rapidly that all of the original cells are gone before any of the replacements have a chance to be assimilated into the new body, but not all at once so as to not raise suspicions about whether I really survive (Plantinga 2007). If I can imagine any of these, then I have the requisite evidence for premise (2). And with that I'd have a compelling argument that I am not identical with Goofy.

More generally, the argument would ultimately show that materialism is false. After all, Goofy was just the best wholly material candidate for being me. But the same arguments would apply just as well to any wholly material object I might be: e.g. put "my brain" in for "Goofy" and you'll see the argument works just as well. So the conclusion we can draw is that I am not identical with any wholly material object. At the very least, I must have some part that isn't material.

> Descartes' argument for immaterialism seems to pull a rabbit out of a hat. The hat is the mere possibility of his existing without being identical with his body. The rabbit is the actuality of his existing without being identical with his body. But this

argument is no magic trick. Because of the Necessity of Identity, if the hat contains the possibility of which he speaks, then the rabbit is already there. And each of us seems to have very good evidence, via our imaginations, that it really is possible for us to exist without being identical with our bodies.

2.7   Or Can They?

So much for Descartes' argument, in its various versions. It's no doubt very clever and raises subtle and fascinating philosophical questions. I don't think the argument succeeds, though. There's a standard reply to the considerations I've adduced on behalf of premise (2), which I don't think is as fatal as it is usually taken to be. But there's another reply, much less discussed, that I think *is* fatal.

A word of introduction before looking at the replies. Premise (2) of each argument claims that a certain possibility exists for *me*; it says that *I* could exist without being identical with Goofy. It's a claim about how a particular thing (the thing that is me) could be, as opposed to a claim about things of a certain kind. In philosophical jargon it's a claim of **de re possibility** ("res" means "thing" in Latin, so the idea is it's a claim about how a particular *thing* could be). Crucially, it's not merely the claim that it's possible for there to be *something or other that is thinking just what I'm thinking*, but which isn't identical with Goofy. That claim wouldn't do the work we need it to do. Indeed, even the claim that it's possible for there to be something or other that is *immaterial* and thinking just what I'm thinking wouldn't do the work we need it to do. (I leave the justification of these claims as exercises for the reader.) This is a crucial point about the argument and its Achilles heel (see Yablo 1990, Zimmerman 1991).

The standard reply dates all the way back to Descartes' contemporary, Antoine Arnauld, and we can put it like this (see Descartes 1641/1996: 107–110). My imagining myself existing without Goofy existing is evidence that I really could exist without Goofy existing only if a certain condition is met. The condition is that I have a "**complete conception** of myself," a knowledge of my essence, and hence of all my essential properties. Otherwise, they say, my success in imagining might be due to my ignorance. I might mistake an impossibility for a possibility because some essential property of mine of which I am ignorant rules out the imagined scenario.

Now: do I have such a complete conception of myself? Do I know, for every property, whether it's an essential property of mine? One reason to think not is that that's a pretty tall order. But there's a more important and specific reason to think not. Assuming I don't *already* know the argument's conclusion—since then I wouldn't need the argument!—there's quite clearly at least one property regarding which I don't know whether it's an essential property of mine. That's the property: being identical with Goofy. I don't know whether it's an essential property of mine because (a) I don't know whether it's a property of mine (remember, I don't yet know the argument's conclusion), and (b) it is a property of mine just in case it's an essential property of mine (that's the very point of Descartes' clever move).

What shall we think of this reply? I don't think it's all that impressive. On the face of it, its requirement that we possess a complete conception is too stringent. Sure, without such a complete conception my imagining *might* be due to my ignorance. But is that all by itself a good reason to think it *is* due to my ignorance? Is it enough to neutralize whatever evidence I get by imagining the scenario? When I look outside and seem to see a mountain I *might* be deceived or dreaming. But is that all by itself a good reason to think I *am* deceived? Is it enough to neutralize whatever evidence I get by looking outside? Not obviously. My experience of a mountain might not be *conclusive* evidence for the actual existence of the mountain, but it's evidence nonetheless and maybe even very good evidence. Imagination stands to possibility as experience stands to actuality. My imagining existing without being identical with Goofy is perhaps not *conclusive* evidence for the possibility of my existing without being identical with Goofy, but it's evidence nonetheless and maybe even very good evidence.

But only if I can in fact imagine that. And I don't see how I can. It's not that I can't imagine a situation in which *someone*, who's always thinking exactly what I'm thinking, is, say, sitting at the breakfast table reading the morning paper, while his bodily parts are being very rapidly and carefully replaced. Indeed, I think I can (easily) imagine there being someone, who's thinking exactly what I'm thinking, is *entirely disembodied*. I just don't see how I'm supposed to imagine *me, in particular,* in either of those situations. What am I supposed to *do* in order to imagine *me* in particular being in that situation?

Think of it this way. Say I start by asking you to imagine that someone, who's always thinking just what you're thinking and looks just like you, is sitting at the breakfast table reading the morning paper, while his bodily parts are being very rapidly and carefully replaced. Done? Ok, I assume you've succeeded. Hold on to that mental image. Next, I want you to imagine *you*, specifically *you*, sitting at the breakfast table reading the morning paper, while your bodily parts are being very rapidly and carefully replaced. Done?

I'm sorry, but I'm afraid I set you up for an impossible task. Did you change anything about the mental image? If you didn't, how is it that you were imagining different scenarios, one more general and the other more specific? If you did, do tell what you changed. Let me guess, you attached a little mental label with your name on it, right next to the original mental image. (That's my guess because that's the best I can do when I try this on myself.) But that can't be sufficient. For one thing, I could have asked you, to begin with, to imagine someone who shared *your name* and who *always wears a dorky label with his name* on his shirt, in which case your little mental label wouldn't take you any further. Ok, maybe you went on to imagine *what it would be like*, from the inside, to undergo the described series of events? But you must have done that the first time around—at least if you succeeded—since you were asked to imagine someone who's *always thinking just what you're thinking*. I challenge you to find something else relevant that you might have changed. I myself can't see what it could be. So I'm dubious that there's anything I can successfully imagine that would justify acceptance of premise (2) of the argument.

Thinking and Imagining (De Re)

To be sure, I am willing to grant that I can *think* about myself in particular, and that I can *introspect* all sorts of things about myself. But I don't think I can *imagine* myself in particular. The reason imagining is different, put more abstractly than what I've already said, is this: imagining represents what's imagined by way of a *correspondence* between an *image*, or *picture*, and the thing imagined. It's by nature a pictorial representation. The trouble is (see Lewis 1986:170–171) that whenever an image or picture corresponds to something, it also corresponds to exactly the same degree to anything that's qualitatively just like that thing. So I can never imagine myself specifically, as opposed to imagining something that's qualitatively just like me.

More cautiously, since I'm not 100% certain that imagining works by pure pictorial representation, I'd say this: the only sort of mental state that is good evidence of genuine possibility is one that works by way of pure pictorial representation (see Segal 2013: 87–95), whether that is or isn't the mental state of imagining. And since pure pictorial representation suffers from the limitation on specificity that I've just mentioned, I can't be in any mental state that is good evidence of the de re possibility claim stated in (2).

There is a problem with Descartes' argument, although it's not the one people usually identify. If I really could imagine *myself* as disembodied or differently embodied, that would give me very good evidence that such a thing is possible, even absent a complete conception of myself. The trouble is that the best I can do is imagine there being someone very much like me who's disembodied or differently bodied, and that just won't do for the purposes of establishing that I'm immaterial.

2.8   The Material World Is Inhospitable to Us

The previous argument contended that the material world was *dispensable* as far as we're concerned: it's possible for us to exist without it. But it didn't suggest that it's *inhospitable* to us. The more successful arguments I'll develop do contend just that. I don't mean that the material world is physically or biologically inhospitable— it's hard to get by sometimes, but life goes on and here we are. I mean *metaphysically* inhospitable. There's a deep mismatch between *our* nature and the nature of the material world. The mismatch is deep enough that even if there is a material world, and even if we causally interact with it, we aren't *part* of it.

Before going any further, I want to stress that the alleged mismatch is between us and the material world *we in fact inhabit*. Unlike the moral and mental arguments I listed above, which contend that no *possible* material configuration could have the moral and mental features we have, the arguments I will give advance the more modest claim that no possible material configuration *in a world relevantly like ours* could be one of us. Any material world that exhibits one of the two features I go on to highlight (fuzziness and flux) is inhospitable to us.

I will build on two facts about the material world: that it's *fuzzy*, and that it's *in flux*. Briefly, what I mean by saying that it's fuzzy is that at least at the level of macroscopic material objects—like Cheerios and chili peppers—things don't have neat and clean boundaries.

Imagine shrinking down to the size of an electron and finding yourself somewhere deep inside a chili pepper sitting on a vine. You look around and there are tons of much larger molecules—molecules that are the stuff of which chili peppers are made. Understandably alarmed by all of this, you decide to make your way out of the pepper. You start traveling as fast as your nano-sized legs can carry you, and you eventually end up squarely outside the pepper. That is, when you look around there's no pepper stuff around you.

Safely outside the pepper, you can now entertain an interesting metaphysical conundrum: Was there a precise time and place at which you departed the pepper? Was there some instant in time before which you were definitely inside the pepper and after which you were definitely outside the pepper? (Ignore your own spatial extent, if you have any: suppose I'm asking about the tip of your nose, which we can assume is itself point sized.) Put it like this: When you got to the "edge," was there a final frontier of atoms, all of which were definitely parts of the pepper, and all atoms beyond which were definitely not parts of the pepper?

Anyone even barely acquainted with the workings of our world at the atomic level would, I venture, answer "No." There was presumably some *period* of time in your journey (however brief) during which the answer to whether you were then inside the pepper would be: *kinda* or *sorta*. You weren't *definitely* inside the pepper then, nor were you *definitely* outside the pepper then. There was no moment at which you went straightaway from being *definitely* inside the pepper to being *definitely* outside the pepper. There's simply no final frontier of pepper particles: regarding a huge number of atoms at the "edges," there's just no definite answer ("Yes" or "No") as to whether it's a part of the pepper. *The pepper stuff tapers off gradually.* There are tons of atoms that are borderline parts of the pepper. And, of course, it's not just the pepper that's like this. Pretty much every macroscopic material object, including human bodies and body parts, is like this. That's what I mean by saying that the material world is fuzzy.

Next, what I mean by saying that the material world is in flux is that at least at the level of macroscopic material objects, and especially *living* material objects, things are regularly gaining and losing parts. Or at least that's how we'd ordinarily describe matters. I will later argue that as a matter of fact nothing *can* gain or lose parts, in which case we'll need to state the point somewhat more delicately. But the scientific facts are uncontroversial. Things like chili peppers are, at any given time, made of tiny particles, very many of which will soon fly off—and then soon thereafter will no longer be near any chili pepper at all—and very many other tiny particles will soon "take their place." The apparent stability of a chili pepper sitting on a vine is illusory, since it's involved in a regular exchange of tiny parts with its environment. And, of course, it's not just the pepper that's like this. Pretty much every macroscopic material object, including human bodies and body parts, is like this. That's what I mean by saying that the material world is in flux.

The two arguments I'm going to develop share this in common: they trade on features of the material world that make it metaphysically inhospitable to us. Those features are its fuzziness and that it's in flux.

2.9   The Argument from Fuzziness

The fuzziness of the material world creates a mismatch between us and that world, since we're *not* fuzzy. There's no place in a fuzzy world for me or you. Or, there are too *many* places for me and you. Either way, there are the wrong number of places.

To see what I mean, let's revisit Goofy. Remember, "Goofy" was my name for your favorite material candidate for being me: as it turned out, or as I stipulated, that was "the human animal sitting in my chair." But the phrase, "the human animal sitting in my chair," like the phrase "the President of the United States," refers to some *thing* only if there's *exactly one* thing to which it refers. That is, only if there's exactly one animal sitting in my chair. But the fuzziness of the material world strongly suggests, as we'll explain shortly, that there's more than one. And if there is more than one human animal sitting in my chair, then the materialist is going to have to be more specific as to which one I am—as you'll see that's just going to be the beginning of the materialist's troubles. If, on the other hand, the fuzziness of the material world can be made compatible with there being exactly one human animal sitting in my chair, that animal is going to be such a peculiar thing that it couldn't possibly be me.

So now: How many human animals *are* sitting in my chair? That depends on what there is in my chair, and what it takes to be a human animal. Let's agree that in my chair right now are a huge number of atoms that are arranged in the shape of a human animal. But if *I* am a human animal—as we are now materialistically assuming—then in addition to all these atoms, there is also in my chair a much larger thing, *me*, that is itself human shaped—and, in fact, is a human animal. What's the relationship between me and the huge number of atoms that are arranged human-wise? Presumably, we don't just happen to be in the same place at the same time. Rather, the atoms—or some specific collection of them—are all *parts* of me. Indeed, they presumably collectively make up or **compose** me. That is to say, not only is each of them part of me but also every part of me overlaps, or shares some part, with at least one of them. They together "cover" me.

Now let's assume that (if materialism is true, then) there is some *precise collection* of atoms that together compose me: that is, let's assume for now that there is some collection of atoms such that every atom in the collection is *definitely* a part of me, any atom not in the collection is *definitely not* a part of me, and (if this doesn't follow from what we've already said) every part of me overlaps at least one of the atoms in the collection. (We'll see soon whether the materialist can avoid the impending challenges by dropping this assumption.) For reasons that will presently become clear, let's call this collection of atoms the "$Goofy_1$-atoms," and the human animal they compose—which, of course, according to the materialist, is *me*—"$Goofy_1$." There's no vagueness at all about $Goofy_1$'s atomic parts—about which atoms are parts of $Goofy_1$ and which aren't—it's all and only the $Goofy_1$-atoms.

If $Goofy_1$ is indeed a human animal, and if the material world is fuzzy (in the way that I've described it), then we seem to be forced to accept the following conclusion: there are, *alongside $Goofy_1$, a huge number of other human animals sitting in my chair*. For example, consider the $Goofy_2$-atoms. This collection of atoms is nearly identical with the $Goofy_1$-atoms with but two exceptions: one of the atoms at the "edge" of $Goofy_1$'s left ear, and which is part of $Goofy_1$ (so it's one of the $Goofy_1$-atoms), is *not* a member of the $Goofy_2$-atoms, and one of the atoms at the "edge" of $Goofy_1$'s right ear, and which is *not* part of $Goofy_1$ (it lies just beyond $Goofy_1$'s boundaries), is a member of the Goofy$_2$-atoms. Let's stipulate that the pair of differentiating atoms are of the same type. There are enough such atoms to go around that this stipulation shouldn't be problematic.

But now given the fuzziness of the material world—i.e. given that the stuff at Goofy$_1$'s boundary tapers off gradually—there is no relevant difference between the Goofy$_1$-atoms and the Goofy$_2$-atoms with respect to whether they should compose a human animal. *There's no sharp cutoff around just the* Goofy$_1$-*atoms that make them more prone to composing a human animal than the* Goofy$_2$-*atoms.* There are exactly as many Goofy$_1$-atoms as there are Goofy$_2$-atoms, and they're exactly the same kinds of atoms. So if the Goofy$_1$-atoms compose something, and that something is a human animal, then it seems ineluctable that the Goofy$_2$-atoms also compose something, and that that something is a human animal. For obvious reasons, its name is "Goofy$_2$."

So there you have it, alongside and almost entirely overlapping Goofy$_1$, there is *another* human animal, Goofy$_2$. It has to be *another* animal, one distinct from Goofy$_1$, because it has different parts. But then, it's not hard to see that there are vastly many *other* collections of atoms that differ from the Goofy$_1$-atoms to exactly the same extent as do the Goofy$_2$-atoms, and that each of these collections composes a human animal all its own. So we end up with vastly many human animals sitting in my chair. The phrase, "the human animal sitting in my chair," turns out not to refer to anything in particular—or to somehow refer indiscriminately to many things—since there are far more than one human animal sitting in my chair! The materialist needs to specify more exactly which of the many human animals in my chair is me: thus, she has specified that it's Goofy$_1$, and not, say, Goofy$_2$. (Figure 2.1, a drawing by Georges Seurat reproduced here in black and white, should help you visualize the fuzziness in Goofy's situation, and the many different candidates for being Goofy.)

Before we go on to discuss just how disastrous this all is for the materialist, I should clear up a possible confusion that might have set in a few paragraphs back. Didn't I say, you might be asking yourself, that it's a consequence of the fuzziness of the pepper that regarding a huge number of atoms at the "edges" there's just no definite answer ("Yes" or "No") as to whether it's a part of the pepper? So how can I *now* be assuming, when it comes to the vast number of human animals sitting in my chair (Goofy$_1$, Goofy$_2$, etc.), that each is composed of some *precise collection* of atoms? Are animals different from peppers? The answer should now be easy to understand: No, animals

Figure 2.1 Georges Seurat (French, 1859–1891), *Madame Seurat, the Artist's Mother (Madame Seurat, mère)*, about 1882–1883, The J. Paul Getty Museum, Los Angeles, 2002.51.

are no different from peppers in this regard, and that's exactly the point. Just as there's no such thing as *the* human animal sitting in my chair, there's no such thing as *the* pepper. The term, "the pepper," is a **vague term**. Where we thought there was just one pepper, there are in fact vastly many massively overlapping peppers, each of which is composed of some precise collection of atoms. There are vastly many candidates for being the referent of "the pepper," and a huge number of atoms at the edges are parts of some of those candidates but not others. So the reason there's no definite answer as to whether those atoms are parts of "the pepper" is that there's no definite answer as to which pepper is *the* pepper—we haven't taken the time to settle which pepper exactly we're referring to, because for all practical purposes, it doesn't matter—not because there is some specific pepper and some specific atom such that there's no definite answer as to whether the latter is part of the former. Or, at least so we are assuming for now.

Now to the disaster for the materialist. I don't think the mere fact that there are vastly many human animals sitting in my chair is a big deal. Again, for all practical purposes, it doesn't matter how many human animals there are in my chair. *Unless, that is, human animals are themselves conscious.* As I've emphasized a number of times, *I* am conscious: I have thoughts, feelings, sensations, and so on. There's some *way it's like to be me*. So if I *am* Goofy$_1$, as we're assuming the materialist maintains, then Goofy$_1$ is conscious. (Remember **Leibniz's Law**.) But, as we've just seen, there are in fact vastly many human animals that almost entirely overlap Goofy$_1$, sitting in my chair. And just as there's nothing to distinguish Goofy$_1$ from Goofy$_2$ with regard to whether it's a human animal—if one is a human animal then the other is—there is nothing to distinguish Goofy$_1$ from Goofy$_2$, or from the vastly many other human animals sitting in my chair, with regard to *whether it's conscious*. If Goofy$_1$ is conscious, then they all are. It's highly implausible that the exchange of one atom, for another atom just like it, could be the difference between having a rich inner life and being "lights out" inside. It's even more implausible that *of the vastly many* human animals who differ from Goofy$_1$ to just the extent that Goofy$_2$ does, *only a handful of them* are conscious.

The upshot: if the materialist is right, *then there are vastly many conscious beings in my chair*. That consequence is evidently false. Perhaps there's nothing incredible about there being very many "computers"—beings, like myself, who can perform *computations*—in my chair, just as there's nothing incredible about it turning out that there are very many computers on my desk. That's just a matter of which tasks and functions a thing can perform. But *conscious beings* are a whole other ball of wax. It's not at all credible that right now in my chair there are very many *distinct people*, each of whom has feelings, experiences, and sensations. So materialism is false.

Let's put the Argument from Fuzziness in premise-conclusion form:

1) If I am a human animal, then I am identical with Goofy$_1$: a being composed of a precise collection of atoms, the Goofy$_1$-atoms
2) If I am identical with Goofy$_1$, then I am conscious if and only if Goofy$_1$ is conscious
3) I am conscious

(Intermediate Conclusion 1) If I am a human animal, then Goofy$_1$ is conscious
4) If Goofy$_1$ is conscious, then so are vastly many other beings that massively overlap with Goofy$_1$ (and so are in my chair)

(Intermediate Conclusion 2) If I am a human animal, then there are vastly many conscious beings that massively overlap with Goofy$_1$ (and so are in my chair)

But,

5) It's not the case that there are vastly many conscious beings in my chair
Therefore,
6) I am not a human animal

Like the argument in §2.9, this one too is valid. There's no way for its five premises to be true but its conclusion false.
And it too is formally valid. It has the following form:

1) If p, then q
2) If q, then r if and only if s
3) r
4) If s, then t
But,
5) It's not the case that t
Therefore,
6) It's not the case that p

Take any five declarative sentences, plug one of them in for "p," another one in for "q," and so on. The conclusion of the resulting argument will follow ineluctably from the premises.

Of course, *a human animal* is just one possible material candidate for being me. It was supposed to be your favorite. You might object that it was never really your favorite or is no longer your favorite. Maybe you'd rather identify me with a human *brain*. Or a human *nervous system*. It doesn't matter. Every plausible material candidate for being identical with me, such as a brain or a nervous system, suffers from the same "fuzzy boundary problem." Identifying me with any of them will still have the consequence that there are vastly many conscious beings in my chair. (Remember, my claim is only about the plausible material candidates *in worlds relevantly like ours*. It might well be possible for there to have been macroscopic, highly complex material objects that have neat and clean boundaries, which are conscious and sit all by themselves in their chairs. But we need to find a plausible candidate for being me in *our world*—which is fuzzy—since that is, after all, where *I* am.)

Indeed, every *implausible* candidate has the same consequence! The philosopher, Roderick Chisholm (1978), once toyed with the idea that he was identical with a single material particle, perhaps lodged deep inside his brain. This has some awkward consequences:

it would make him much older than we had thought, and it would be strange that he has no recollection of ever floating around outside a human brain. Worse still, it wouldn't actually address the crux of our present difficulty. (Not that Chisholm suggested otherwise; he was contending with the fact that the material world is in flux, not the fact that it's fuzzy.) An atom might not have fuzzy boundaries, but now we have an even more straightforward reason to think there's vastly many conscious beings in my chair: there are, after all, vastly many atoms (and vastly many of each element represented in the human body) in my chair, with nothing to make one more fitting to be conscious than any other.

So if you accept the five premises, you don't have much of a choice but to reject materialism. I take it (2) and (3) are entirely uncontroversial. Premise (2) follows from the unexceptionable Leibniz's Law (as long as there is a property of being conscious). And if you're running this argument "on yourself," you better not deny (3). There are really only three controversial claims in this argument—captured in premises (1), (4), and (5). What follows are defenses of each, starting with premise (4).

> The Argument from Fuzziness starts by assuming that if you're a material object, then you're made of some definite collection of parts. But then given the fuzziness of the material world, there are countless other objects in your chair, each also made of some definite collection of parts, that are just like you in every possible way that could matter for whether a thing is conscious: if you're conscious, then so is each of them. But you are conscious. So if we accept that you're a material object, we'll also have to accept that there are countless other conscious beings in your chair. But that's absurd, and we shouldn't accept it. Instead, we should deny that we're material objects.

2.10   What Goes for One Goofy Goes for All

At the heart of the Argument from Fuzziness is the idea that since Goofy$_1$ and Goofy$_2$ (and a host of other animals in the chair) are so similar—differing only in the identity of the single atom that distinguishes between them—then if the former is conscious, then it stands to reason that the latter is as well. This is the essence of premise (4). I've already spoken in its favor, and now I want to respond to an objection to it. Some materialists might object with the following speech[3]:

Consider a house: say, your house, sitting in your yard. Pretend for the moment that the house has perfectly neat and clean boundaries, even at the atomic level. Still, we might suppose there are more houses in your yard than we thought, for the following, simpler reason.

What does it take to be a house? Presumably, it's a combination of being able to function in a certain way (a house of cards isn't actually a house) and being shaped a certain way (a car is not a house even though you can, and some people do, live in it). But we don't expect perfection in either regard. Even a house with a missing window is a house.

Aha! Then wouldn't the part of your fully intact house that is "the-house-minus-the-window-upstairs" *itself* be a house? You'd have at least two houses in your yard, one a very large part of the other (one has the upstairs window as a part, one doesn't). And you can see that continuing this line of thought will land us in an abundance of houses in your yard, and mine too.

But even *you*—who just presented the Argument from Fuzziness—didn't think to raise *this* issue. You got riled up only by the *fuzziness* of such things as houses and peppers. So, you must be thinking something like this. Being a house is a **border-sensitive property**: having it isn't just a matter of its bearer's *function and shape*, but also a matter of what *its bearer's surroundings* are like, and in particular a matter of what's going on *at its border*. Something can be disqualified from being a house because of what it's attached to. In particular, a house-shaped domicile still won't be a house if, say, it's a very large part of some other object that's also a house-shaped domicile. That's why the-house-minus-the-window-upstairs doesn't count as a house.

I'm going to interrupt to note that the hypothetical materialist delivering this speech is neglecting an alternative explanation for what I might be thinking, namely, that there simply is no object that is the-house-minus-the-window-upstairs, that although the collection of atoms that are arranged in the shape of my house do compose something (a house), the collection of all of those atoms *except for the "window atoms"* don't compose anything at all. But since this speech was directed at me, the hypothetical materialist was right to neglect the alternative explanation. As far as I'm concerned, if there are any houses at all, then any collection of atoms whatsoever composes something.

On top of that, the alternative explanation seems to just push the question back one step. Presumably, the reason one of the collections composes something and the other doesn't is that the one would compose a house (if it composed anything at all) and the other would compose a rather more bizarre object, a house-minus-a-window and not a house. But that's just what we're trying to explain: why wouldn't the house-minus-a-window also be a house? So let's allow the speech to continue.

Well, being conscious is also like that. It's a border-sensitive property, and so *by its very nature* it cannot be possessed by anything that so massively overlaps *another* conscious being that they nearly share a boundary. Thus, although there are vastly many animals that almost entirely overlap and are relevantly similar to Goofy$_1$, it's not true that Goofy$_1$ is conscious just in case all of the other animals are. To the contrary: Goofy$_1$ is conscious just in case all of the other animals *aren't*. So I have no reason to accept premise (4).

I was nodding along with this speech until the final paragraph. I am happy to grant that being a house is border sensitive. And I would even grant that *if* being conscious were like *that*, then there'd be no reason to accept premise (4), and there would even be reason to deny it. But I don't think it's even remotely plausible that being conscious is border sensitive. I don't think it's in any way a matter of how its bearer's surroundings are. (At least not *constitutively*: maybe as a matter of contingent fact, nothing can be consciously aware for too long unless it's supported by a steady stream of nutrients. But that's no part of what it is to *say* that someone is conscious.)

To make this more precise, let's bring to the fore a helpful distinction I mentioned earlier in passing, the distinction between intrinsic and extrinsic properties.

Extrinsic properties, like being an uncle, are possessed at least partly in virtue of how something other than its bearer (and its bearer's parts) is.

Intrinsic properties, like being spherical, aren't.

Intrinsic properties never differ between possible duplicates; extrinsic properties sometimes do.

It strikes me as downright obvious that:

Intrinsicality of Consciousness: The property of being conscious is intrinsic

Indeed, I cannot think of a clearer instance of a non-trivial intrinsic property than the property, being conscious. [Size and shape are generally thought to be some of the clearest instances of non-trivial intrinsic properties. I just assumed as much when I gave the example of being spherical. But I have my doubts about the intrinsicality of size (Segal 2016), and Skow (2007) has cast doubt on the intrinsicality of shape.] After all, that property says of a thing *that there's some way it's like to be that thing*. If God were to instruct Gabriel to duplicate me, and Gabriel created a being that was very much like me but for the fact that it was "lights out" for him—such that there was nothing it was like to be him—then I would think Gabriel would have failed miserably. Sure, that being might have *appeared* to the rest of the world to be a duplicate of me. But it wouldn't *be* a duplicate of me (Hawthorne 2004). Indeed, it wouldn't be anything close to a duplicate of me. Again, being able to perform computations, or some other mental function, might turn out to be extrinsic. But having an "inner life" is a whole other ball of wax.

The intrinsicality of consciousness is a bedrock datum for me. Whether a thing is conscious or unconscious can't be a matter of how it relates to other things, in the way that being an uncle is. A thing can't fail to be conscious just in virtue of having the wrong neighbors or relatives. As it turns out, even the real-life philosopher upon whose views the above speech was modeled agrees in spirit, if not in letter, with this bedrock datum. For Sider (2003) concedes that there is another feature in the nearby vicinity of being conscious, the feature of being conscious*, which *is* intrinsic. And being conscious* is, even by his lights, what makes for the difference between a rich inner life and having the inner life of a doorknob. In effect, being conscious is just a matter of having the feature of being conscious* together with satisfying the "no neighbor" condition. So what distinguishes Sider from me (in this regard) is just the meaning of "being conscious"—I think it picks out the intrinsic feature whose existence we both agree about, while he thinks it picks out the combination of *that* feature with satisfying the "no neighbor" condition. But this semantic dispute is a mere distraction from my argument for immaterialism. I can grant Sider the semantic claim and then just reformulate the entire argument in terms of being conscious*, as opposed to being conscious. That is, I can simply replace all occurrences of "conscious" with "conscious*."

Consider it done. (Relabel the steps of the argument (1*) through (6*).) Now (4*) is secure. The only premise that might have been made less plausible by the reformulation is (5*), which now says "It's not the case that there are vastly many conscious* beings in my chair." You might ask: Is this as plausible as the original (5), which said "It's not the case that there are vastly many conscious beings in my chair"? Do we have firm opinions about consciousness*, in the way we do about consciousness? Well, it's good you raised the issue, since in any case I wanted to add a defense of premise (5)/(5*), and this is a perfect opportunity.

> A materialist might challenge premise (4) by suggesting that being conscious is relevantly like being a house. Both properties, by their very nature, impose certain conditions on what's going on at the border of the objects that have them. Just as it's conceptually impossible for my house and my-house-minus-the-window-upstairs to be houses, it's conceptually impossible for both Goofy$_1$ and Goofy$_2$ to be conscious.

But this is a bad analogy. Being conscious isn't at all like being a house. Being a house is highly extrinsic; being conscious is intrinsic. Saying of someone that there's something it's like to be her is clearly to say something about *her*, not about who or what she's connected to.

2.11 Who Says There Aren't Vastly Many Conscious Beings in My Chair?

My reason to begin with for thinking (5) was true was *not* that it was a conceptual truth, that its denial was *incoherent*, in the way that it is perhaps incoherent, if being a house is border sensitive, for there to be vastly many massively overlapping houses in my yard. Nor did my reason for thinking it true have anything to do with what we'd be willing to *say*; in particular, my reason was *not* that we'd be loathe, in the ordinary business of life, to utter such things as "there are vastly many conscious beings in my chair." To rely on the former would be dialectically unwise, as we've seen, because it would undermine my justification for premise (4). To rely on the latter would be to lean in our metaphysical inquiries far too heavily for my taste on what we are and are not prepared to *say* in our unreflective moods. My reason is rather that the denial of (5) is radically at odds with what we assume as a matter of course, whether explicitly or implicitly, in our practical and moral reasoning.

If I'm about to decide whether to go bungee jumping, I might naturally find myself reasoning as follows:

(A) There's a potential for a really exciting thrill; on the other hand, there's also the risk of death or serious injury; but the potentially adverse outcome would directly impact only me (and the ground!), and so at least I have no *ethical* obligations to weigh against the potential benefit (other than whatever ethical obligations I have to myself, and whatever ethical obligations I have to my nearest and dearest who might suffer indirectly as a result of my death or injury); it's nothing at all like deciding to go bungee jumping under the following condition: if I incur death or serious injury, then millions of others will likewise suffer death or serious injury.

Similar things might run through my mind in cases that *do* involve straightforwardly ethical considerations. Suppose I'm contemplating donating a kidney. I might naturally find myself reasoning as follows:

(B) The recipient stands to gain a whole lot; on the other hand, I'll suffer a lot of discomfort, and there's a small chance of death or serious injury, but the discomfort will be suffered only by me, and the potential for death or serious injury would directly impact only me, and so there are no ethical considerations *against* donating to weigh against the ethical considerations in *favor* of donating (other than whatever ethical obligations I have to myself, and whatever ethical obligations I have to my nearest and dearest who might suffer indirectly as a result of my suffering, death, or injury); it's nothing at all like deciding to donate a kidney under the following condition: millions of others will automatically suffer whatever discomfort I do, and in the unlikely event that I incur death or serious injury, then millions of others will likewise suffer death or serious injury.

And while we're talking about donating a kidney: suppose I decide to donate a kidney and I've been told to choose which of two total strangers, both in need of a kidney, will receive it. Here's something I would *never* think to myself (and even if someone raised it as a possibility, I'd reject it as preposterous):

(C) I should like to know which of the two is *fatter*, or better yet, if there's some way of measuring the surface area and thickness of their skin, I should like to know which of them has the thicker skin; all else (age, health, etc.) being equal, I'd like my kidney to go to the one with the thicker skin.

In reasoning in accordance with (A) and (B), and refusing to reason in accordance with (C), I am implicitly assuming the truth of (5), and of (5*) just the same. If there were vastly many conscious beings in my chair, then there most certainly *would* be ethical considerations, vastly many very weighty ones, to weigh against the potential benefit to myself of bungee jumping, and there most certainly *would* be ethical considerations, vastly many very weighty ones, to weigh against the ethical considerations in favor of donating a kidney, and the corpulence or thick skin of the kidney recipient most certainly *would* be an ethically relevant factor.

Deciding to bungee jump in perfectly ordinary circumstances would be *just like* deciding to go bungee jumping under the condition that: if I incur death or serious injury, then millions of other conscious beings will likewise suffer death or serious injury—for all the conscious beings who massively overlap me will share my fate.

Deciding to donate a kidney in perfectly ordinary circumstances would be *just like* deciding to donate a kidney under the condition that: millions of others will automatically suffer whatever discomfort I do—for presumably all the conscious beings who massively overlap me will suffer if I do, and in the unlikely event that I incur death or serious injury, millions of others will likewise suffer death or serious injury—for all the conscious beings who massively overlap me will share my fate.

And if all else between the two candidate kidney recipients were equal, then I certainly *should* take account of how fat or thick-skinned each one is; for donating to the fatter/thicker-skinned one would be a way of saving *more* conscious beings. Presumably, each of these conscious beings has an equally valuable life (we've stipulated that all else is equal). Even if a full-blown consequentialism isn't true, it seems clear that if I am confronted with a choice between saving *n* conscious beings or *m* conscious beings—where *n* is greater than *m*—then as long as all else is equal and no one's rights are being violated, I am duty-bound to save *n* conscious beings (cf. Taurek 1977). In the case I've proposed, all else *is* equal and no one's rights are being violated, so I ought to donate the kidney to the fatter fellow (Simon 2017b).

> Denying (5) gives ethical valence to many courses of action that are ethically neutral; it gives other courses of action the opposite ethical valence of the one they have, and it makes certain factors ethically relevant when they're ethically irrelevant. Mutatis mutandis for denying (5*). Our everyday practical and moral reasoning involves a tacit commitment to (5)/(5*).

2.12   Might I Be Vague?

WARNING! THIS AND THE NEXT SECTION ARE PRETTY TECHNICAL–THEY'RE THE MOST TECHNICAL PART OF THIS CHAPTER. FEEL FREE TO SKIP THEM, ESPECIALLY IF PREMISE (1) ALREADY SEEMS RIGHT TO YOU.

I've completed my defense of all of the premises other than (1). I can provide a defense of premise (1) once we've laid out the alternative to it. It'll turn out, as I argue in the next section, that it doesn't matter for the success of the argument whether my defense of (1) is right or not. But I can't provide a defense of that *either* until we've laid out the alternative.

What *is* the alternative to (1)? If I am a human animal, but I'm not identical with anything composed of a precise collection of atoms, then what? Presumably, I'm still composed of atoms. Again, it's not plausible to think that I'm a human animal, located where there are lots of atoms that are arranged human-wise, but that I'm not made up of any of them. So if (1) is false, it must be because I'm identical with Goofy—of whom we can now speak again—a being composed of an *im*precise collection of atoms. Or, if it's hard to wrap your head around what it means for a collection to be imprecise (it's hard for me to wrap my head around it, too!), we can put the relevant consequence this way: there are atoms that are definitely parts of Goofy, there are atoms that are definitely not parts of Goofy, and there are atoms—like the one that is a member of the Goofy$_1$-atoms but not the Goofy$_2$-atoms, or the one that is a member of the Goofy$_2$-atoms but not the Goofy$_1$-atoms, and all of the "penumbral atoms"—such that they are neither definitely parts of Goofy nor definitely not parts of Goofy. In short, *it's indeterminate whether they're part of Goofy.* What Goofy *is* is a vague matter. He is (i.e. I am, if the materialist is right) what we might call a **vague object**.

> A thing is a **vague object** if there is something that is neither definitely a part of it nor definitely not a part of it.

I take it that if Goofy exists, then so do each of Goofy$_1$, Goofy$_2$, and so on. It would be very surprising if only the vague object existed— a metaphysically peculiar beast—and not the more metaphysically tractable precise objects. Since all of these objects exist, we can ask about the *relationship* between them. What's Goofy's relationship to Goofy$_1$, Goofy$_2$, and so on? Well, Goofy doesn't seem to be definitely identical with Goofy$_1$, for they're not even definitely composed of the same atoms. By the same token, Goofy doesn't seem to be definitely *not* identical with Goofy$_1$, for they're not definitely composed of different atoms. So Goofy is neither definitely identical with Goofy$_1$, nor definitely not identical with Goofy$_1$: *it's indeterminate whether Goofy is identical with Goofy$_1$.* And, of course, by the same token, it's indeterminate whether Goofy is identical with Goofy$_2$. And so on. That is, if Goofy is a vague object, then he is indeterminately identical with each Goofy$_n$. The converse is also true: if Goofy is indeterminately identical with each Goofy$_n$, then Goofy is a vague object. I will therefore treat the claim that Goofy is a vague object as interchangeable with the claim that Goofy is indeterminately identical with each Goofy$_n$ (*pace* Tye 1990, Wilson 2013).

In sum, the alternative to (1) is this:

(1′) If I am a human animal, then I am identical with Goofy, a being of which the following is true:
    (a) It is indeterminate whether Goofy is identical with Goofy$_1$
    (b) It is indeterminate whether Goofy is identical with Goofy$_2$
    (c) ...

Now that the alternative is on the table, we can offer the following defense of (1)[4]: on the one hand, the alternative to (1) requires that there are cases of indeterminate, or vague, identity; on the other hand, **vague identity** leads to incoherence; so, the alternative to (1) is incoherent. By elimination, (1) must be true.

Technically, it's not (1′) that's incoherent; it's what (1′) says is true *if I am a human animal* that's incoherent. But the materialist can hardly fault me for assuming that materialism *doesn't* land us in incoherence.

Here's a more careful way to put my point: either (1) is true or (1′) is true. If (1) is true, then per the argument I've given above, I am not a human animal; if (1′) is true, then per the argument I'm about to give, I am not a human animal, since the conjunction of (1′) and my being a human animal implies something incoherent. So, I am not a human animal, whether or not (1) is true.

Why should I think that vague identity leads to incoherence? This in turn can be answered in two ways. First way: vague identity, at least as it's being countenanced in (1′), requires that there be vagueness *in the world*, and not just in how we *represent* the world.

We get how there could be vagueness regarding whether Bill is bald. The word "bald" isn't perfectly determinate in meaning, since there are a range of equally good candidate meanings for the word "bald" (differing in regard to precisely how many hairs it takes to not be bald), and we've never wasted our time settling on just one of them. If you have zero hairs, you're definitely bald, since there's no good candidate meaning of the word "bald" according to which you can have zero hairs and not be bald. If you have 100,000 hairs, you're definitely not bald, since there's no candidate meaning of the word "bald" according to which you can have 100,000 hairs and still be bald. But there are lots of intermediate cases in which some of the good candidate meanings for "bald" would count the case as bald and some of the good candidate meanings for "bald" would count the case as not bald.

However, "identical with" doesn't seem to be like the word "bald," in this respect. There isn't a range of equally good candidate meanings for "identical with." As a matter of fact, it seems to be as clear and precise a piece of English terminology as there is, with just one candidate meaning. And the name "Goofy$_1$," also has just one candidate meaning: we've specified exactly which atoms compose it. So where does the indeterminacy as to whether Goofy is identical with $Goofy_1$ come from? You might very naturally suggest that it arises from the indeterminacy in the referent of the word "Goofy," in much the same way that there is indeterminacy in the meaning of the word "bald," and in the referent of "the Sahara desert." After all, each of the $Goofy_n$s is an equally good candidate to be the thing referred to by "Goofy," and maybe, I've never wasted my time settling on just one of them. But this can't be what's going on here. Notice that given materialism, I have another way of referring to Goofy. I can just use the first-person pronoun, "I," and thereby cut out any reference to Goofy at all. That is, (1'), the alternative to (1), implies this simpler claim:

(1″) If I am a human animal, then:
    (a) It is indeterminate whether I am identical with $Goofy_1$
    (b) It is indeterminate whether I am identical with $Goofy_2$
    (c) ...

These indeterminacy claims are puzzling indeed. I'm somehow supposed to think that it's indeterminate whether *I* am identical with $Goofy_1$. But the first-person pronoun, as it figures in a thought, is perfectly determinate in meaning. It refers to the thinker of that thought. And each thought has just one thinker. Even if there *were* many thinking animals in my chair, they wouldn't literally share the very same thoughts: no two thinkers literally share a thought. (The many thinking animals might all be thinking the same thing, but that's not to say that there's just one act of thinking that somehow belongs to all of them.) But even setting that aside, the reply now

---

Thinking vs. Speaking

If I went ahead and *uttered* the sentence "I am identical with $Goofy_1$," then since each of the $Goofy_n$s are plausibly making the same utterance—they're producing the very same sequence of air vibrations—then it's reasonable to assume that there are indeed a number of equally good candidates for being the referent of the word "I" that each one utters. That's why I've stuck with the case in which I merely think the thought to myself.

under consideration seeks to limit the number of thinkers in my chair
to one. So then there's only one thinker *there* to be the thinker of my
thought and hence to be the referent of the first-person pronoun in
my thought. So the first-person pronoun, as it figures in my thought,
can only refer to the lone thinker in my chair.

But I've already noted that the words "is identical with" and
"Goofy$_1$" are also perfectly determinate in meaning. So the fact that
it's indeterminate whether I am identical with Goofy$_1$ can't be traced
to any indecision or imprecision in how we represent the situation.
It must be that the indecision or imprecision is in the situation we're
representing. It would be as if the *world* hasn't made up its mind
about where exactly I am and what my exact parts are—a phenomenon sometimes called **ontic vagueness**. And it's far from clear that
that makes any sense.

> **Ontic vagueness** is vagueness that is due neither to our ignorance
> nor to the imprecision of our representations, but to the nature
> of the thing we're representing

That's one way to support the idea that vague identity lands us in
incoherence. A second, very elegant and apparently more general
way goes via Leibniz's Law (Evans 1978). Remember, according to
that law, for any things x and y, if x is identical with y, then for any
feature F, x has F if and only if y has F. Consider now the following feature: being indeterminately identical with Goofy$_1$. According
to (1′), it's indeterminate whether Goofy is identical with Goofy$_1$.
So Goofy has that very feature. But it's *not* indeterminate whether
Goofy$_1$ is identical with Goofy$_1$. That's an instance of a general truth:
for anything whatsoever x, it's definitely the case that x is identical
with x (and so it's not indeterminate). So Goofy$_1$ *lacks* the feature,
being indeterminately identical with Goofy$_1$. But then Leibniz's Law
allows us to infer that it's not the case that Goofy is identical with
Goofy$_1$. Full Stop. And that, conflicts with what (1′) says, i.e. that it's
indeterminate whether that's the case.

Even worse, everything we assumed in this argument is definitely
the case. Leibniz's Law is *definitely true*. If (1′) is true, then it's *definitely the case* that Goofy has the feature, being indeterminately identical with Goofy$_1$. And it's *definitely the case* that Goofy$_1$ lacks that
feature. So we can conclude from this argument that if (1′) is true,
then it's *definitely* not the case that Goofy is identical with Goofy$_1$.
And that consequence of (1′) is plainly inconsistent with what (1′)

itself says. That is, (1′), with its claim of indeterminate identity between Goofy and Goofy$_1$, contradicts itself. The notion of vague identity isn't just metaphysically suspect; it's logically untenable.

> If premise (1) is false, then materialism implies that I am a vague object. If I'm a vague object, then I'm indeterminately identical with certain other (non-vague) objects. But the idea of my being indeterminately identical with another thing is both metaphysically suspect and logically untenable. So the materialist better not deny (1).

2.13   It Won't Help If I'm Vague

I think the defense of (1) that I presented constitutes a strong case in its favor. I acknowledge, however, that the case is not knock-down.[5] But, as it turns out, it *doesn't matter whether the arguments I've adduced against (1′) and in favor of (1) succeed.* Even if vague objects are perfectly upstanding, and perfectly capable of being conscious, that makes no real difference to my argument. I can, with some added modifications, use the same argument, but with (1′) instead of (1).

The reason is that *consciousness isn't vague.* There's no such thing as someone being *kinda, sorta* "lights out." There's either some way it's like to be you, or there isn't. Period. Sometimes we get woozy or lightheaded. But that's not a case in which it's indeterminate *whether* we're conscious. It's perfectly determinate *that* we're conscious when we feel woozy. We feel woozy after all and determinately so. It's the *character* of our experience that's fuzzy, not its *existence.* Likewise, we might sometimes get intoxicated to the point that we're "in and out." But that's not a case in which there's some moment in time at which it's indeterminate whether it's "lights out." Some moments we're "in," and then, it's definitely not "lights out"; some moments we're out, and then, it's definitely "lights out." So here's the bottom line, put in terms of the property, being conscious:

> Consciousness Isn't Vague: For anything x (and any time t, at t) either x definitely has the feature, being conscious, or x definitely lacks the feature, being conscious

Since I am conscious, it's not the case that I'm definitely not conscious, so I am *definitely* conscious (duh, I could have told you that!).

OK, so let's start the argument again, this time using (1') instead of (1) and then replacing "conscious" with "definitely conscious."

(1') If I am a human animal, then I am identical with Goofy, a being of which the following is true:
  (d) It is indeterminate whether Goofy is identical with $Goofy_1$
  (e) It is indeterminate whether Goofy is identical with $Goofy_2$
  (f) ...
(2') If I am identical with Goofy, then I am definitely conscious if and only if Goofy is definitely conscious
(3') I am definitely conscious

First notice that from these three premises, we can infer:

(3.1') If I am a human animal, then Goofy is definitely conscious

Next, notice that from (1') itself, we know a lot about the relationship between Goofy and each of $Goofy_1$, $Goofy_2$, etc. In fact, we know enough to infer from (3.1'), together with the fact that consciousness isn't vague, that:

(3.2') If I am a human animal, then $Goofy_1$ is definitely conscious

Indeed, we know enough to infer from (3.1'), together with the fact that consciousness isn't vague, the stronger claim that:

(3.3') If I am a human animal, then $Goofy_1$ is definitely conscious, **and** $Goofy_2$ is definitely conscious **and** ...

How do these inferences go? What licenses them is a very plausible variation of Leibniz's Law, customized for the case of vagueness. First, a piece of terminology. Let's say that

> "a feature F is determinacy-involving" = F is the feature **being definitely G** or F is the feature **being definitely not G** or F is the feature **being indeterminately G** [for some substitution of a predicate for "G"]

Less formally, a feature that's determinacy-involving is one that, as it were, says something about determinacy, even if what it says is that things are indeterminate. This is as opposed to ordinary features, which say nothing at all about determinacy or indeterminacy.

Features like being indeterminately identical with Bob, or being definitely bald, are determinacy-involving. I want to set these aside, because they're troublesome. Let's call any feature that *isn't* determinacy-involving, "standard." Then, we can put the variation of Leibniz's Law as follows:

> **Leibniz's Law for Indeterminacy:** For any things x and y, if x is (at least) indeterminately identical with y, then for any standard feature F, x definitely has F only if it's not the case that y definitely lacks F.

Think of an example. Take the feature, being bald. That's a standard feature. So, Leibniz's Law for Indeterminacy rules out a case like the following: Bill is definitely bald (he definitely has the feature, being bald), Bob is definitely not bald (he definitely lacks the feature, being bald), and yet it's indeterminate whether Bill and Bob are identical. That certainly seems like the kind of thing that *should* be ruled out. They're *definitely* not identical if what one definitely *is* the other definitely *isn't*.

Notice that Leibniz's Law for Indeterminacy doesn't rule out vague identity as such (the way Leibniz's Law does). It's custom tailored so as *not* to rule it out. (That's why this reply is independent of what I said above about vague identity being incoherent.) What follows according to the revised law from the fact that Goofy$_1$ definitely has the feature, being identical with Goofy$_1$, together with the fact that Goofy is indeterminately identical with Goofy$_1$, is just that it's *not* the case that Goofy *definitely* lacks the feature, being identical with Goofy$_1$. That's as it should be; indeed, that follows from just the fact that Goofy is indeterminately identical with Goofy$_1$. Of course, it doesn't follow from those facts, according to the revised law, that Goofy definitely has the feature, being identical with Goofy$_1$; that's also as it should be or at least as it's intended. And *nothing at all follows*, according to the revised law, from the fact that Goofy definitely has the feature, being indeterminately identical with Goofy$_1$, together with the fact that Goofy is indeterminately identical with Goofy$_1$, since being indeterminately identical with Goofy$_1$ is determinacy-involving and so isn't a standard feature.

But now consider what *does* follow from the revised law. The feature, being conscious, like the feature, being bald, is a standard feature. So from the fact that Goofy definitely has the feature, being conscious, together with the fact that Goofy is indeterminately identical with Goofy$_1$, it follows that it's *not* the case that Goofy$_1$ definitely *lacks* the feature, being conscious. But here's the kicker: given that consciousness isn't vague, it then follows that *Goofy$_1$ definitely* *has the feature*, being conscious. Of course, by the same token, it follows that Goofy$_2$ definitely has the feature, being conscious. And so on. That is, definite consciousness *trickles down* from Goofy to each of the precise candidates with which he's indeterminately identical. The trickle starts by requiring them each to be at least indeterminately conscious (that is, not *definitely not* conscious). But given that consciousness isn't vague, for each one, there's no stable stopping point for them short of being *definitely* conscious.

So, far from *helping* the materialist avoid the woes of the many conscious beings in my chair, the alternative that identifies me with a vague object that is indeterminately identical with each of the precise candidates only exacerbates her woes. For one thing, it allows us to cut out one of the argument's premises. We can just replace (4), which was a *premise*, with (3.3′), which we've *inferred* from (1′) through (3′). We don't need to *assume* anything additional to get the vastly many conscious beings; they come along for free! For another thing, we have as many conscious beings as in the original version, *plus one more*. We have all the precise Goofy$_n$s—who are all definitely distinct from one another, and all definitely conscious—and on top of them, we now have Goofy himself![6]

> Even if premise (1) *is* false, the Argument from Fuzziness will remain essentially unaffected. Even if I'm a vague object, I'm still definitely conscious. But then, each of the things I'm indeterminately identical with is either indeterminately conscious or definitely conscious. But nothing can be indeterminately conscious. So, yet again, each of the vastly many humanoid things in my chair is definitely conscious. It turns out that whether (1) is true or not, the materialist is stuck with far too many (definitely) conscious beings in my chair.

2.14 Argument from Fuzziness: Taking Stock

I've finished my defense of the Argument from Fuzziness. There were a lot of moves with a substantial amount of give-and-take, so let me summarize the main ideas. The materialist has two choices. She can identify me with just one of vastly many human beings in my chair, each composed of a precise collection of atoms, but then she is faced with vastly many conscious beings in my chair. Alternatively, she can identify me with a vague object, which is indeterminately identical with each of the things composed of a precise collection of atoms. But that isn't obviously consistent, and it isn't obviously consistent with the fact that I have the feature of being conscious, and most importantly, given that I *do* have that feature and that that feature cannot be vague, the alternative equally leads to vastly many conscious beings in my chair. So either way there are vastly many conscious beings in my chair. And there being vastly many conscious beings in my chair (and in yours) is morally preposterous: it has me sizing up things I shouldn't be sizing up—like people's waist size and the supposedly enormous ethical price of purely altruistic acts.

2.15   Argument from Flux

The Argument from Fuzziness exploited a *synchronic* mismatch between us and the material world, i.e. a mismatch *at a given time*. The Argument from Flux will exploit a *diachronic* mismatch, i.e. a mismatch that comes to the fore *over a stretch of time*. The mismatch is essentially this.

(1) Each of us persists over time—on average we exist for around 70–80 years (ignoring any afterlife we might have)
     And,
(2) As we persist, we remain fairly "localized" in space—we don't find ourselves at some point in time directly and simultaneously touching objects that are as far apart as New York is from Sydney, say.

    (The alternative to (2) probably seems so ludicrous that it's not clear to you why I'm even bothering to say this. It will soon become clear why.)

But no actual macroscopic material object, no good material candidate for being *one of us*, does both of those things. That is, no such object persists for long stretches of time while remaining fairly localized in space. The reason for that fact about macroscopic material objects is a conjunction of two further facts. One is the "phenomenon of flux" that I described earlier: as I said, pretty much every actual macroscopic material object is involved in a regular exchange of tiny parts with its environment. When it comes to living organisms, this exchange is nearly constant and very thoroughgoing. Focusing specifically on the case most relevant to me:

(3) Within a relatively short period of time, many of the atoms that right now compose Goofy will be scattered throughout Israel; within a somewhat longer period of time, but still much

shorter than 70 years, the overwhelming majority will be scattered throughout the atmosphere; and within a somewhat longer period of time than that, they will form a spherical shell whose diameter far exceeds the distance between New York and Sydney.

Given (3), the only way that Goofy could persist for 70–80 years, all the while remaining fairly localized in space—that is, the only way that (1) and (2) could be true, if I'm identical with Goofy—is if Goofy could be made of different parts at different times. That is, if Goofy himself could be composed of certain atoms right now, but then later be composed of those atoms that spatially and functionally replace the atoms that have flown off. But, the second, metaphysical fact precludes this:

(4) Nothing is composed of different parts at different times.

It follows from (3) and (4) that, *unlike me*, no actual macroscopic material object manages to persist for long stretches of time while remaining fairly localized in space. Any actual macroscopic material object that *does* manage to persist for long stretches of time—if such there be—won't hold its shape (whether that be feline, canine, or humanoid) for very long and will instead spread out throughout the atmosphere.

From our four premises, it follows that I am not identical with Goofy. Of course, Goofy is just one material candidate for being me. But, as with the other arguments we've examined, it won't matter much which material candidate you propose. Every plausible material candidate for being identical with me, such as a brain or a nervous system, suffers from the same "problem of flux." So our four premises imply the falsity of materialism.

I think (4) is really the only contentious thing I've said in this whole section. It shouldn't be very controversial that we exist on this Earth for an average of 70–80 years, and it shouldn't be very controversial that we do so *on* this Earth, not *spread throughout the atmosphere*, and the phenomenon of flux is an uncontroversial empirical fact. But (4) is understandably going to raise eyebrows. In fact, it would be natural to infer its *denial* from all of the uncontroversial things I've pointed to.

That, however, would be a mistake. As we shall see there is a *compelling argument* for (4). And (4) is *consistent* with all of the uncontroversial things I've pointed to. It's just not consistent with all of those things *taken together with materialism*. The moral to draw is that we're immaterial, not that there's some problem with what seems to be an utterly compelling argument.

> The Argument from Flux exploits the fact that while each of us persists and remains relatively localized, no macroscopic material object does that. And the reason no macroscopic material object does that is a combination of two further facts: one, the empirically observed phenomenon of flux and, two, the metaphysical fact that nothing can be composed of different parts at different times. The metaphysical fact is the only piece of the argument that really needs defending. Providing such a defense will be the task of the next section.

2.16 Nothing Can Gain or Lose Parts

There are at least a couple different arguments for (4). One is direct and unified, but it relies on a non-obvious metaphysical principle (van Inwagen 1990: 77–78). A second is indirect and piecemeal but is also more intuitive and can be grasped more easily. I will present the second one.

To understand its overall structure, it'll help to introduce some terms. Say that "x undergoes at t a pure loss of part(s)" means that at t, x loses some part or parts without their being replaced. If God just annihilated Fido's ear at 10 AM—and nothing else happened at that moment to Fido—that would be a clear case of Fido undergoing at 10 AM a pure loss of parts. Likewise, say that "x undergoes at t a pure gain of part(s)" means that at t, x gains some part or parts without losing any of the ones he had beforehand.

The argument I rely on here is indirect and piecemeal in the sense that it consists of "sub-arguments" for the intermediate conclusions that:

> (4.1) Nothing can undergo any pure loss of parts
> (4.2) Nothing can undergo any pure gain of parts

And then, it assumes that if those conclusions are true, then

> (4.3) Nothing can lose and gain parts at the same time

How very strange it would be if there was some *absolute necessity* that precluded pure losses and pure gains but allowed for instantaneous exchanges, as if there were some absolutely necessary laws of conservation of *number* of parts! I assume there is no such law.

From (4.1) to (4.3), it follows that nothing can ever change its parts; from which it follows that nothing ever *does* change its parts; from which (4) would seem to follow.

That's the overall structure. What remains to explain are the sub-arguments for (4.1) and (4.2). But they are perfectly analogous to each other—no one could reasonably reject one but not the other—so I will just provide the argument for (4.1). Indeed, I will provide an argument for just a *particular instance* of (4.1): that is, I will take a specific example in which it might seem that something underwent a pure loss of parts and show that it *couldn't* have undergone a pure loss of parts. Since there's nothing special about the chosen example, it'll be clear that the point holds universally.

Consider this (hopefully fictional) story, involving Goofy. On January 1, 2030, God decides that Goofy needs only nine fingers. Who needs a second ring finger? God only knows. So at 10:30 AM on that New Years' Day, God just *annihilates* Goofy's right ring finger. Boom. Gone, along with all of its constituent atoms. If anything can undergo a pure loss of parts and survive, then Goofy can survive the annihilation of his right ring finger. So let's assume that Goofy *does* survive this divine operation and see where it leads.

Contradiction is where it leads! The trouble is that Goofy can't *become* the thing made of all the rest of the body parts, since there already *was* something, something *else*—call it "Goof"—made of all of the rest of the body parts before the divine operation. And two things can't *become* one thing; for if they are ever one thing, then at that point, they have all the same properties (remember Leibniz's Law!), including the properties that say who they were and will be identical with.

We can put it even more straightforwardly, and without appeal to Leibniz's Law, if we time-stamp various characters in the story.

First character: let "Goofy-at-10" be the name Goofy has at 10 AM. That is, suppose we point at 10 AM to Goofy and say "let that human animal be named 'Goofy-at-10.'"

Second character: let "Goof-at-10" be the name of *the thing that is all of Goofy-at-10 except his right ring finger*. That is, suppose we point at 10 AM in the direction of Goofy and say "let the thing that is now composed of all and only those atoms that are (a) parts of Goofy-at-10 but (b) not parts of Goofy-at-10's right ring finger, be named 'Goof-at-10.'"

Third character: since we're assuming that Goofy survived the divine operation, we can allow ourselves the liberty of referring to the human animal who's standing there at 11 AM as "Goofy-at-11." That is, suppose we point at 11 AM in the direction of the human animal standing there and say "let *that* human animal be named 'Goofy-at-11.'" (The fact that we've used "Goofy" as part of his name is not really to assume that Goofy-at-10 is identical with Goofy-at-11. We'll still need to make that assumption explicit. But it's a natural name to use, given that assumption.)

Fourth character: finally, since nothing at all happened to Goof-at-10—the operation was performed on something attached to Goof-at-10, not to any part of him—we can comfortably assume that Goof-at-10 survived and is right there at the end, made of exactly the same parts as before. So we can allow ourselves the liberty of referring to the human animal who's standing there at 11 AM and who looks just like Goof-at-10, "Goof-at-11." (Again, the fact that we've used "Goof" as part of his name is not really to assume that Goof-at-10 is identical with Goof-at-11. We'll still need to make that assumption explicit. But it's a natural name to use, given that assumption.)

I've written as if there are four characters in this story. But plausibly there are just two: Goofy and Goof. That's because some of the names, like "Goof-at-10" and "Goof-at-11," are names for the same thing. Nothing problematic there. The problem, though, is that *if Goofy survives the divine operation*, then there's just *one character*. And that's not possible; if anything here is clear, it's clear that Goofy-at-10 and Goof-at-10 are different characters. One of them has a right ring finger as a part at 10 AM and one of them doesn't!

Let's put the derivation of a contradiction in premise-conclusion form (here "$x = y$" means "x is identical with y" or "x is one and the same thing as y," and "$x \neq y$" means "x is not identical with y" or "x and y are two things"):

A. Goof-at-10 $\neq$ Goofy-at-10 (they have different parts)
B. Goof-at-10 = Goof-at-11 (nothing happened to Goof)
C. Goof-at-11 = Goofy-at-11 (there's only one human animal standing there at the end)
D. Goofy-at-11 = Goofy-at-10 (supposition that Goofy survives the loss of his finger)
E. Goof-at-10 = Goofy-at-10 (from B, C, D)
F. Contradiction! (A and E)

Step E is justified by the **transitivity of identity** (employed twice): if a = b, and b = c, it follows that a = c. This can in turn be derived from Leibniz's Law. (Hint: consider the property, being an *x* such that *x* = c.) But it need not be. It's perfectly obvious on its own. Given what identity is—the relation of being one and the same thing—it's quite clearly impossible for a to be identical with b, and for b to be identical with c, but for a to fail to be identical with c.

So (A), (B), and (C), and (D) lead to a contradiction. I've already spoken in favor of (A) and (B). In favor of (C)—and as against someone who would claim that there are two human animals there after the operation, made of exactly the same parts and located in exactly the same place—we can make a number of points. First, if not for the difficulty we're now discussing, no one would ever dream of saying that there are two distinct human animals, made of exactly the same parts and located in exactly the same place, every time someone loses a finger. That should give one pause before rejecting (C). Of course, it's probably also true that, if not for the difficulty we're now discussing, no one would ever dream of denying that Goofy can survive the loss of his finger. So this consideration only takes us so far. But in addition, we should note that relying on a denial of (C) *as a way to avoid my conclusion* actually requires you to accept the even more absurd claim that right now in my chair are not just two but *millions* of distinct animals, *made of exactly the same parts and located in exactly the same place*. After all, Goofy has apparently been losing tiny parts on a fairly regular basis. And if that appearance matches the reality, and if you want to maintain the coherence of that possibility by embracing "co-location," then there is going to be *an extra human animal (made of exactly the same parts as Goofy and in the exact same place as Goofy) for every time Goofy lost a part and survived*! Aside from this being perfectly absurd, it also means that the "the problem of very many conscious beings in my chair" is going to be made even worse. Now, having nothing whatsoever to do with the fuzziness of the material world—even if all of Goofy's boundaries were crystal clear—there'd still be very many conscious beings in my chair. For now, there is *no difference at all* between Goofy and all of the other human animals that share exactly the same parts, and so nothing could possibly explain why just Goofy is conscious while the rest aren't. So we best not deny (C).

The only remaining culprit is (D). So we should deny it. That is, we should conclude that Goofy didn't survive the loss of his right ring finger. But if this argument works, it works for everything, not just Goofy; it shows that nothing undergoes a pure loss of parts. And if it works, it shows not just that as a matter of fact nothing undergoes a pure loss of parts, but rather, as (4.1) says, that nothing *can* undergo a pure loss of parts. After all, if instead of focusing on a single example, the premises were turned into universal generalizations about this *sort* of case, then all of the rest of the premises other than (D) would be necessarily true, not just contingently so. So, the suitably generalized (D) couldn't possibly be true. Otherwise, it would be possible for there to be a true contradiction, and that's not possible.

As I said, the argument for (4.2) is exactly parallel. (I leave this as a fun exercise for the reader.) And I will not provide any further defense of (4.3).[7] So that wraps up my argument for (4) and with it my argument against my being identical with some macroscopic material object. Since that's the only kind of object I could plausibly be if I'm a material object at all, I conclude—now on the grounds of flux rather than fuzziness—that I'm not a material object.

> The claim that nothing can be made of different parts at different times might strike you as wholly implausible. Perhaps it is, at first glance. But reflection on what losing and gaining parts would actually involve reveals the exact opposite to be true. The claim that something *could* be made of different parts at different times has the consequence that two things could become one thing or that one thing could become two things. And those consequences aren't just wholly implausible. They're absurd.

2.17   Conclusion

I have considered three arguments against materialism: the Argument from Conceivability, the Argument from Fuzziness, and the Argument from Flux. As I see things, the first one is good but ultimately fails. The second and third arguments are not only good but are also ultimately successful.

My conviction that the latter two arguments succeed is what leads me to accept not just immaterialism but pure immaterialism—the view that we are wholly immaterial (§2.1). For if I have any material parts at all, then presumably I have a *macroscopic* material object, such as a human animal, or a human brain, as a part. (It's not a plausible view that I am composed of an immaterial soul and a single atom; it's probably even less plausible than the view that I am identical with an atom. That's probably why *no one*, not even Chisholm (1978), seriously entertains it.) But this can't be, for the very same reason that I can't be *identical* with any such macroscopic material object. I'd be fuzzy, and I'm not; I'd either be short-lived or soon spread very thin, and I'm neither of those.

It's worth re-emphasizing that it *doesn't* follow from any of the arguments I've considered that any possible being who's like me—with my mental and moral life—would have to be immaterial, let alone wholly immaterial. As far as the arguments I've considered go, there might well be a possible version of me—who thinks and freely decides and has moral worth in just the same way I do—but is a macroscopic material object in a world in which such things have clear boundaries and stable careers. Indeed, there might well be a possible version of me who shares my mental and moral life, who inhabits a world just like ours (with all of its fuzziness and flux) but who is a *microscopic* material object that holds radically mistaken views about his age and past or even a *macroscopic* material object in such a world who holds radically mistaken views about the number of conscious beings in his chair, about what considerations are ethically relevant, and about his lifespan or shape.

However, those are nothing more than skeptical possibilities for *me*. What the arguments I've considered show is this: unless I'm radically mistaken about many fundamental matters, then *I* am no part of the material world. And, of course, there are all the other arguments I mentioned but didn't explore, some of which do attempt to establish that any possible being who's like me, with my mental and moral life, would have to be immaterial (though perhaps not wholly immaterial). But I've already gone on long enough, and the conclusion about *me* (and you) is what interests me anyway.

Notes

1   Swinburne (2019, 30–31) ultimately defines a 'physical property' as one 'which (of logical necessity) always makes an event of a substance having that property an event to which no one substance can have privileged access by experiencing it'. This, as best as I can tell, has the extremely awkward consequence that the property, being immaterial, is itself a physical property.

The most promising alternative is to define 'physical feature' in terms of *physics* or *physical theory* (see Wilson 2006, Ney 2008). But even if this approach manages to overcome the various difficulties it confronts, (a) I think its correctness is best explained by the correctness of the definition I go on to give (via the link: physics deals in completely general laws), and (b) whether or not that's the case, a physics-based definition *also* has the consequence that the feature, being material, says nothing about how the thing is in itself.

2   For some further metaphysical arguments I don't have space to discuss, see Swinburne (2007) (and closely related 2013, 2019), Hawthorne (2007), Zimmerman (2010), Schneider (2012), and Robinson (2016).

3   Part of this speech is modeled on Sider (2003), which is a reply to Merricks (1998).

4   There's another defense, which basically goes as follows (see Zimmerman 2010): On the one hand, the alternative to (1) says that I am a vague object; on the other hand, I have certain features—such as the feature, being conscious—that no vague object could have; so, the alternative to (1) is false. By elimination, (1) must be true.

5   David Lewis (1988) contends, rightly in my view, that Evans' argument succeeds only if its target is the claim that the world itself can be vague (and not just our descriptions of the world). If that's right, there aren't two *independent* arguments against vague identity; instead, the Evans argument shows that *vague identity in the world* isn't just metaphysically suspect, it's logically untenable.

6   Alright, maybe not. It's true that for each of the $Goofy_n$, it's indeterminate whether Goofy is identical with *it*. But maybe it's not indeterminate whether Goofy is identical with *some one of them or other*; it's not as though Goofy might be identical with Mars. Goofy is definitely *one* of them, it's just indeterminate which one. So then we'd end up with exactly the same number of conscious beings as in the original version of the argument. Cold comfort, of course.

7   I should add that (4.1) would be problematic enough for the materialist, even without (4.2) or (4.3). In the actual world, given how the "exchange of parts" actually happens, Goofy won't survive for very long if he can't survive a pure loss of parts. There are plenty of times when there's a time lag, even if only very brief, between when parts 'fly off' of Goofy and when new parts are 'assimilated'.

First Round of Replies

Chapter 3

Fuzzy Edges and Amputations

Eric T. Olson

Contents

3.1 Aaron's Antimaterialist Arguments

Aaron's case for our having a soul is completely unlike the traditional arguments given by the likes of Plato, Descartes, and Leibniz. His thought is that we must be immaterial because the physical world is "metaphysically inhospitable" to us. By this he means that no material thing could have the place in the world that we have. Only an immaterial thing could.

He gives two arguments of this sort. The "fuzziness argument" says that because of our fuzzy edges, there are far too many material things for any of them to be you or me. Any material person would be one of billions and trillions of overlapping people thinking the

DOI: 10.4324/9781003032908-5

same things. Yet that's not how it is with us: there aren't billions and trillions of overlapping people sitting here now and thinking these thoughts. It follows that we're not material things.

The "flux argument" says that because of metabolic turnover, no material thing could have anything like the sort of career or history that you and I have: it could never be first a child and later an adult, for instance. Because each of *us* is first a child and later an adult, it follows once again that we're not material things.

I'll state these arguments in my own way, but my statements are meant to be equivalent to Aaron's. I'll then try to show that although they present real worries for materialism, they're no reason to give it up.

3.2   The Fuzziness Argument

Suppose for the sake of argument that I'm a material thing. I'm made of atoms. A lot of them: more than there are grains of sand in all the earth's deserts and beaches put together. But it's impossible to say exactly which atoms they are. I seem to extend out to my skin. My skin, though, is not a completely sharp boundary: there are atoms that we can't confidently classify either as parts of it, and thus as parts of me, or as not parts. And although sometimes this may be due to ignorance about the precise details and further investigation would resolve the matter, in many cases there seems to be just no saying.

Aaron assumes that if I'm made of atoms, there must be a precise collection of them composing me at each moment. We may not always be able to know whether a given atom is a part of me, but the question always has a definite answer, knowable or not: every atom in the universe is now either a part of me or not a part. I'll examine this assumption in due course, but let's accept it for the time being.

Now take an atom that's a part of me even though we can't be sure that it is, and consider all my current atoms *except* that one. Aaron says these atoms make up a material thing of their own. And although that thing is indistinguishable from me for all practical purposes, it's not me: it's smaller by one atom. Now consider all the atoms that are parts of me together with one that's *not* a part, even though, again, we can't tell that it's not. They too compose a material thing, one very slightly bigger than me. That gives us three different things: me, a thing that's an atom smaller than me, and a thing that's an atom bigger.

You can see where this is going: for *every* atom that's a part of me but not obviously a part, there's a thing just like me only without it, and for every atom that's not a part of me but not obviously so, there's a thing just like me only including it. What looks like just one philosopher is really a great horde of them—at least as many as there are atoms that we can't classify either as parts or me or as non-parts—differing by just one atom on the surface of their skin.

These beings all share the same sense organs and nervous system. Nothing could make just one of them conscious and intelligent and the others not: simply having one peripheral atom more or less, Aaron says, can't make the difference between having a mental life and not having one. So given that *I* have a mental life, they too must each have a mental life like mine. They think my thoughts, enjoy my pleasures, and suffer my pains. This will be the case no matter what material thing I am: even if I don't extend all the way to my skin but am really only a brain, there will still be trillions of atoms that no one could confidently count either as parts of me or as not parts.

So my being a material thing, Aaron says, implies that there are a vast number of philosophers sitting here writing. But there aren't: there's only me. I must therefore be an immaterial thing. That would avoid the problem: because an immaterial soul has no parts or fuzzy edges, it doesn't overlap with a vast number of thinking beings just like it only larger or smaller by only one tiny peripheral part. My being the only philosopher here requires me to be immaterial.

We could summarize the argument like this:

1. If I'm a material thing, there is a precise collection of atoms that now compose me.
2. Whatever atoms now compose me, there are many other precise collections, differing from mine by just one peripheral atom, that each compose a different thing.
3. Anything that now differs from me by just one peripheral atom is now thinking my thoughts. So,
4. If I'm a material thing, there are many different things now thinking my thoughts (from 1, 2, and 3).
5. There is only one thing now thinking my thoughts. So,
6. I'm not a material thing (from 4 and 5).

And the same, of course, goes for the rest of us.

This means that we must be *entirely* immaterial. If I had both a soul and a body as parts, there would be a vast number of philosophers here, each made up of my soul and one of the candidates, so to speak, for being my body. The only way to avoid this conclusion (given the argument's premises) is to deny that I have any material parts at all.

> The fuzziness argument says that any material person would be one of a great horde of people, each differing from the others by only a single atom. Being physically so similar, they would all think exactly alike. Yet each of us is not one of a great horde of people all thinking exactly alike. It follows that we must be immaterial.

3.3   The Atomic Composition Principle

That's the fuzziness argument. Its premises are 1, 2, 3, and 5. Let's look first at 1. It says that if I'm a material thing, I must have sharp boundaries: I must be made of a precise collection of atoms. Why is that? Didn't we begin with the thought that complex material things *don't* have sharp boundaries? Call a thing with sharp boundaries a *precise object*. A thing is a precise object if everything is (at a given time) either definitely a part of it or definitely not a part of it. And call a thing without sharp boundaries a *vague object*: some things are neither definitely parts of it nor definitely not parts. 1 says that I must be a sharp object. Why could I not instead be a vague object?

Aaron says this wouldn't solve the problem (§2.13): even if *I* were vague, there would still be many precise objects now thinking my thoughts. Why is that? Well, my being vague would mean that although certain atoms are definitely parts of me—call them *the definite atoms*—others are not definitely parts of but not definitely not parts either. They're borderline cases of parts. Call them *the borderline atoms*. So I'm "sort of" made up of just the definite atoms, but I'm also sort of made up of the definite atoms together with the borderline atoms.

But then, Aaron says, there will be a precise object definitely made up of the definite atoms together with all but one of the borderline atoms. (What I called the borderline atoms are only borderline parts of *me*. They're definitely parts of this precise object.) There will be another precise object definitely made up of all the definite atoms together with all but some other of the borderline atoms. And for every borderline atom, there will be a precise object made up of the definite atoms and all the borderline atoms except that one.

As Aaron notes, the relation between these precise objects and me will be messy. None of them *definitely* has different parts from me: every atom belonging to one of them is at least to some degree a part of me too, and every atom that's definitely mine is a part of each of them. So perhaps none of them is definitely different from me, even if none is definitely the same as me either. But the important point is that each of them is definitely different from the others, as they're all definitely made of different atoms.

Because each of these precise objects differs from me by at most a single borderline atom, they're all mentally just like me. As before, what looks like just one philosopher is really a great horde of them. Aaron concludes that we can't avoid that repugnant consequence just by denying premise 1 and taking me to be a vague object: that only makes the problem more complicated.

This reasoning makes an important assumption: that a vague object with fuzzy edges would have to overlap with a lot of precise objects. For any atoms that are borderline parts of me, there must be a precise object made up of those atoms together with those that are definitely parts of me. More generally, Aaron seems to be assuming that *any* atoms, no matter what their nature or arrangement, must always make up a precise object. Call this the *atomic composition principle*:

The atomic composition principle
For any atoms, there is an object such that each of those atoms is definitely a part of it and every other atom is definitely not a part of it.

(A more precise statement is given in the Glossary.) That's how we got all those precise philosophers, each composed of all my atoms (or of all the atoms that aren't definitely not mine) minus one on my periphery. Without this principle there would be no apparent reason to suppose that all my atoms plus or minus one make up anything at all. And if they don't, there may be only one philosopher here, just as it seems. (I'll return to this thought in §3.6). So the fuzziness argument stands or falls with the atomic composition principle.

The central premise of the fuzziness argument is that for any collection of atoms, there is a material thing made up of exactly those atoms: the atomic composition principle. This is what generates the vast number of beings just like me only bigger or smaller by a single atom.

3.4 The Neat-and-Tidy Picture

Let's examine the atomic composition principle more closely. Aaron doesn't explicitly argue for it; he expects us to find it obvious. And many others, materialists included, accept it too. It's part of a certain metaphysical picture of the material world. Let me try to sketch this picture.[1]

Think of the Great Plains. We know that it extends from the Mississippi River to the Rocky Mountains. (Ignore its northern and southern boundaries.) But where is it *exactly*? Which stones along the western bank of the Mississippi belong to it, and which ones belong to its surroundings? And where is the line dividing the mountains from the plains? These questions seem to have no answers. If a crew of surveyors were to draw a precise boundary around the Great Plains, they would have to make a lot of arbitrary decisions. If another crew were to carry out the same task independently, there's no chance that the two boundaries would be the same.

Is this because the Great Plains is a fuzzy region having *no* precise boundary? In that case both crews would have got it wrong, as they would both have drawn a sharp line. Yet it seems that both might have done their job perfectly. There are simply many different but equally good answers to the question, "Where do the Great Plains begin?" That's not to say that just any boundary would be correct: it would be wrong to put Baltimore inside the Great Plains or Omaha outside it. There are plenty of incorrect boundaries. But there's no uniquely correct one.

Now a single region can't have two different boundaries: it can't both include and not include a certain stone, for example. So it seems that each correct boundary around the Great Plains must correspond to a different region that is, so to speak, a candidate for being the Great Plains. All these candidates satisfy the description "the area between the Mississippi and the Rockies." Our use of the name "the Great Plains" simply doesn't distinguish them. The reason we can't say exactly where the Great Plains begin is that we haven't bothered to choose among the candidates: we haven't attached the name to a single precise region. And it would be pointless to do so, because it makes no practical difference which region we choose, as long as it stretches roughly from the Mississippi to the Rockies. (And the terms "the Mississippi" and "the Rockies" are imprecise in the same way.) Our talk of the Great Plains refers ambiguously to many different regions, and each of our imaginary survey crews has done its job correctly by drawing the boundary of one of them. So the Great Plains doesn't really have fuzzy edges. It appears to only because many different things with sharp edges are equally good candidates for being the Great Plains.

That's the picture behind the atomic composition principle. Aaron applies this picture to the physical world generally. What looks like a single material thing with fuzzy edges, he says, is really a vast number of precise objects differing very slightly in their peripheral atoms. For every correct way of drawing a sharp boundary around a complex material thing, there's a thing having that boundary. So the reason we're unable to say exactly where my boundary (or that of my body) lies is that we haven't bothered to attach the term "Eric" (or "Eric's body") to just one precise object. We use it to refer ambiguously to many overlapping objects, just as we do with the term "the Great Plains."

This means that vagueness is not "out there in the world", but only in our language. The objects themselves are completely sharp, and our inability to describe them precisely—to say exactly which atoms make them up—is due only to the loose connection between those objects and the words we use to talk about them.

This picture sees the world as metaphysically neat and tidy. Everything in it has a sharp boundary. But it's also rather crowded: that's why combining it with materialism leads to the conclusion that there are billions and trillions of philosophers sitting here and writing this. We might call that combination **crowded materialism**—as opposed to Aaron's "crowded immaterialism."

> The atomic composition principle is part of a metaphysically neat and tidy picture, according to which all material things have precise boundaries. If we can't say exactly where the Great Plains begin and end, it's because there are a vast number of equally good candidates for being the Great Plains and we haven't attached that name to just one of them. Vagueness lies not in the world, but in our description of it. This is the picture behind the fuzziness argument.

3.5   Crowded Materialism

Aaron thinks crowded materialism gives us too many people. If that's what follows from our being material things, he says, we can only conclude that we're immaterial. But no one can maintain this fastidious attitude across the board. If brooms and hats were material things, it would follow by the same reasoning that there were too many of them as well. Yet Aaron doesn't take brooms and hats to be immaterial. Why does the fuzziness argument work for you and me but not for hats?

Presumably he's willing to tolerate a surfeit of *ordinary* material things. If we ask how many chairs there are in my office, for example, he'll say there are two ways of answering. The "strict and pedantic" answer is billions and trillions. But what we usually want to know in asking the question is how many *nonoverlapping* chairs I've got, to which the answer is four.

When chairs share nearly all their atoms, the thought goes, we count them as one. There are four chairs in my office in that there are at least four (in the strict and pedantic sense), and every other chair in my office shares most of its atoms with one of those four. It's this "loose and ordinary" number of chairs, not the strict and pedantic number, that's of interest to the estates and facilities management department of my university. In fact it's the number we care about for every purpose apart from the metaphysics of material things. So whatever the strict and pedantic number of chairs may be, in the ordinary sense that matters there are just four.

Aaron is happy to say this about chairs, but not about ourselves: he insists that there really is, in the strict and pedantic sense, just one philosopher here. Why the difference? It's not as if we can *see* that there's just one philosopher. Everything would appear just the same if there were billions and trillions, sharing all but a few atoms. It would seem to each of them as if he were the only one. A large number of *nonoverlapping* philosophers crammed into my office would of course look different, but no one can distinguish between one philosopher and a trillion overlapping ones: as with chairs, we can detect only the loose and ordinary number. How do we know, then, that the strict and pedantic number of philosophers here is any less than the strict and pedantic number of chairs?

Here Aaron appeals to practical and moral judgments. When he goes bungee jumping on Sundays, he risks his own neck but no one else's. Yet crowded materialism would mean that breaking his neck would break the necks of billions and trillions of other philosophers. But surely, he says, in deciding whether bungee jumping is a good idea, he need only consider himself (and his family and a few other close associates), not billions and trillions of others.

Likewise, crowded materialism implies that if I donate a kidney, the number of people who benefit will depend on the physical size of the recipient: if I give it to a big man of 180 kg, I'll benefit far more people (in the strict and pedantic sense) than if I give it to a small man of 60 kg. And the more people our actions benefit, other things being equal, the better. So large people ought to be first in line for organ transplants. But your size is obviously irrelevant to whether you ought to be given a transplant. Aaron infers from this that only one person risks his neck when he makes his Sunday jump, and only one would get my donated kidney. What seems like just one person really is just one.

But however sensible this may sound, it assumes that these judgments are based on the strict and pedantic number of people and not the loose and ordinary one. If you're considering an action that might harm a certain number of people, it clearly matters how many: harming a billion people is worse than harming just one. But is it worse if those billion people share all but a single atom? We may wonder. Why is it not the loose and ordinary number that matters morally and practically? That would make crowded materialism compatible with our ordinary moral and practical judgments. Aaron thinks that harming a billion overlapping people is not like harming one person, but like harming a billion nonoverlapping people. But that's far from obvious, and he gives no argument for it.

It may be that when people overlap in a way that gives them the same nervous system, their pleasure and suffering is the same. If both Aaron and I break our necks jumping, it's a double tragedy: there's twice as much suffering as there would be if only one of us did. (Imagine that we both survive, badly damaged.) But if two people sharing all but a single atom break their neck—the neck they share—it's not twice as bad, because their suffering is the same. It's not just that they suffer in the same way, but that there's only one pain sensation that they both feel, located in their shared brain. There's only one feeling of despair, one fear of never recovering, and one regret at not having double-checked the knots. There could hardly be trillions of pain sensations, fears, and so on just because the borderline atoms in their skin make it the case that there are, in the strict and pedantic sense, trillions of people there. And maybe what matters morally is not the strict and pedantic number of suffering people, but the amount of suffering.

I don't know whether this is right. But any friend of the neat-and-tidy picture will need to say something rather like it about the value of material things. Imagine that Aaron's jump this Sunday passes off safely, but his watch—a cherished heirloom handed down through generations of Segals—falls into the gorge below and is lost. Aaron must accept that what looks like just one watch is really a vast number of them, because there's no saying exactly which atoms make it up. Yet that doesn't seem to make his loss any worse. Nor is it any worse to lose a bigger watch than a smaller one, even though it means losing far more watches. If he had lost two *nonoverlapping* watches, one handed down from his mother's side and one from his father's, that would have been twice as bad. But two heirlooms sharing all but a single atom have no more value than one. When it comes to material things, it's the loose and ordinary number that we care about, not the strict and pedantic number.

And if that's how it is with watches, why not with ourselves? Why should we care about the strict and pedantic number of people when in every other case we care only about the loose and ordinary number?

> Combining the neat-and-tidy picture with materialism implies that what looks like just one philosopher is really a vast number of them differing from each other only imperceptibly: "crowded materialism". But this is not as bad as it seems. It suggests that we count massively overlapping people as one for ordinary purposes. In that case it's this "loose and ordinary" number of people that we care about, not the "strict and pedantic" number.

3.6   The Rough-and-Messy Picture

Aaron argues that if materialism is true, there are far more people than we thought. I've tried to show that even if that's right, we're still correct about the loose and ordinary number of people, and that might be what we actually care about. But materialists needn't accept the original implication: they can maintain that even in the strict and pedantic sense there's only one philosopher here. They can reject the neat-and-tidy picture.

The fuzziness argument says that if I'm a material thing, I'm made of atoms; but whatever atoms these are, there are other collections of atoms just like them only with one more atom or one less.

Further—and this is the crucial step—each of these other collections makes up a material thing of its own. And because their difference from me is so trivial, these other things think just as I do, giving a great horde of philosophers. This assumes that for any atoms whatever, there is something made up of exactly them: the atomic composition principle. Without this principle, there's no reason to suppose that all my atoms plus or minus one make up something different from me. But that principle is not obvious or compelling. I doubt whether all my atoms plus one make up anything at all: I think the only human-sized material thing here is me.

The fundamental point of disagreement between Aaron and me is about what it takes for smaller things to make up bigger ones.[2] If we had some smaller things, what would we have to do to get them to compose something bigger? Imagine three objects having no parts of their own, arranged like this:

Then there might be some larger things—**composite** objects—having some of these simple objects as parts. How many such things? Here are three possible answers:

1. There is a thing made up of A and B, one made up of A and C, one made up of B and C, and one made up of A, B, and C.
2. There is a thing made up of A and B but no other composite object.
3. There are no objects other than A, B, and C. None of them is a part of anything larger.

(I use the words "thing" and "object" interchangeably as completely general count nouns. Everything is a thing and an object.) Other answers are also possible—that there's a thing composed of A and C and one composed of B and C, but nothing made up of A and B or of A, B, and C, for example—but I'll ignore them.

These answers are mutually inconsistent: at most one of them can be true. The first says that there are four composite objects, the second that there's one, and the third that there are none; and obviously there can't be both four composite objects and only one, or one and also none. And it seems that one of these answers (or one of the others that I've set aside) must be true. There must be *some* number of things having A, B, or C as parts, even if that number is zero, just as every person must have some number of children. None of these answers is either trivially true or trivially false. No principle of logic can take us from a statement about things without parts to a statement about things with parts. For this reason philosophers disagree.

Aaron appears to accept answer 1. More generally, he thinks that smaller things *always* make up something bigger, no matter what their nature or arrangement. If we ask what we'd have to do to get smaller things to make up a bigger one, his answer is nothing: it suffices simply for them to exist. Composition, we might say, is automatic or universal or unrestricted:

> **Unrestricted composition**
> Any things whatever always make up something bigger.

This follows from the atomic composition principle of §3.3 (which adds to it the claim that all composite objects are precise: nothing is ever a borderline part of anything.)

This gives us a world crammed full of material things, including a great horde of human animals sitting here and writing this, differing from each other by only a single atom—and many more differing by two atoms or three or seventeen. That's the foundation the fuzziness argument is built on.

The principle implies further that there's a thing made up of your atoms and mine, composed of two physical organisms many miles apart. There's a thing made up of your atoms, my left foot, and the sun. And there are billions and trillions of objects that are equally good candidates for being each of those things, differing from one another by only a single atom. Finally, it implies that this animal—my body—is made up of what we might call "**arbitrary undetached parts**": there is, for example, such a thing as all of me but my left pinky. As we'll see, this is a crucial premise in Aaron's

---

If the number of my atoms is n, the number of material things made up of some or all of them, according to unrestricted composition, is $2^n - 1$—the number of subsets of the atoms apart from the empty set. Seeing as n is around 7×10^{27}, that's a *really* big number.

second argument for immaterialism. Abstract though it may seem, unrestricted composition is the principle that leads Aaron to think that we must be immaterial.

I don't accept the principle. I deny that just any arbitrary atoms make up something bigger. Again, I doubt whether the atoms making me up plus one more on my periphery make up anything. Nor do your atoms together with mine. It's not just that they don't make up a "real object" or a "genuine thing": they don't make up anything at all. Atoms don't automatically make up a bigger thing. Some do and some don't: it depends on their nature and arrangement.

For this reason I reject the second premise of the fuzziness argument: I deny that whatever atoms compose me, there are other collections, differing from mine by only one atom, that each make up another being. There aren't a vast number of overlapping philosophers writing this.

Now I can't say exactly which atoms make me up. There are some that we can't classify either as parts of me or as non-parts, no matter how thoroughly we investigate. As I see it, none of these atoms are *definitely* parts of me, but none are definitely *not* parts of me either. They're borderline cases. That's why we're uncertain about them. I'm a vague object with fuzzy boundaries. So I also reject the first premise of the fuzziness argument: I deny that if I'm a material thing, there's a precise collection of atoms composing me.

Aaron thinks materialism gives us too many people because it implies that I'm composed of a precise collection of atoms, there are many different precise collections arranged here in human form, and every such collection composes a person. *I* think I'm composed of an *im*precise collection of atoms, and no other atoms arranged here in human form compose anything at all. There's only me. I described Aaron's picture as neat and tidy. We might call mine "rough and messy." There's no consensus on which picture is right, and the topic is a very hard one. Although I prefer the rough-and-messy picture, I concede that it faces two serious difficulties.

First: though it may sound sensible to suppose that some things compose bigger ones and others don't—that something about the way my atoms are arranged makes them compose a bigger thing and something about the way my atoms and yours are arranged, or all my atoms plus one, prevents them from doing so—it's hard to say what this something is. What does it take for smaller things to make up something bigger? You might think it's some sort of physical bonding: that things compose something just if they're physically attached in a certain way (van Inwagen 1990: §6). That would imply that there is something made up of A and B in the diagram above but nothing made up of any of the other simple objects, because only A and B are attached. But I can't accept this answer, because many of my own atoms are in a liquid state and not attached. The reason I didn't say how many objects have A, B, or C as parts is that I don't know the answer.[3]

Second, the rough-and-messy picture has the troubling implication that there is vagueness in the things themselves and not just in our description of them as the neat-and-tidy picture has it (van Inwagen 1990: §17). Suppose atoms compose something if, and only if, they meet a certain condition, whatever it may be. And suppose some atoms meet that condition and some don't. My current atoms meet it and thus compose something, and yours do too. Your atoms together with mine, I claim, don't meet it, nor do all my atoms plus one: that's why there's nothing made up of your atoms together with mine or of all my atoms plus one. But this condition is likely to have borderline cases. There will be atoms that don't definitely meet it, yet don't definitely fail to meet it either: atoms that only "sort of" meet the condition for composing something.

Imagine that my next bungee jump goes badly wrong and I have a fatal accident. My remains are cremated and my ashes are scattered at sea. Before the jump my atoms make up something, and after my cremation they don't. (Ignore, for now, the fact that I'm composed of different atoms at different times.) At some point my atoms cease to make up anything bigger. But there doesn't seem to be any precise instant when this happens. There is a period when my atoms neither definitely compose something nor definitely don't, because they're a borderline case of meeting the condition for composition. This will be so whatever that condition is, as long as my atoms satisfy it while I'm alive but not after my cremation.

Because I exist only as long as my atoms compose something, it follows that there is no precise instant when I stop existing. There must be a time when I neither definitely exist nor definitely don't exist. And this vagueness will not be in any way due to our description of the situation. It's not as if there's something there and the rules governing the word "exist" aren't precise enough to tell us whether it applies to that thing, as in ordinary cases of vagueness. The rules governing the term "the Great Plains" aren't precise enough to tell us exactly which piece of land it applies to. Likewise, the rules for the word "tall" don't specify a precise minimum height that a tall person has to be. But there's no imprecision in the rules about how to use the word "exist": it simply applies to everything there is. It doesn't mark off two classes of things, those that exist and those that don't, leaving room for borderline cases. There *are* no things that don't exist. There couldn't be. (What about dragons? Aren't they things that don't exist? No: it's not that there *are* dragons, and they fail to satisfy the conditions for existing in the way that Napoleon fails to satisfy the conditions for being tall. There simply are no dragons.) Whatever there is, exists. If there were *any* object composed of my atoms, it would have to exist. The trouble is that it's indeterminate whether there is any such object, as opposed to only individual atoms. There's sort of an object there and sort of not. Nor is it a borderline case of being an object as opposed to a non-object: again, everything is an object. The vagueness is in the world itself and not in our description of it.

During the period when my atoms are a borderline case of composing a bigger thing, then, I appear to be in a condition intermediate between existence and nonexistence. But the very idea of a condition intermediate between existence and nonexistence is profoundly mysterious. We know what it is to be in a condition intermediate between being tall and not being tall: to be sort of tall and sort of not tall. But how could something sort of exist and sort of not exist?

It's tempting to answer that it couldn't: existence cannot be indeterminate. It doesn't admit of borderline cases. But if some atoms met the condition for composing something and others didn't, that condition *would* allow borderline cases, and it would be indeterminate whether a composite object exists. It looks as if the only way to avoid vague or borderline existence is to say that *all* atoms must meet the condition for composing something: composition must be unrestricted.

There is in fact another way to avoid vague existence, namely to say that there is *no* composition. Smaller things never make up anything bigger, and nothing is a part of anything else (van Inwagen 1990: 72–73). The only material things are those without parts: individual quarks and electrons, for example. But this is no help in defending materialism against the fuzziness argument, because if you and I are material things, we have many parts: I could hardly be an individual quark or electron. A materialist who rejected composition would have to deny her own existence. And no one can deny her own existence and be right about it.

So the rough-and-messy picture says that when my atoms disperse after my death, they stop composing anything; but because this dispersal is a gradual process, there's a period when they only "sort of" compose something: a case of borderline existence. How does the neat-and-tidy picture avoid this troubling consequence? That's a complicated story. But the picture suggests that the atoms making me up when I die always compose something, even after my ashes have been scattered: that follows from unrestricted composition. Presumably those atoms always compose the *same* thing. So my body will exist for billions of years, though not as a connected object: it simply changes from a physical organism to a thin cloud as my atoms disperse.[4] As we'll see, that's precisely Aaron's view.

> Materialists can resist the fuzziness argument by rejecting the atomic composition principle and the neat-and-tidy picture. They can deny that all my atoms but one make up anything at all. Not just any atoms make up a bigger thing; it depends on how they're arranged. But this "rough-and-messy" picture has the troubling implication that there is vagueness in the world and not just in our way of describing it: specifically that there can be borderline cases of existence.

3.7 Why the Fuzziness Argument Doesn't Support Immaterialism

Aaron argues that materialism leads to the unwelcome conclusion that what looks like one person is really many of them differing by just a single atom. I've given two responses. First, this wouldn't be as bad as it sounds: there would still be only one person there in the sense that matters practically. Second, we can avoid it by rejecting the neat-and-tidy picture on which any atoms whatever make up a bigger thing. We can say instead that there is nothing made up of all my atoms but one, and I really am the only person here.

I'll make one more point about the fuzziness argument. The argument claims that materialism gives us too many material things for any of them to be you or me. But if this is a problem, it's not one that can be solved by taking us to be immaterial. In fact that would only compound the problem. My being immaterial would not make the great horde of material thinkers go away, or make its members any less conscious or intelligent. It would only increase its size by adding yet another thinker: an immaterial one. That there are billions and trillions of material beings now thinking my thoughts is no easier to believe on the assumption that I'm an immaterial thing than it is on the assumption that I'm material. If we want to avoid that conclusion, we'll need to deny that each person shares her mental life with a great horde of other beings. We'll need to argue either that those other beings don't exist (as the rough-and-messy picture has it), or that they don't think. But simply saying that you and I are immaterial does neither of these things.

Here's another way of making the point. Recall that dualism consists of three principles (§1.4): there are thinking things, there are material things, and nothing is both thinking and material. Two claims follow from this:

1. We are immaterial.
2. Material things (such as our bodies) never think.

The second claim is independent of the first: our being immaterial doesn't rule out there being material thinkers as well. And the first claim's appeal depends on the second: no one would suppose that each of us is a thinking soul attached to a thinking body, so that what looks like one person is really at least two, one immaterial and the other material. (How could I ever know whether I was the immaterial thinker or one of the material ones?) So if you want to argue that we're immaterial, you'll need to argue that material things don't think.

Yet the fuzziness argument supports only the first claim. It provides no evidence for the second. Of course, premise 5 of the argument *says* that there's only one thinker of my thoughts, and that together with the claim that I'm immaterial implies that my body doesn't think. But that premise is precisely what's now in question: given the neat-and-tidy picture that the argument presupposes, it looks wrong, unless material things never think. That's what Aaron has to argue for. But if we could establish that material things never think, it would imply straightaway that we're not material, because it's evident that *we* think. (That I think is not something I could be wrong about: I couldn't mistakenly think that I think.) In that case we'd have no need of the fuzziness argument.

This is not to say that the argument is of no value. It poses an awkward problem for materialists: they need to choose between crowded materialism and the rough-and-messy picture. (Other options may be available, but they're no better.) If you don't like either of these—which would be understandable—that may be a reason to explore alternatives to materialism: to ask seriously whether it's possible for material things to think. But without an account of why they can't, immaterialism will remain unsatisfying.

> Our being immaterial has no attraction if material things like our bodies can think: in that case there will again be far too many thinkers for any of them to be you or me. But the fuzziness argument gives no account of why material things can't think. And if we had such an account, it would imply all by itself that we're immaterial, and we'd have no need of the fuzziness argument. So the argument cannot defeat materialism.

3.8   The Flux Argument

Our discussion of the fuzziness argument will help in assessing Aaron's second objection to materialism: the flux argument. It says that no material thing could ever be first a child and later an adult. Given that each of *us* was once a child and is now an adult, it follows that we're not material things.

The argument's main premise is that nothing can have different parts at different times. It's not just that nothing can change *all* its parts: nothing can change any part at all. Whatever is a part of an object at one time must be a part of it whenever that object exists.

Now if I'm a material thing, I'm made of atoms. And I'm constantly taking in oxygen and expelling carbon dioxide through respiration. But if nothing can change its parts, the result of my exhaling a carbon atom can't be me with one atom less: it can only be someone else. He'll look like me and remember what I did this morning. He'll *think* he's me. But he can't be, because he and I have different parts. What looks like one philosopher constantly changing his parts must really be a series of different beings, which don't change their parts, rapidly succeeding one another.

What happens to me, then, when I exhale an atom (assuming materialism)? Given that nothing can change its parts, that atom must be a part of me whenever I exist. So I would seem to exist for as long as my atoms do. When I exhale an atom, I begin to disperse. I cease to be a connected object. Instead I become composed of many atoms arranged in human form together with one free-floating atom. By this time tomorrow, one or two per cent of my atoms will be dispersed throughout the local atmosphere and sewage system, but they'll remain parts of me. In a year's time I'll be nothing but a thin cloud spread out across the northern hemisphere.

For most of my past I've been likewise dispersed. I came into being when my atoms were created. When the solar system was formed four and a half billion years ago, I became confined to this planet. Over the past year or so more and more of my atoms have become arranged in human form, so that I'm now a conscious human being. But not for long: even as I write this, I'm dispersing again. By a cosmic coincidence, my atoms might one day come to be arranged in human form once more, but most likely I'll remain an undistinguished cloud until the end of the world.

So if I'm made of atoms, I was never a child. There was once a child with my name—a great number of them in succession, in fact—but none of them was me, because they all had different parts from me. And I'll never be an old man. Though with any luck there will be a long sequence of old men bearing my name and having memories of writing this book, none of them will be me.

But surely I *was* once a child. That's true, Aaron argues, only if I'm not made of atoms. *My body* is made of atoms: what looks like one physical organism really is a series of different organisms rapidly succeeding one another. And the same is true of any other material thing. But not me. I can only be a wholly immaterial thing with no parts to be dispersed.

> The flux argument claims that no material thing could be first a child and then an adult. That's because nothing can have different parts at different times. Given that I was once a child and am now an adult, I must have lived as a human being for many years without losing or gaining any parts. But because of metabolic turnover, no material thing can do that. It follows that I must be an immaterial thing.

3.9   The Amputation Paradox

The main premise of the flux argument is that nothing can change its parts. That's very counterintuitive. Why couldn't I have different parts at different times?

Aaron's answer might be called the *amputation paradox*. It starts with the plausible claim that nothing can change its parts unless it can survive the loss of a part, making it smaller. Why can't something get smaller by losing a part? Well, think about how that could happen. Imagine that some arbitrary part of me—my left pinky, say—is amputated. Here's me (or my body, if you prefer) with the finger attached:

F is my finger, and FC is "all of me but that finger": my **finger complement**, made up of all my atoms except those in my left pinky. And here's the situation after my finger is amputated:

Has the amputation made me any smaller? It doesn't look like it. It seems to have merely detached my finger from the rest of me. I may have changed from a connected object that's all in one piece to a disconnected object in two pieces. Or I may have ceased to exist altogether. But it doesn't look as if I first have something as a part and then exist without having it as a part. In fact it doesn't look as if *anything* has shrunk by losing a part.

Suppose for the sake of argument that I did become smaller, so that my finger is not a part of me after the amputation. In that case I must be first made up of my finger and my finger complement and then made up of just my finger complement. But what does it mean to say that I'm "made up of just my finger complement"? What is the relation, after the amputation, between my finger complement and me? There appears to be no difference between us then: we're in exactly the same place; we have the same physical properties; we're made up of the same atoms. Not even God could tell us apart. How could the operation squeeze two material things into the same location? If my finger stops being a part of me, the result must be that I *am* my finger complement: we become one and the same.

So the only way I could lose a finger is by coming to be a thing that was previously only a part of me. My finger complement and I must be first two things and then one thing. But that's logically impossible: a thing and another thing can never become a thing and itself. We can see the problem by noting that after the operation (supposing, again, that I survive it without a left pinky), my finger complement and I have different histories. I once had a left pinky as a part, but my finger complement didn't. The amputation makes *me* smaller, but not my finger complement. But if we were the same thing after the amputation, then that one thing would have both previously had a left pinky (because it's me and I had one) and not had one (because it's my finger complement, which never had one). I would have got smaller and yet not got smaller. If I got smaller and my finger complement didn't, we must be two different things. So I can't become my finger complement. Yet that's what would have to happen for me to shrink by losing a finger. It follows that I can't shrink.

The argument proceeds by *reductio ad absurdum*—that is, by deriving a contradiction from the assumption that I get smaller:

1. Suppose I become smaller by losing a finger. Then
2. My finger complement and I are one and the same after the operation (from 1, given the reasoning above). But
3. My finger complement and I are not one and the same after the operation (because we have different histories).

Because 3 contradicts 2, we infer that the initial assumption is false:

4. I don't become smaller by losing a finger.

And as none of this reasoning turns on any special features of me or my finger or finger complement, it implies that nothing can ever lose *any* part. More generally, nothing can have different parts at different times. It follows that I can be a philosopher for many years despite metabolic turnover only if I have no parts at all. And in that case I must be an immaterial soul.

> The amputation paradox purports to show that nothing can get smaller by losing a part. If I were to get smaller by losing a finger, that would make me the same thing as my finger complement, the thing formerly made up of all my parts outside my finger. But because my finger complement has a different history from me, we can't be the same thing. So I can't get smaller by losing a part. More generally, I can't have different parts at different times.

3.10 Heraclitean Materialism and the Rough-and-Messy Picture Again

What can the materialist say about the flux argument? The most obvious responses parallel my remarks about the fuzziness argument. One is to accept that nothing can change its parts, so that what looks like one person living for many years is really a series of different people rapidly succeeding one another: call this "**Heraclitean materialism**" after the ancient Greek philosopher Heraclitus, who held a more extreme version of it. And we could try to argue that this is not as bad as it seems, just as I tried to do for crowded materialism.

Even if strictly speaking we were never children, it needn't follow that we're completely deluded about our pasts. There's still something right in saying that I was once a child. There was a certain child (or a series of them) that I, and no one else, now relate to in a special way. I can remember things that happened to him. I bear scars from his injuries. There's a special sort of causal connection between him and me: I exist now because he existed then, and I've inherited many of his properties: my eye color, my genetic makeup, my interest in abstract questions, and so on. We could sum all this up by saying that he and I are **temporal counterparts** (Goswick 2013: 377–380; see also Olson 2006: 395–398).

Things would appear just the same to me whether the beings who bore my name in the past were really me or only my temporal counterparts: I'd remember their adventures just the same either way. No one can tell the difference between a single persisting person and a series of temporal counterparts. When people are temporal counterparts of each other, we call them by the same name. When we speak of the number of children in my family, we count temporal counterparts as one, just as we do for children sharing most of their atoms according to crowded materialism. I use the word "I" to refer not just to myself but to my temporal counterparts too. That makes the ordinary statement that I was once a child true as long as there's a child among my temporal counterparts. So even on Heraclitean materialism, there's a perfectly good sense in which I *was* once a child.

To adapt the terms I used earlier, you could say that I was once a child in a loose and ordinary sense, even if in the strict and pedantic sense I wasn't. And again, you could argue that it's the loose and ordinary sense that matters practically. I'm responsible for the actions of my past temporal counterparts: if one of them made a mistake, I'm the one who now has to apologize. If one of my past counterparts made a promise to a past counterpart of yours, it's me who has a duty to keep it, and it's you that I have the duty to. I have a special, selfish reason to care about what happens to my future temporal counterparts that doesn't apply to anyone else: looking out for number one means looking out for my future temporal counterparts.

That's the sort of thing I'd say if I accepted that things can never change their parts. I'd say it before giving up materialism. But I'd rather try to show that things *can* change their parts. I'll propose a solution to the amputation paradox.

The paradox arises because there seems to be no acceptable way of describing the relation, after the amputation of my finger, between my finger complement and me: it can't be me, because we have different histories, yet it can't be anything other than me because we're made of just the same atoms at the same time.

All this assumes that there is actually such a thing as my finger complement. Why suppose that? There are, of course, certain atoms that are parts of me but not parts of my left pinky. But why must those atoms make up a bigger thing? Only, it seems, because any atoms whatever, no matter what their nature or arrangement, must always make up something. The amputation paradox presupposes unrestricted composition. If some atoms don't make up anything at all, it's doubtful whether all my atoms save those in my finger do. My finger complement would be an "**arbitrary, undetached part.**" If there were such a thing, there would also be a thing composed of all my atoms plus or minus one on my periphery, and I'd be one of a great horde of overlapping philosophers. That's precisely the sort of thing we can avoid by adopting the rough-and-messy picture of §3.6.

But if there's no such thing as my finger complement, what occupies the box marked "FC" in the "before" diagram—the region that I occupy minus the one containing my left pinky? Well, nothing *exactly* occupies it. It's occupied by a lot of individual atoms. Before the amputation, I'm composed of certain atoms x, y, and z together with my finger, like this:

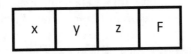

(The number of my atoms outside my left pinky is of course more than three, but that was all my department's art budget would stretch to. The point is the same whether it's three or 10^{27}.) Afterwards that box is occupied not by my finger complement but by me, so that I'm made up of just x, y, and z:

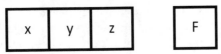

The paradox arises only if x, y, and z by themselves make up something before the amputation. But we needn't assume that.[5]

In fact we can turn the amputation paradox into an argument against unrestricted composition and the neat-and-tidy picture. Start with the premise that it's possible for a thing to get smaller by losing a part: for example, I can survive the loss of a finger. That certainly looks right, and it's as good a starting point as any for a philosophical argument. But if there were such a thing as my finger complement, it would be impossible for me to shrink by losing a finger, for the reason Aaron gives (it would make me one and the same as something that was previously only a part of me, which is logically impossible). It follows, contrary to unrestricted composition, that some atoms don't make up anything bigger: all my atoms except those in my finger don't.

> One materialist response to the flux argument is to accept that although in the strict sense I was never a child, I *was* once a child in the loose sense of being psychologically and causally continuous with one. A second is to dispute the premise that nothing can change its parts. We can do this by giving up unrestricted composition and the neat-and-tidy picture.

3.11   Why the Flux Argument Doesn't Support Immaterialism

The flux argument says, again, that because nothing can change its parts, *I* can't change *my* parts. But no material thing could be first a child and later an adult without changing its parts. Because I was once a child, I must therefore be an immaterial thing. I've discussed two replies. The first conceded that I was never *really* a child but argued that this is not as bad as it looks. The second tried to show that things *can* change their parts. But even if both these replies are mistaken, the flux argument doesn't actually support the claim that we're immaterial.

Given the facts about metabolic turnover, the argument implies that what looks like just one human animal is really a series of different animals rapidly succeeding one another. If those animals are conscious and intelligent like me, their belief that they were once children (in the strict and pedantic sense) is mistaken. That looks just as bad as saying that I myself was never a child. But we can't avoid it simply by adding to these material thinkers an *im*material one that really was once a child. If the flux argument presents a problem for materialism, it's not one that can be solved just by taking ourselves to be immaterial.

You might suppose that if I'm immaterial, I can know at least that *I* was once a child (in whatever sense a wholly immaterial thing can be a child), even if the material thinkers are mistaken about whether they were. But that's doubtful. The suggestion is that there are at least two beings now thinking my thoughts: an immaterial soul that was once a child, and a material thing that's now an animal but has spent most of the past five billion years as a scattered cloud of atoms. How could I know that I'm the soul and not the animal? Everything would appear just the same to me either way. If I were the animal, I'd still have memories of walking to the office this morning, agreeing to write this book two years ago, and once being second runner-up in the egg-and-spoon race. The animal will find the flux argument just as convincing as the soul does. If he follows Aaron's reasoning, he'll come to believe that, because he was once a child—which he believes for the same reason I believe this about myself—he must be wholly immaterial. But of course he'll be wrong about this. And given the evidence available to me, that could be my own situation. Even if I *were* immaterial, I could never know it. The flux argument gives me no reason to suppose that I'm a soul.

Immaterialists will of course object to my assumption that any material thing is conscious or intelligent. They'll say that the only thinker here is the soul. And given that *I* think, I must be that soul. But the flux argument provides no support for this. We'll need some other reason to suppose that material things never think—not even human animals with healthy brains. And if we had such a reason, we could infer straightaway that we must be immaterial and we'd have no need of the flux argument. In other words, the flux argument can't enable us to know that we're immaterial unless it's combined with some other reason (such as the "mill" argument of §1.9) to suppose that material things never think. But such a reason would enable us to know that we're immaterial even without the flux argument.

So the flux argument cannot establish immaterialism. Like the fuzziness argument, it can only make trouble for materialism. Materialists must either accept that we were never really children or else solve the amputation paradox—that is, show how things can change their parts. (Again, other options may be available, but they're no more attractive.) If you don't like either of these, that's a reason to explore alternatives to materialism. But if you want to argue that we have a soul, you'll need to argue that material things never think, and here the flux argument is no help.

> For the flux argument to show that I'm immaterial, it must give me a reason to suppose that I'm not the physical organism sitting here. But for all the argument says, that organism thinks just as I do, in which case I have no such reason. I can know that I'm immaterial only if I can know that material things never think. But the flux argument gives no reason to suppose that material things don't think. And if we had such a reason, we'd have no need of the flux argument.

Notes

1   The sketch is adapted from Lewis (1986: 212f).
2   The classic discussion of this topic is van Inwagen (1990): see especially §§2 and 3.
3   For a fascinating proposal, see van Inwagen (1990: §9).
4   Most friends of the neat-and-tidy picture avoid this consequence by saying that material things are not actually composed of atoms but of "temporal parts" of atoms. This offers a response to Aaron's flux argument as well. But I can't say any more about it here. For details, see Sider (2001: §4.9) and Olson (2007: ch. 6 and §7.3).
5   This reasoning is from van Inwagen (1984). For other proposed solutions to the paradox, see Olson (2006, 2007: 153–164).

Chapter 4

A Sane Soul-Hypothesis and the Sane Materialist Alternative

Aaron Segal

Contents

4.1 Where We Part Ways

There's quite a lot that I agree with in Eric's wonderfully lucid opening statement. I agree that using the word "mind" to frame and conduct the debate about what we are is ill-advised and can only lead to confusion (§1.5); that Descartes' argument for immaterialism from what we can imagine is unsuccessful (§1.8); that Leibniz's Mill argument for the impossibility of a material thinking thing is unsuccessful (§1.9); that the so-called Interaction Problem is not all by itself much of a problem for immaterialism (§1.10); and much else besides. There's so much that I agree with that I was *almost* able to read through the first ten sections without finding a substantial point of disagreement. Almost but not quite. I disagree with a number of things Eric says about what we *seem* to be (§1.6), and so I will begin with my thoughts on that, before turning to his Duplication Argument (§1.11).

DOI: 10.4324/9781003032908-6

4.2   The Appearances

In my own opening statement, I spent a good deal of time disput-
ing arguments that materialism is the default view, the view that is
innocent until proven guilty. But there was one such argument that I
only mentioned but did not discuss. That was the argument from the
appearances. The thought behind this argument is that we *seem* to be
material. In just the same perceptual way that the knife blade seems
to be made of metal or the house seems to be made of bricks, we
seem to be made of matter. These allegedly materialist appearances
are both first personal and third personal. *You* appear to yourself to
be material—say, when you look in the mirror and see a flesh-and-
blood human being, and *your friends and family* appear to you to
be material—say, when you sit down to dinner with them and everyone's stuffing their faces.

Or so goes the thought. Eric develops and refines this thought. One
of the important refinements he makes is this: it's not quite right, he
says, that we seem to be material, in the sense of being *wholly* material. The appearances don't rule out our *also* having an immaterial
part, à la **compound immaterialism**. Rather, the thought is, we seem
to be *at least partly* material. I'll return to this important refinement
in a moment. So refined, though, Eric endorses this thought. But he
doesn't make much of it. He thinks that even though it's true that we
uniformly appear to ourselves and others to be at least partly material, those appearances provide very little reason, if any, to think we
are at least partly material.

I disagree with him on both counts. On the one hand, if the
appearances are as Eric says, then they would constitute a good reason to think we are in fact at least partly material. That is, they
would constitute a good reason to think that the view I hold, according to which we are *wholly* immaterial, is false. Or, at least they
would constitute a good reason to take the falsity of my view as the
default—a good reason to deny my view, absent any considerations
in its favor. (Of course, I think there *are* considerations in its favor,
the ones I adduced at the first stage. But it's still important to figure
out whether there's any default, because (a) not everyone, alas, will
find my arguments convincing, and (b) that'll determine the baseline,
i.e. how much work my arguments have to do—where the needle
starts determines how far the needle has to move to get to the immaterialist side.)

On the other hand, I disagree with Eric about what the appearances are. I don't think we appear to be even partly material. It's not

that I think we appear to be *im*material, let alone wholly immaterial. I just think the appearances we have are indifferent to the question of our materiality.

Eric has already laid the groundwork for this claim. Recall the refinement. The appearances are indifferent between materialism and compound immaterialism, Eric notes, because things would seem the same either way. It's worth quoting Eric here, because he puts the point so nicely:

> The senses can't detect things that are invisible and intangible ... A partly material thing will look and feel the same as a wholly material one. So although sense perception doesn't give the appearance that we have a soul, it doesn't give the appearance that we don't have one either. If we did have a soul, there is no reason to expect that fact to make any difference to our sensory experience.

Exactly. Things would seem the same whether materialism or compound immaterialism were true.

But the same can be said for compound immaterialism and pure immaterialism: things would seem the same either way. Suppose there are two planets as much like Earth as the following stipulations allow. One is inhabited by human people whose nature is the same as what compound immaterialism says our nature is, and the other inhabited by human people whose nature is what pure immaterialism says our nature is. (If materialism is true, neither of these planets is *exactly* like Earth.) Now, on both of these planets, whenever and wherever there is a human person, there is an immaterial soul and a body that are intimately connected with each other: there is a two-way, direct, and immediate causal connection between the soul and the body. And the causal connection between them, we can stipulate, is exactly the same on the two planets. The only difference between the planets concerns whether the human *people* have their bodies as *parts* ("the human people are compound," we might say) or merely as *appendages* ("the human people are wholly immaterial," we might say). But that's a rather subtle, *metaphysical* difference, and there's no reason to expect it to make a *sensory* difference. Indeed, the external senses (sight, smell, etc.) can detect only bodies and their movements; the internal senses (introspection, memory, etc.) can detect only mental states and episodes; putting these together, one can perhaps detect causal relationships between bodily movements and mental episodes (like when you detect that your decision to stand up caused your body to get up from the chair). But nothing else seems detectable through the senses. And all of those things that *are* detectable are *exactly the same* for "the compound human people" and "the wholly immaterial human people." Their bodies do the very same things, they think the very same thoughts, and the causal connections between their bodies and souls are the very same. So, no human person on either planet could tell, just by looking or feeling, which planet he was on. Not only is there no reason to expect the subtle metaphysical difference between the two to make a sensory difference, there is a reason to think that it *can't* make any such difference.

The bottom line is that things would seem the same whether pure immaterialism or compound immaterialism were true, and, as Eric has pointed out, things would seem the same whether compound immaterialism or materialism were true. So things would seem the same regardless of which of the *three* views were true. That's why I say the appearances are indifferent to the question of our materiality—and so we have no sensory evidence for, or against, materialism.

Two points are worth noting about this argument. The first is about the principle that Eric and I are both tacitly assuming, which is roughly this: if things *would* seem sensorily to us just as they actually do even if compound immaterialism or pure immaterialism were true, then we have no sensory evidence for materialism. But this principle isn't quite right. If it were right, then so would a principle that said this: if things would seem sensorily to you just as they actually do even if you were in the Matrix, then you have no sensory evidence for the existence of your house. But of course you have such sensory evidence, despite the fact that things would seem just as they do even if you were in the Matrix. Just because you *could* be living in the Matrix, and things *would* seem just the same, doesn't mean that your senses don't represent the world in a way that's incompatible with your being in the Matrix, nor does it mean that you have no sensory evidence for the existence of your house. It just means that your sensory evidence *isn't airtight*, that it *could* mislead.

There is a true principle in the neighborhood, though, that will do just fine for my purposes. It's not just that the appearances *would* be the same even if compound immaterialism or pure immaterialism were true, it's that they *should* be the same: the appearances make no representations one way or the other. (Note the difference from the

Matrix case, in which the appearances had by those in the Matrix do (mis)represent reality in a way that's inconsistent with their being in the Matrix.) For convenience, let's say that "appearance X is neutral between P and Q" means that P and Q are incompatible, and X doesn't represent the world as being P rather than Q or Q rather than P. Then, the principle I'm appealing to is this: if appearance X is neutral between P and Q, then X is not sensory evidence for one rather than the other. I think this principle is rather obviously true.

And the structure of my argument is rather simple:

(1) Ordinary appearances are neutral between materialism and compound immaterialism (our senses are blind to, and hence silent on, whether there are intangible and invisible things, as Eric pointed out)

(2) Ordinary appearances are neutral between compound immaterialism and pure immaterialism (our senses are blind to, and hence silent on, the subtle metaphysical difference between these two views)

Hence,

(3) Ordinary appearances are neutral between materialism and pure immaterialism (if X is neutral between P and Q, and X is neutral between Q and R, then X is neutral between P and R)

One might raise the following objection to both premises (1) and (2): the senses, psychology has supposedly taught us, *add* lots of information—i.e. they aren't "silent" on matters—to which they are strictly "blind." So, while ordinary appearances might well be *blind* to the difference between materialism and compound immaterialism, and to the difference between compound immaterialism and pure immaterialism, that doesn't mean they are *silent* on either one of those. Fair enough. But here we should note the following: whatever the senses are adding provides no sensory *evidence* for the view they speak in favor of; sensory evidence comes from what the senses detect, not from what they superimpose. So we can simply ignore the information added by our senses when figuring out what the appearances provide evidence for.

(4) If appearance X is neutral between P and Q, then X is not sensory evidence for one rather than the other (the principle)
Hence,
(5) Ordinary appearances are not sensory evidence for materialism over pure immaterialism

The second point worth noting is that my claim is about the ordinary appearances we *in fact have*. There are *possible* appearances that could tell *against* materialism. Suppose I'm lying in my hospital bed, deathly ill but totally lucid, and all of the sudden, it seems to me that I'm floating near the ceiling, looking down from above at my body and at all of the doctors hovering around me; I notice that the cardiologist is wearing a hat and embroidered in the top—in a location I couldn't possibly see from my hospital bed—it says "from your Aunt Nancy"; shortly thereafter, it seems again that I'm lying in my hospital bed, surrounded by my doctors, and I ask the cardiologist, "Do you have an Aunt Nancy?"; shocked by both my impudence and my intimate knowledge, she responds, "Why, yes, but howsoever did you know?!?" Some people report things like this happening to them. If so, they have pretty damn good sensory evidence that they are at least partly immaterial. If they were wholly material, after all, I'd want to know how they managed to perceive the room from above without the aid of a periscope. (As I noted in §2.5, some philosophers rely on just such reports of near-death or out-of-body experiences in arguing against materialism.) Now, I am dubious of such reports. Maybe they're true; maybe not. But there's nothing impossible about them. So there are at least possible appearances that could tell against materialism, even if they're not the ones we usually, or ever, have. Not so for possible appearances that could tell *in favor* of materialism. For the reasons I gave above, there don't seem to be any possible appearances—of the *kind* we currently have—that would specifically support materialism. Of course, if God were to give us a sixth sense, that could directly detect our nature, then we could have sensory evidence that supported materialism. But that would not be an appearance of the kind we currently have.

> Materialists sometimes argue that they have the senses on their side. It seems to me the exact opposite. The appearances we in fact have are likely indifferent to our materiality, and certainly provide no support for materialism. On the other hand, there are at the very least possible appearances, of the same kind that we

have, which would support immaterialism, but none that would support materialism. If anyone has the senses on their side, it's the immaterialists. Although probably no one does.

4.3 Faux-Mentality

The first argument for materialism that Eric develops and actually espouses is the Duplication Argument. (As I said above, he develops but doesn't seem to put much stock in the "Interaction Problem." As we both seem to agree, there isn't much of a problem there. Since I have nothing substantive to add to what Eric said about it, I simply recommend rereading his excellent discussion.) Here's how I'd summarize the argument: if we were to make a perfect atom-for-atom physical duplicate of your body, we would expect it to at the very least have *some* mental life, to not be *comatose*, for example. That expectation would be based on our experience: we never find human beings with severe mental defects without brain defects. Since you have no brain defects, neither would your atom-for-atom duplicate. On the other hand, we wouldn't expect the duplicate to come along with a soul. A body is one thing, a soul is another thing. So we'd expect the duplicate to be a "soulless body." And immaterialism implies that a soulless body would have no mental life whatsoever, that it *would* just lie there comatose. So immaterialism's prediction about your physical duplicate is known, based on our experience, to be false. A theory that makes false predictions is false. Hence, immaterialism is false.

At the end of the day, Eric concedes that the "duplication argument is not conclusive." Being inconclusive, I should note, isn't much of a mark against the argument, since almost no philosophical argument is conclusive. To my mind, though, the argument is *very* far from being conclusive. The first major problem with the argument is that it portrays immaterialism as much stronger and much weirder than it is. The argument assumes that if immaterialism is true, then a soulless body would have no mental life whatsoever. To appreciate what's intended, here's Eric: "… they'd be alive, but unconscious and unresponsive. Immaterialism implies that a physical organism is like a radio. A radio can't produce sound by itself; it can only receive signals from a transmitter … When it receives no such signals, it's comatose." Yes, *comatose*. But immaterialism implies no such thing. Consider a computer. Or, better, a really sophisticated android (i.e. a humanoid robot). The following seems like a real possibility, something that's true for all we know: the android looks and behaves just like a human and even engages in all sorts of things that are very much like *thinking*—computations, calculations, and concatenations—but it's "lights out" inside the android. There isn't anything it's like *to be* the android, the way there's something it's like to be you. Given that supposition, I'd say that the appearance of mentality in the android is just that: an appearance. That is, if indeed computers and androids have no "inner life," then they don't *really* think at all, any more than a thermostat does. But they do a whole lot that is very much like thinking. *It's not as though they're comatose.* They might speak Russian fluently; though they don't actually understand Russian, since they don't understand anything at all. They might tend to choose jazz at the jukebox, though they don't actually prefer jazz, since they don't prefer anything at all. We might put this by saying that, under the supposition that it's "lights out," the android has **faux-mentality**—it's a lot like mentality, but it's not the genuine article. (Note well! This is not at all the same as the distinction that Eric mentions between "higher mental powers" and "lower mental powers." It's the difference between bona fide mental powers, and ones that merely look to be.)

Now not only does it seem like there's a real possibility of a sophisticated android having faux-mentality, it seems that such a possibility is clearly consistent with immaterialism. Immaterialism in no way implies that it's impossible for a soulless material object to have *faux*-mentality. (I don't even think it implies that it's *impossible* for a soulless material object to have genuine mentality; it only implies or strongly suggests that none in fact do. We'll set that point aside for now and return to it below.) In particular, it in no way implies that it's impossible for a soulless *android* to have faux-mentality.

But by the same token, it in no way implies that it's impossible for a soulless *human organism* to have *faux*-mentality. Human organisms are no less capable in general, and no less capable of faux-mentality in particular, than are sophisticated androids. So, the fact that we've never found a soulless human organism who was comatose or suffered from severe dementia but was physically indistinguishable from the organism that is your body is really neither here nor there. Even if we could somehow find a soulless human organism that was physically indistinguishable from your body, I wouldn't expect to find it *comatose* just because immaterialism is true. I'd expect it to be no less faux-mentally capable than a really sophisticated android.

So the claim about immaterialism's implications is wrong. And the argument can't be rehabilitated by simply weakening that claim. Say we had replaced the sentence about immaterialism's implications with the following sentence: "Immaterialism implies that a perfect physical duplicate of you without a soul would have no *genuine* mental life." I'd be willing to go along with that. But then for the argument's reasoning to be valid—in order for it not to be fallacious—the step in the argument about what we *would* expect would have to be adjusted likewise, i.e. as saying that "we'd expect such a physical duplicate to have a *genuine* mental life like yours." But, supposing as we are that the physical duplicate would be soulless, I'd expect no such thing, and no one who isn't already a materialist should expect any such thing. There's simply no independent evidence—that is, independent of the question of whether materialism is true—that a soulless perfect physical duplicate of you would have a *genuine* mental life. The only evidence that Eric cites, the only such evidence there *is*, comes from people with *observable* mental defects. But observable mental defects will be defects even in one's faux-mental life; they will be things like an inability to string together a sentence or recognize one's children. It's true that we never see anything like that without some physical defects in the brain. But that supports only the claim that a perfect physical duplicate of you would be faux-mentally indistinguishable from you, not that he'd be genuinely–mentally indistinguishable from you. We simply can't peer into someone else's head to see if their mentality is genuine. Of course, I *do* assume that your mentality is genuine but only because I assume you are a soul.

> The Duplication Argument fails because it gets immaterialism's implications wrong. Once we get clear on the distinction between faux mentality and the real thing, we can see that immaterialism's implications for the case Eric envisages are much less radical than the Duplication Argument would have us believe.

4.4 Materialism Is No Better Off

That's the first big problem with the argument. It has to do with what immaterialism says a soulless duplicate would be like. The second big problem has to do with whether we'd expect the duplicate to be soulless in the first place. Remember, the argument assumes that since the body is one thing and the soul is another thing, we'd *expect* your physical duplicate to be soulless. But what exactly is meant by this? In general, our expectations are, and should be, influenced heavily by our experience. My expectation that the sun will rise tomorrow, or that the next pot of water I put on the stove will boil, is due to my experience with previous days and other pots of water. So if Eric says that we'd expect your physical duplicate to be soulless, here's what I'd ask first: given what background information is that supposed to be our expectation?

One option would be that it's supposed to be our expectation, *even given all of our prior experience, including our experience with the mental capacities of other human beings.* But if that's what's meant, then the claim that we would expect the duplicate to be soulless is pretty implausible—at least if "we" includes us immaterialists. We immaterialists who have had experience with the mental capacities of other human beings might well reasonably expect any duplicate of you to come along with a soul. After all, we could turn the Duplication Argument on its head. Experience has taught us—as the argument itself assumes—that human beings with severe mental defects always have physical defects in the brain. And the argument also assumes that a human being with no soul would, according to immaterialism, have severe mental defects—indeed, so severe as to have no mental life at all. (Let's set aside my objection from the last section; if that objection succeeds, there's no need for this one.) But you have no physical brain defects. So, we immaterialists should conclude that your physical duplicate must come along with a soul after all. That is, that's what we should expect.

Sure, the duplicating machine wasn't *designed* to produce souls or attach them to physical objects. But it might well end up doing just that, in a consistent and predictable way. Your car engine wasn't *designed* to produce noxious exhaust fumes, and yet it ends up doing just that, in a consistent and predictable way. The reason is that there are certain laws of nature that connect what the engine was designed to do (produce controlled combustion) with the production of noxious exhaust fumes. In just the same way, we might suppose, it's simply a law of nature that whenever there is a material object that exhibits a certain degree of functional complexity, it gets hooked up with a particular soul. By the immaterialist's lights, that's exactly what we'll have learned from our vast experience with the mental capacities of other human beings. So, the duplicating machine does the physical duplication. Nature takes care of the rest.

Eric concedes that this *could* be what would happen if we were to perform the experiment. But he contends that it's a convoluted, inelegant hypothesis. You might ask yourself, though, how does that constitute an objection to the reply I've just given? My point was that given everything we know from experience, we immaterialists *should* expect your physical duplicate to come along with a soul, and so one of Eric's premises is just false. Why does the *complexity* of my suggestion matter one way or the other?

I think Eric's point can be put this way: the premise in the argument that we'd expect your physical duplicate to be soulless was meant as a claim about what we'd expect *without* the benefit of our knowledge from experience. If we knew nothing about the correlation between mental and physical states, and we asked ourselves whether the duplication of your body would thereby duplicate your soul, our answer, our so-called a priori expectation, would be *no*. A body is one thing, a soul is another thing. The simplest, least convoluted hypothesis about what would happen is that there'd be no soul and therefore (if immaterialism were true) no mental life. So, when we discover through experience that your duplicate *would* have a mental life, that counts against immaterialism. It counts against immaterialism in the same way that the existence of horrible suffering counts against theism: we wouldn't expect such suffering if theism were true, while we would if atheism were true.

But notice an important point about the case of suffering and its bearing on theism vs. atheism. The argument works only if we assume that there's a *difference* between theism and atheism regarding whether we'd expect horrible suffering. If horrible suffering would be equally unexpected given atheism, then the existence of horrible suffering wouldn't tell in favor of atheism over theism. So, in order for Eric's argument to work, it has to be the case that there's a difference between materialism and immaterialism regarding whether we'd expect—*expect a priori*—that your duplicate would have a mental life. And I don't think there is any such difference between materialism and immaterialism. At least not between immaterialism and what is *far and away the best way to fill out the materialistic view*.

Here's why. As Eric helpfully points out (§1.5), the question of what mentality is—of what mental *features* are, and whether they are themselves just complex physical features—is distinct from the question we are debating in this book. Materialism, as understood in our debate, in no way implies that mental features just are physical features.

Mental Features

Before we start discussing the relationship between mental features and physical features, we should ask: what's meant by "mental feature"? It's much easier to answer that question than to answer the parallel question regarding "physical feature" (see my discussion in §2.3). As I'm using the term, a feature is by definition mental just in case it can be had only by a thinker or a thought. Thus, the features, being conscious, and feeling happy, and being a yummy chocolatey experience, are all mental features.

We could each be physical—having some shape and size and being made of matter—but also have some other features that are not themselves physical features. And that's good news for materialism, since mental features—some of them, at any rate—certainly don't seem to be physical features. They don't even seem to be *necessitated* by a thing's physical features. Eric repeatedly notes that "We have only the faintest understanding of how physical activities of any sort could be mental activities. Perhaps we can't even conceive of a material thing's thinking by virtue of its physical workings." Indeed. A number of philosophers (Jackson 1994, Chalmers 1996) maintain that we can go further—and correctly, in my view. They argue that we can actually see that nothing *could* think just in virtue of its physical workings. Physical workings are one thing, mental phenomena another. A specification of the positions and movements and causal dispositions of all of a thing's parts, no matter how many parts it has and no matter how complex their arrangement, is insufficient to explain or entail that the thing is having a yummy chocolatey experience. There's a manifest gap between the two: the former is simply the wrong *kind* of feature to pin down the latter with absolute necessity. So, if a material object thinks at all, then its thinking is not some complex physical feature, but rather *another* feature it has—another *fundamental* feature it has—alongside its physical features. This view is known as **property dualism**, so-called because it says there are (at least) two kinds of properties (i.e. features), physical properties and mental properties, and no property is of both kinds.

Because **property dualism** is compelling, materialists would do well to accept it. But then they have no business employing the

Property Dualism

There are two pesky definitional issues about "property dualism" that I should put on the table. First, the term can be used for the slightly weaker claim that *some* mental properties aren't physical and *some* physical properties aren't mental. The difference between that weaker claim and the stronger one I stated above won't matter for our purposes, so feel free to have either formulation in mind.

Second, and more importantly: property dualism goes further than just saying that mental features aren't *themselves* physical features (and physical features aren't themselves mental features). It says that mental features aren't necessarily *settled* by a thing's physical features (and physical features aren't even settled by a thing's mental features). That is, there could be physical duplicates—two objects that are alike in all physical respects—that are not mental duplicates (and mental duplicates that are not physical duplicates). To use the fancy philosophical term, property dualism says that mental features don't **supervene** on physical features.

We can stick with the initial simple formulation of property dualism if we stretch the meaning of "physical feature" a bit. If we let any (non-trivial) feature that's settled by a thing's physical features count, at least by extension, as itself a physical feature, then saying that every mental feature is a physical feature (in the extended sense) comes to the same thing as saying that of necessity any two physical duplicates are mental duplicates. And so *denying*, as property dualism does, that every mental feature is a physical feature (in the extended sense) comes to the same thing as denying that of necessity any two physical duplicates are mental duplicates. Adopting this linguistic convention will keep my formulations simpler when I later discuss alternatives to property dualism. But you should be sure to keep in mind what's meant.

duplication argument against immaterialism, since their own view fares no better. If we put your body in the duplicator and pressed the duplicating button 25 times, we'd end up with 25 human bodies that are physically indistinguishable from yours. If we knew nothing from experience about the correlation between mental and physical states, but we assumed that property dualism was true, what should we expect the mental lives of these 25 duplicates to be like? Well, I don't know what we *should* expect, but I know what we *shouldn't* expect: we shouldn't expect them *all* to be thinking the very same thing; indeed, we probably shouldn't even expect them *all* to be thinking, period. (By "thinking" I mean real thinking, not faux-thinking. As should be clear from what I said above, I certainly *would* expect all thousand to be at least faux-thinking the same thing.)

Think of it this way. Suppose we had a scale model generator, rather than a duplicator. If you put your body in the generator and press the button, it's guaranteed to produce a model of your body, made perfectly to scale. Beyond that, it makes no guarantees. (Buyer beware!) Now, if we went ahead and put your body in the generator and pressed the button, what should we expect the *size* of the output to be? Should we expect it to be the size of a thumbnail, or a turkey, or a colossus, or what? The answer, pretty clearly, is that there's no particular size at all we should expect it to be. Shape is one thing, size another. And if we had 25 different such scale model generators, made by different manufacturers, and we put your body successively in each one of them, we definitely *shouldn't* expect that all 25 outputs will be the same size. Again, shape is one thing, size is another. Likewise, if property dualism is true, physical features are one thing, mental features another. We really shouldn't expect one to go with the other, let alone correlate so well.

But they do. That's what we've learned from experience. And so, even though property dualism tells us we shouldn't expect it, we do assume that if we physically duplicated your body, the duplicate would also have a mental life, and one just like yours. So a property-dualist materialism and immaterialism are in the very same boat here. The former no less than the latter would have us expect the world to be different from how it turned out to be. So the world's turning out that way can't support the former over the latter.

If the duplication argument presents a serious challenge to immaterialism, then the analogous argument presents an equally serious challenge to a property-dualist materialism. I take it that a materialist adherent of property dualism won't think the latter challenge is very serious at all. After all, just because mental features and physical features are *different* doesn't mean they can't be *lawfully wed*. The correlations between the mental and the physical, a property dualist will say, are basic, brute, and bedrock; they are captured by fundamental **psycho-physical laws** (Chalmers 1996). Just like the fundamental **physical laws**, the fundamental psycho-physical laws are, well, fundamental—they're not true in virtue of some deeper connection between the physical and the mental. (Whether the existence of these laws requires some Supreme Being, like God, is a general question about laws of nature, whether physical or psycho-physical. If it does require them, then the existence of a Supreme Being will have to be part of the solution; if not, not. But there's nothing new here. Physical laws give rise to the same two options.) But then an immaterialist can and should say an analogous thing about the body and the soul. Just because the body and the soul are different doesn't mean they can't be lawfully wed. The fact that whenever there's a body (or a brain) of a certain level of complexity, it gets a soul to have and to hold is basic, brute, and bedrock; it's captured by a fundamental psycho-physical law. My point now isn't just that an immaterialist *can* offer that response. I've already noted that, and Eric has already granted it. My point now is that a materialist who puts her best foot forward will have to offer *substantially the same response*, if she has any response at all.

> On top of the problem that the Duplication Argument imputes to immaterialism implications that it doesn't have, a materialist who wields the argument against immaterialism confronts an additional problem. The problem is that an analogous and equally strong argument can be levelled against the most plausible materialistic view: one that takes property dualism on board.

4.5   Creation Ex Nihilo?

I gather Eric thinks that an immaterialist is in a worse position than a materialist—even a property-dualist materialist—since a property-dualist materialist will be able to get by with just the emergence of novel *features*, while an immaterialist will need to take on board the creation of novel *substances*, i.e. souls. And, Eric says (§1.15), the creation of novel substances is *extravagant*. It would involve things coming into existence ex nihilo, a phenomenon unknown anywhere else in nature; what's worse, it would involve ordinary material things like brains or organisms, lacking in any other evident superpowers, causing those things to come into existence from nothing.

This is an interesting point. If immaterialism in fact implies that (a) souls come into existence out of nothing, and that (b) your soul came into existence only as a result of your body reaching a certain level of complexity, then immaterialism does seem to (a′) make us (and all other souls) a rather special sort of thing, and (b′) give our bodies some rather special powers.

The first thing I would note in reply is that we already knew that we (and all other thinking things) were rather special. Both the materialist and immaterialist agree that we (and all other thinking things) have rather special *abilities*: the ability to think and everything that comes along with that. And the immaterialist already thinks that we (and all other thinking things) are rather special in our makeup: none of us is made of matter. If we immaterialists had to accept that we were also special in another way, I don't know how much that should come as news.

And though our bodies would have the power to bring something into existence out of nothing, that "power" would be very different from the power of God, or even a wizard, to do the same. It's not a power that our bodies could *choose* to exercise or not—our bodies have no choice in the matter, because they have no mental life. Their having that "power" would mean nothing more than this: given the actual psycho-physical laws, whenever and wherever a material object reaches a certain level of complexity, a soul comes into existence and gets hooked up to it. If God exists, then God might well be creating those souls in accordance with the laws; otherwise, this process would happen by itself. Either way, I'm not sure how much more extravagance any of this adds to the fact that souls are coming into existence ex nihilo in the first place. God is already supposed to be able to create ex nihilo, so if God is creating the souls, this would add no more extravagance at all. If God isn't involved, there'd be no *agent* at all creating the souls—the body would be no more of an agent than the sun is in growing trees.

But the second thing I would note is that it's not obvious that immaterialism really does imply that souls are brought into existence by brains or organisms, let alone brought into existence out of nothing. Most contemporary immaterialists do indeed think that I came into existence around the same time as my body or brain (see Taliaferro 1994, Swinburne 1997, Hasker 1999, Zimmerman 2010). But it can be denied. One way to deny it is pretty flatfooted and old-fashioned: Perhaps I have been in existence, *as a thinking thing*, for a very long time. It's just that when my body reached a certain level of complexity, I came to be "hooked up" to that particular body. Plato seems to have held this view. The view does have the awkward consequence that I have existed as a thinking thing for much longer than I remember. (Plato, in his *Meno*, actually embraces this consequence, since it accounts in his view for our ability to know a priori truths about such things as mathematics and philosophy. In his view, we're just recalling the truths that we learned before becoming embodied, when we promptly and sadly forgot them. I told you it was old-fashioned!)

Another way to deny it, which is less old-fashioned and doesn't have that awkward consequence, is to say that I have been in *existence* for a very long time—much longer than my body (or brain)—but that I only came to be a thinking thing at a certain point in the development of my body (or brain). Other respectable metaphysical views have us existing for just as long and undergoing transformations no less radical than this. For example, according to one prominent view, *anything* that *ever* exists, always existed and always will exist (Williamson 2013). Nothing really goes into or out of existence. What looks like going into and out of existence is just a matter of going from being **abstract** (with no causal powers, and no location, like a feature) to being **concrete** (with causal powers, and a particular location, like a person) and back again. An immaterialist who goes this route need not maintain that any of us has undergone a transformation so radical as from the abstract to the concrete: just from the unthinking to the thinking. Moving to a view much closer to home: **animalism**—the version of materialism that Eric himself endorses, and what I've been using as a stand-in for materialism simpliciter (§2.6)—says that each of us is a human organism. Quite plausibly, animalism has as a consequence that each of us was once an unthinking fetus (Olson 1997, ch. 4). So according to that very prominent version of materialism, each of us has undergone a transformation from an unthinking thing to a thinking thing.

It's true that animalism doesn't say that we've existed for a very long time before our bodies did. But as the Argument from Flux is meant to establish, a consistent materialism can't really avoid that conclusion. Indeed, it leads to a far worse conclusion: if I manage to exist at all for more than a few seconds, then I've existed for a very long time, *and for all but a few seconds of that existence,* I've been an unthinking spherical shell. So an immaterialist who goes this route is still in a much better position than a materialist.

We're back to where we were at the end of the previous section: the Duplication Argument's challenge to immaterialism is hardly more daunting, if at all, than the challenge it presents to materialism.

Immaterialism seems to be committed to the extravagant idea that my body managed to create me *ex nihilo*. It's not clear how extravagant this idea really is. But in any case, immaterialism isn't committed to it. Immaterialism is consistent with my having existed long before my body; and it's consistent with a non-old-fashioned kind of such pre-existence. Whether I in fact pre-existed my body, and if so, whether I did so in an old-fashioned way, are beyond me.

4.6   Who's Doing the Thinking?

Once you see how I think the Duplication Argument's challenge can be met—with basic, brute, and bedrock, laws that connect the states of certain physical things with the mental states and mental capacities (and perhaps existence) of certain souls—you should be able to predict how I'm going to address the Remote Control Argument. Recall the argument: intoxication makes you woozy, brain injuries usually have crippling cognitive consequences, and anesthesia knocks you out completely. All of that is uncontroversial. But, Eric says,

> Immaterialism implies that the relation between the body and the soul is like that between a remote-control drone and its operator. Changes in the body may affect its ability to communicate with the soul, but not the soul's ability to function.

Immaterialism implies no such thing, though. And the commitments I've just taken on in addition to immaterialism imply precisely the opposite. Changes in the body most certainly can and do affect the soul's ability to function; they do so in a predictable and regular way, in accordance with the psycho-physical laws of our world. And so it is that intoxication, brain injury, and anesthesia can render a person unconscious or incapacitated.

Eric calls this proposal "electric dualism," as it suggests that the body provides the soul not just with *information* but also with something analogous to *electricity*. He is dissatisfied with electric dualism for two reasons. One reason is that it allegedly involves mysteries. I will return to this complaint in §4.7, where I examine the broader "mystery charge." The second reason is as follows: according to electric dualism, in order for a soul to think, it needs to be hooked up to a properly functioning body. The body and the soul are both necessary for thinking. So what makes it the case, Eric asks, that it's the body that's enabling the soul to think, rather than it being the soul that's enabling the body to think or them cooperating so that the thing made of both the body and the soul thinks (what he calls "**cooperative dualism**")? In short: if a properly functioning body is necessary for thinking, why, according to the immaterialist, is it playing second (mental) fiddle to the soul? Eric thinks there's no good answer to this question. And saying instead that the body thinks, or that the soul doesn't think, would spell the end of immaterialism.

I'm frankly perplexed by the question. It seems to reflect a rather large gap between our views of what thinking is. But before I get to that, let me make two smaller points. First, it doesn't follow from my proposal that a soul needs to be hooked up to a properly functioning body in order to think. What follows is that *if* it's hooked up to a certain body, then that body needs to be properly functioning in order for the soul to think. (I suspect Eric is being unduly influenced by his own analogy to electricity. Yes, when it comes to a light bulb, it's not just that once it's hooked up to a certain power source, the power source needs to be properly functioning for the light bulb to go on; it's that without being hooked up to a power source it won't go on at all. But the analogy to electricity was Eric's, not mine.) My proposal is consistent with there being a soul that can think just fine before being hooked up to a body, or despite having never been hooked up with a body, or having been "unhooked" from a body it was once hooked up to. Perhaps that's what happens when we die. (See §4.5 for two ways in which I might have preexisted my body, one that has me thinking then and one that doesn't. As I said, which of these ways is right, if either of them is, is beyond me. So I wouldn't want my proposal to rule out the possibility of my having been a thinking thing before my body came into existence.)

Second, even if we suppose it's true that, given the actual psycho-physical laws, souls *can't* think without being hooked up to a properly functioning body, there's still a sense in which souls *can* think without being hooked up to a properly functioning body: namely, if the psycho-physical laws had been different. The psycho-physical laws that connect bodily states to soul states are not only basic, brute, and bedrock, but they are also presumably **contingent**. That is, the psycho-physical laws could have been different, or there could have been no such laws at all. So a soul's need for a properly functioning body is a conditional need: conditional upon certain laws, which could have failed to obtain. Souls don't *really* need bodies to think, not absolutely speaking, anyway.

This is very different from Eric's case of the conjoined twins, Lefta and Rita, who play the guitar together. Remember the case: Lefta presses the strings against the neck of the instrument in the appropriate sequence while Rita strums. There's no possible scenario in which only one of these activities gets done, and it counts as playing the guitar. (Strumming without pressing might come close but still doesn't amount to playing.) Each one is contributing something that's absolutely necessary for there to be guitar playing going on. Not so in the case of the body's activities, the soul's activities, and thinking. The latter case is much more like the case—as a certain kind of materialist would describe it—of a thinking human animal attached to and completely dependent on a ventilator. If the ventilator malfunctions or goes, so does the human animal and with him his ability to think. But no one is thereby tempted to suggest that rather than the ventilator enabling the human animal to think, it's the human animal enabling the ventilator to think, or that it's the thing made of the human animal and the ventilator that's doing the thinking![1] One good reason no one is tempted to suggest either of these things is that the human animal needs the ventilator in order to think only because of certain contingent facts about the body's need for oxygen. If God were to miraculously suspend the need for cellular respiration—if He were to facilitate the cells going about their business without converting oxygen to carbon dioxide—then the ventilator's activity wouldn't be necessary for the thinking to be going on. It's not just that the ventilator could be dispensed with; it's that what the ventilator is *doing*, i.e. supplying the cells with oxygen, could be dispensed with, and the person could go on thinking just as before. That's a very clear indication that the ventilator's activity isn't itself part of the thinking that's going on, and hence, that the ventilator is not actually doing any thinking itself. Mutatis mutandis for the body's activity, according to the sort of immaterialism I'm defending.

But even if we suppose it's true that, as a matter of absolute necessity, souls *can't* think without being hooked up to a properly functioning body, I am still perplexed by Eric's question. For the sake of illustration, suppose God exists, and that nothing can happen without God willing that it happens. So, if a volcano is erupting right now, God has to have willed that it erupt right now. If you're boiling up a pot of noodles right now, God has to have willed that you boil up a pot of noodles right now. And if I'm thinking right now, God has to have willed that I think right now. So as a matter of absolute necessity, I can't think without God willing that I'm thinking. Indeed, as a matter of absolute necessity, I can't think a given thought without God willing that I think *that thought*.

Now, ask yourself, does it follow just from these supposed facts alone that whenever I think something, it's really God and me *thinking that thought together* (or, even more radically, that only God is really thinking that thought)? Does it follow just from these supposed facts alone that when something tastes chocolatey to me, something tastes chocolatey to God as well (or, even more radically, that the thing tastes chocolatey only to God)? It doesn't seem to follow, and I would be perplexed if someone asked why we don't say those things instead. God's act of willing seems nothing more than a *necessary precondition* for *my* thinking and tasting, not *part and parcel* of them. This is perfectly obvious when it comes to volcanic eruptions and God's willing them to erupt. No one thinks it follows—from the supposition that volcanoes can't erupt unless God wills that they do—that whenever volcanoes erupt, God and the volcanoes are erupting together (or, even more radically, that only God is erupting!), and no one even thinks to *ask* why we shouldn't say those things instead.

So why should Eric's question arise about the activities of a properly functioning body but not about the divine will? The latter is just as necessary for my thinking as the former (supposing God exists); so the former can be just as extraneous to my thinking as the latter (supposing immaterialism is true).

Or so I say. Perhaps Eric would in fact suggest that God counts as thinking my thoughts, supposing that His willing is necessary for me to think. Thinking, I hear Eric continuing, isn't like an volcanic eruption—it's like boiling up a pot of noodles. Ask yourself: does it follow, from the fact that you can't boil up a pot of noodles without God having willed that it be done, that whenever you boil up a pot of noodles, God and you are boiling it up together? Here, I'm not so sure that the answer is "no." At the very least, I wouldn't be perplexed by someone who asked why God is playing second fiddle—seen as just an enabler rather than an actual player—when He seems to be playing no less an important role than you are.

So, which is it? Is thinking like an volcanic eruption, or is it like boiling a pot of noodles? Of course, it's like each of them, in different ways. The real question then is which way is *relevant* for our discussion. We have to ask why, on the one hand, no one suggests that whenever a volcano erupts, God and the volcano are erupting together, and on the other hand, some might suggest—even *I* might suggest—that whenever you boil up a pot of noodles, God and you are boiling it up together. I think the distinction is this: boiling up a pot of noodles is *entirely a matter of causing something to be the case* (the "something" is the pot of noodles coming to a boil). It doesn't matter how you do the job—you could light a fire, turn on an induction stove, leave the pot on the hood of a car in Death Valley, or use magical powers—as long as the job gets done. And supposing you can't boil a pot of noodles without God willing that you do (and willing that the pot boil), God is plausibly doing at least as much to get the job done as you are. But erupting isn't like that. Erupting, like vomiting, is at least partly a matter of having one's insides end up on one's outside; a little more technically, it's at least partly a matter of a thing undergoing specific internal changes, in the spatial configuration of its parts, in the temperature distribution among those parts, and still other changes. (Grammarians recognize the difference we're noting between boiling up a pot of noodles and erupting. "Boiling," as it's used in the phrase "boiling up a pot of noodles," is said to be a *transitive verb*; "erupting" is said to be an *intransitive verb*.) Since God's insides obviously don't end up on His outside, we're not tempted to suggest that God erupts, even supposing His activity is necessary for a volcano to erupt.

So now the question we have to ask is this: is thinking entirely a matter of causing something to be the case? Or, to give a little more leeway to the other side, is thinking purely a matter of its causes and effects? Is it sufficient to be in a state that tends to be brought about by such and such and tends to in turn bring about this and that? According to a number of views in philosophy of mind, the answer is yes.

> **Analytic behaviorism** says that to have a mental property (such as being in pain) is to be disposed to behave in certain ways (such as wincing, screaming, or taking painkillers) in certain circumstances.
>
> (Ryle 1949, Malcolm 1968)

It's all a matter of input/output, without any regard for the processes going on inside the thinker or even whether there are any processes going on inside. A less crude descendant of that view, **functionalism**, recognizes the importance for thinking of the particular processes going on inside the thinker (Putnam 1967). Thus, a black box that just happened to cause the right output in response to the right input wouldn't thereby count as thinking.

According to **functionalism,** to be in a given mental state (such as pain) is to be in a state that occupies a certain "node" in a causal network, some of whose "nodes" are behaviors (such as wincing and screaming) and some of which are stimuli (such as toe stubbings and torture chambers), but others of whose "nodes" are still other mental states (such as a desire for relief).
(see Levin 2018 for elaboration)

But what makes any of those other states *mental* states, and the particular mental states they are, is still the fact that they're causing certain kinds of things and being caused by certain other kinds of things. In short, it's their causal roles.

If I found either analytical behaviorism or functionalism appealing, then I could appreciate the force of Eric's question. After all, given the lawful correlations I've granted between soul states and brain states, it's true that for any soul state that plays a certain causal role, there will be a correlating brain state that plausibly plays much the same role. So if the soul states are mental, why not the brain ones? But as I have hopefully made clear at a number of points, I have little sympathy for any view that makes thinking purely a matter of being in a state that plays a certain causal role. Property dualism is compelling in large part because there is an evident gap between thinking, on the one hand, and the causal dispositions of a thing, on the other hand. Allowing myself to speak as a materialist for the moment: two different material things could be functionally indistinguishable and yet differ mentally. Perhaps one of them is "lights out," and the other is actually conscious. Using the terminology from §4.3, we would say that the first one has mere faux-mentality, while the second has the genuine article. Or maybe both of them are conscious and differ only in being "color spectrum inverts" (Block 1978): when one of them sees blue, the other sees red, and vice versa. They can both distinguish the color of the stripes on an American flag from that of the field behind the stars, and both of them will call the stripes "red" and the field "blue," and both of them will group the color of the stripes with the color of blood and not with the color of the sky, but all their visual seemings will be systematically color inverted. These possibilities, assuming as I do that they really are possible, refute both analytical behaviorism and functionalism.

For our purposes, thinking is like volcanic eruption, not like boiling a pot of noodles. And so whether the divine will or a properly functioning brain is necessary for a soul to think, that's no reason at all to suggest that God or the body is itself thinking the soul's thoughts together with it.

> Eric asks why, given electric dualism, the body is playing second mental fiddle to the soul. Given that the body is necessary for the soul to think, why is it just the soul that's thinking, rather than just the body, or the two of them together? There are a number of answers: first, the body isn't necessary for the soul to think; second, even if it were true that, given the actual psycho-physical laws, the body *is* necessary for the soul to think, that necessity is conditional. If the laws had been different, and they could have been, then the body could have been dispensed with and the soul would have been able to think just fine. Third and finally, even if the body and its activities were absolutely necessary for the soul to think, that wouldn't be a good reason to think the body is itself thinking; not, at any rate, according to the most plausible views in the philosophy of mind.

4.7   Surplus Mysteries?

In addition to the "thinking body objection," Eric argues that electric dualism—and immaterialism just as such—leaves us with surplus mysteries, *more* mysteries than we'd be left with given materialism. And that all by itself is a reason, Eric thinks, that we should be materialists.

Electric dualism in particular leaves us with a mystery about how and why the soul's thinking depends on the body's activities. That is, one question confronting the electric dualist is:

(1) How is it possible for a material thing to *produce* thinking (in an immaterial thing)?

As Eric sees it, this question presents the electric dualist with a mystery.

And then immaterialism just as such leaves us with still further mysteries. Eric makes much of immaterialism's supposed implication that it is impossible for a material thing to think. This leads him to ask the immaterialist:

(2) Why is it impossible for a material object to think?

As Eric sees it, this question presents the immaterialist with a second mystery.

Finally, there's the question for the immaterialist of how an immaterial thing *does* manage to think:

(3) How is it possible for an immaterial thing to think?

As Eric sees it, this question presents the immaterialist with a third mystery.

It's true, Eric acknowledges, that it's a mystery how *anything* manages to think. That is, the materialist faces the analogous question:

(4) How is it possible for a material thing to think?

And this question, Eric agrees, presents the materialist with her own mystery. So in effect (3) and (4) "cancel each other out." But the immaterialist has surplus mysteries in questions (1) and (2). (As Eric nicely points out, the materialist also faces question (1), sans the parenthetical qualification, but this is not an *additional* question for the materialist. According to the materialist, there's no difference between producing thinking and engaging in thinking. So there's no *surplus* mystery in (1), beyond the mystery in (4).)

My way with these supposedly surplus mysteries will be brisk, maybe even brusque. My answer to question (2) is straightforward: it's *not* impossible for a material object to think. Or, at least I'm not committed to the impossibility of a thinking material thing. Immaterialism *itself* implies no such thing. For immaterialism is a view about what we are: it says that we are at least partly immaterial. It's also the case that we think. It follows as a matter of logic from these two facts that some immaterial things *do* think. But nothing follows from these two facts about what *doesn't* think, let alone what *can't* think.

You might say that even if immaterialism itself doesn't imply that no material thing can think, the *arguments* for immaterialism do. But neither of the arguments *I* endorsed for immaterialism implies that material objects *can't* think; neither of them even implies that no actual material objects *do* think. (A more general point: I am aware of no argument for immaterialism that implies that material objects can't think, which doesn't also *explain* why material objects can't think. In §2.5, I listed a good number of arguments that suggest one or other mental feature we couldn't have if we were material. But they of course don't just suggest these things and leave it at that. They provide reasons for thinking these things are true—reasons such as *every material thing has parts, and nothing that's made of parts could have a unified point of view* (Hasker 1999). Each of these reasons, if true, also serves to *explain why* no material thing can think.)

You might say, though, that even if I didn't assume or logically imply that nothing material thinks, I did conclude something that's *plausible only if* no actual material thing thinks. For I concluded that Goofy doesn't think, and that neither do any of the other human organisms massively overlapping Goofy: the reasoning being that if any of them thinks, then they all do, and all of them thinking would have unpalatable moral and practical consequences. By the same token, as I pointed out, I would conclude the same regarding any and all of the candidates for being my brain: none of them thinks, since if any of them thinks, then they all do, and all of them thinking would have unpalatable moral and practical consequences. But it's hardly plausible that there are *other* actual material things that think, just not human brains or bodies. If *any* actual material thing thinks, then some of those things do. And so I am committed to there being no actual material things that think.

That much seems right to me. But I'm not sure how that's supposed to leave me with a mystery. After asking question (2), Eric added parenthetically "Or if it is possible for a material thing to think, the mystery is why our bodies don't in fact do so." I don't see how that's a mystery at all. The thought seems to be that if it's even so much as *possible* for our bodies (or bodies like ours) to think, then we should expect our bodies to *actually* think. But why should we expect that? It's not as though we expect every possibility to be actual. (That would anyways be impossible, since different possibilities are incompatible.) Just as I think it's possible for a human body to think, I think it's possible for an electron to think: I don't believe **panpsychism** is *impossible*.

> **Panpsychism** says that the mental pervades the whole of reality: everything, including water and air, thinks.

But should I therefore expect panpsychism to be *true*? Is it mysterious that no electrons think? I don't see why it would be.

I suspect that behind Eric's claim of mystery lies one of two things. Perhaps he is simply assuming one of the views in the philosophy of mind, such as behaviorism or functionalism, that makes thinking purely a matter of being in a state that plays a certain causal role.

Given such a view, it would in fact be mysterious that we think but not our bodies, since we're both in states that play much the same role. Indeed, it wouldn't just be mysterious, it would be pretty clearly false. I've already said, though, why I don't think any such view is true.

Alternatively, perhaps Eric means by "mystery" something much weaker than what I mean by it. Indeed, one gets the distinct impression that any brute fact, any fact that doesn't have an explanation, counts by Eric's lights as a mystery. In order for a fact to be a mystery, in Eric's sense, there's no need for it to run counter to what we think should or could be the case: no requirement that it flouts our expectations, and certainly, no need for it to strike us as impossible. Otherwise, how could it be *both* a mystery for the immaterialist that it's impossible (according to immaterialism) for a material thing to think (question 2) *and* a mystery for the materialist that it's possible (according to materialism) for a material thing to think (question 4)? It can't be that both the possibility and the impossibility of a material thing thinking run counter to our expectations. Each is just the negation of the other, so if one of them runs counter to our expectations, then the other must be just what we expected!

Now, given Eric's attenuated sense of "mystery," I'm willing to concede that there's a "mystery," in *that* sense, in it being the case that no material thing thinks. But we need to remember what that means. It just means that there's no deeper explanation for the fact that no material thing thinks. The same goes for question (1). I've repeatedly stated that the fundamental psycho-physical laws—that underlie the causal connections between bodily states and soul states—are themselves basic, brute, bedrock. So if the meaning of question (1) is, "What explains the fact that my body's physical states affect my mental states?" then my answer is that the fundamental psycho-physical laws explain that fact. If the meaning of the question is, "What explains the fundamental psycho-physical laws?" then my answer is that nothing does, that those laws are fundamental and that's the end of it. (Or, at least nothing beyond what might be required to explain *any* law. If a Supreme Being is required to explain the physical laws, then the same will go for the psycho-physical laws; if not, not.) So there's no surplus *mystery*; at most, there's just some surplus *bruteness*.

How much should that extra bruteness bother me? How much should that keep you up at night if you've agreed with me until now? Very little, I think. At most, that extra bruteness could serve as a tie-breaker; if there were no compelling arguments on either side, or if the views were otherwise equally matched, perhaps we should incline toward the theory that leaves fewer things brute. But that's not at all the situation we found ourselves in. As I see matters, there are at least two compelling arguments for immaterialism—the Argument from Fuzziness and the Argument from Flux—and no compelling arguments for materialism. Evidently, we should be immaterialists and learn to live with a little more about the world that has no deeper explanation.

By way of analogy, consider a debate, not about materialism but about how *many* concrete things there are. One side (the **pluralist**) claims there are *a lot*, and the other side (the **monist**) makes the quixotic claim that there's really *just one*, and more specifically that all of the apparently distinct concrete things really do exist *but are all identical with each other*. The Moon and the Suez Canal, for instance, are really just one thing, multiply located and diversely manifest. Now suppose that the pluralist supports her view with some compelling arguments—it shouldn't be hard to come up with Leibniz's Law-style arguments for the distinctness of the Moon and the Suez Canal! And suppose further that the monist *has* no compelling arguments. All he's got is the following point: there are countless *correlations* between the states of all of the apparently distinct concrete things. The states of the Moon, for example, are in fact highly correlated with the states of the Suez Canal—as we all witnessed when the Ever Given was finally dislodged. And while the pluralist can explain the fact that they are so correlated by invoking fundamental physical laws (in the case of the Moon and the Suez Canal, it's the Law of Universal Gravitation), she has no further explanation for those fundamental physical laws. But the monist has an explanation for the fact that the Moon and the Suez Canal are "connected": the explanation is that they are one and the same thing. It's true, even the monist might have to grant that there's no explanation for the fact that *these* particular states (the Suez-ish height of water) of the Moon/Suez Canal are correlated with *those* particular states (the Moon-ish position relative to the Earth) of the Moon/Suez Canal, but at least he has an explanation for the fact that what goes on with "one" affects what goes on with the "other." So, the pluralist has to accept some extra bruteness. How much should that extra bruteness bother her? Very little, I think. If the dialectical situation is as I've described it, we should *obviously* be pluralists and learn to live with a little more about the world that has no deeper explanation. We should do the same regarding immaterialism, if we need to.

> Eric argues that immaterialism leaves us with more mysteries than materialism. But neither immaterialism itself nor the arguments I rely on for immaterialism leaves us with more mysteries. At worst they leave us with more bruteness. And the cost of that extra bruteness—if there is any extra bruteness—pales in comparison to the price that's exacted from the materialist by the Argument from Fuzziness and the Argument from Flux.

4.8   Physicalism and Idealism

But I don't even think we need to live with more about the world that has no deeper explanation. To appreciate why, it'll help to reflect first on a recurring theme so far.

You may have noticed that I have leaned at various junctures on property dualism. I appealed to it explicitly in arguing that materialism is no better off than immaterialism in contending with the Duplication Argument and in addressing Eric's objection to the body playing second mental fiddle, and it was just beneath the surface in my own reply to the Duplication Argument (employing a distinction between faux-mentality and genuine mentality). I think there's a more general point to be made here: if you already accept property dualism, which many materialists do, then there's no good objection to immaterialism that isn't an objection to your own view (see Lycan 2013 for a similar idea). What's more, looking back at my arguments *for* immaterialism, you might detect its fingerprints at various points in the Argument from Fuzziness. (Think about what a functionalist in the philosophy of mind would say about my conviction that being conscious is intrinsic and non-vague.) Other philosophers have provided still other arguments for immaterialism that rely essentially on property dualism (see Zimmerman 2010, Schneider 2012). It's fair to say that the debate over materialism will and should look quite different depending on whether the materialist side has conceded the truth of property dualism.

Eric might legitimately refuse to concede any such thing.

> **Physicalism** says that every feature—or at least every mental feature—just is a physical feature.

Perhaps Eric endorses not just materialism but materialism in conjunction with physicalism. Or, even if Eric doesn't *endorse* any such specific combination, he might well wish to remain *neutral* as between physicalism and property dualism. After all, whatever difficulties physicalism faces, it also has a number of advantages, not the least of which is that it provides him a tidy reply to the Duplication Argument, and it provides him with a straightforward answer to his question (4): a material thing can think because a material thing can have physical properties. (Physicalism isn't available to a pure immaterialist such as myself. Since each of us has plenty of mental features but, according to pure immaterialism, no physical features—or at least no intrinsic physical features, which could plausibly be identified with a mental feature—it can't be true that every mental feature is a physical feature.)

Physicalism

As with my statement of property dualism, what's intended in my statement of physicalism is the extended sense of the term "physical feature," according to which any (non-trivial) feature that's settled by a thing's physical features counts, at least by extension, as itself a physical feature. So to say, as physicalism does, that every mental feature is a physical feature (in the extended sense) is to make the apparently weaker claim that of necessity any two physical duplicates are mental duplicates. But it's still true that physicalism isn't available to a pure immaterialist such as myself. After all, you and I are *trivially* physical duplicates, since neither of us has any physical features, and yet we differ in our mental features.

Now, I'm not really out to convince Eric. I'm not really even out to convince you, the reader. I'm out to figure out what I should believe. And since I'm convinced by the objections to physicalism, I don't mind assuming its falsity and going from there. I can't help but have the nagging feeling, though, that I should revisit the possibility of physicalist materialism—that is, the specific combination of materialism and physicalism—since that view has an elegant simplicity that I seem unable to achieve once I give up on physicalism (and then on materialism).

In truth, however, I too can achieve an equal measure of elegant simplicity. If I had been more precise in my earlier discussions, I would have leaned not on property dualism, in particular, but on the mere denial of physicalism. That's all that was required both in my responses to Eric's arguments and in developing my own arguments. The denial of physicalism says that some mental feature is not a physical feature. That's consistent with property dualism, which says *that*, and *also* goes on to say that, some physical feature is not a mental feature. But the denial of physicalism doesn't *entail* property dualism. For the denial of physicalism is also consistent with idealism.

Idealism says that every feature—including every physical feature—is a mental feature.

(Segal and Goldschmidt 2017)

Idealism 2.0

Analogously to my statements of property dualism and physicalism, what's intended is an extended sense of the term "mental feature," according to which any (non-trivial) feature that's settled by a thing's mental features counts, at least by extension, as itself a mental feature. So to say, as idealism does, that every physical feature is a mental feature (in the extended sense) is to make the apparently weaker claim that of necessity any two mental duplicates are physical duplicates.

I mentioned idealism, and gave a rough-and-ready characterization of it, early on in the debate. You might wonder how the more precise definition I've just given connects with my earlier rough-and-ready characterization, that "the material world is at best second-class: it's a mere shadow of the *real* world, an idea in a mind or minds." Well, it connects in the following way. If we ask how it could *be* that every physical feature is a mental feature—how it could be that having a mass of 5 kg, say, is a mental feature (whether in the original sense or in the extended sense)—there seems to be just one plausible answer: that the feature of having a mass of 5 kg is just the feature, *being the idea* of having a mass of 5 kg. So then, a chair that has a mass of 5 kg, and so has the feature of having a mass of 5 kg, also has the feature, *being the idea* of having a mass of 5 kg. But anything that has *that* feature *is itself just an idea*—perhaps in a Supreme Mind. The more precise definition has the rough-and-ready one as a consequence.

Note that the counterpart, or mirror image, of a physicalist materialism is not a *property-dualist* immaterialism but an *idealist* immaterialism. Just as a materialist (and only a materialist) can maintain that every mental feature is a physical feature (**physicalist materialism**), so too an immaterialist (and only an immaterialist) can maintain that every physical feature is a mental feature (**idealist immaterialism**).[2] And just as physicalist materialism provides a ready answer to Eric's question (4), idealist immaterialism also provides ready answers to (1) and (2). The answer to (1) is that the phenomenon of a material thing producing thinking in an immaterial thing is nothing other than one thought in an immaterial thing (since that's what a material thing *is*) producing another thought in an immaterial thing. Nothing mysterious there. Likewise, the answer to (2) is that material objects can't think because they are themselves thoughts (in an immaterial thing), and thoughts can't themselves think. Nothing mysterious there. So, there's no surplus of mysteries, or even of brute facts, given idealist immaterialism.

You might suggest that now the unanswered (3) saddles an immaterialist with an extra brute fact. But the physicalist answer to (4) ("a material thing can think because a material thing can have physical properties") merely invites the follow-up question: "How is it possible for a material thing to have physical properties? How is it possible for *anything* to have physical properties." (Just think about it for a while. Everything can start to seem pretty mysterious if you think about it long enough.) And answering that question with "That's its job, damn it!" is ultimately no more illuminating than providing the very same answer to question (3).

Of course, Eric might find idealism wholly implausible. I'd beg to differ (Segal and Goldschmidt 2017). I'd also return the favor; physicalism seems to me wholly implausible. Be that as it may, the bottom line is this: if we compare apples to apples, materialism has no advantage over immaterialism. If we combine each of them with property dualism and then compare, they both have roughly equal quantities of bruteness. If we compare physicalist materialism with idealist immaterialism, we reduce the quantity of bruteness on both sides in equal measure. Either way, we have roughly the same number of apples.

So while we should anyway believe immaterialism, we are lucky not to have to pay any real price for doing so.

I argued in the previous section that if immaterialism saddles us with extra bruteness, the cost of that bruteness pales in comparison to the price that's exacted from the materialist by the Argument from Fuzziness and the Argument from Flux. In this final section I argued that immaterialism doesn't actually saddle us with extra bruteness. When each of materialism and immaterialism is conjoined with property dualism, they both have roughly equal amounts of bruteness. And while the conjunction of materialism and physicalism manages to avoid much of the bruteness, so does the conjunction of immaterialism and idealism, and by equal measure.

Notes

1   Alright, maybe not *no one*. See Clark and Chalmers (1998). Cf. Stapleford and Wentzell (2019) for a powerful reply.
2   Only an immaterialist can maintain that every physical feature is a mental feature, because the conjunction of materialism about us with the claim that every physical feature is a mental feature--and hence that material things are nothing but ideas--has the consequence that *we* are nothing but ideas. Could I be just an idea? That seems pretty hard to swallow. (Although see Lebens (2015, 2017), and Goldschmidt and Lebens (2020), for a defense of so-called Hasidic Idealism.)

Second Round of Replies

Chapter 5

The Appearances and the Evidence

Eric T. Olson

Contents

5.1   Appearances One More Time

I can address only a few of the many forceful points Aaron makes in his reply. Start with the question of whether we *seem*, in ordinary experience, to be material or immaterial. By "ordinary experience" I mean the way things appear to all of us, as opposed to any special experience that scientists or other experts may have. Which view looks right on the face of it? Which would you be more likely to accept before considering philosophical or scientific arguments, religious teachings, or other specialist knowledge?

The question is about what ordinary experience tells us. It's not whether that experience is *evidence* for our being material or immaterial. Evidence is information bearing on the truth or falsity of a proposition. If money was stolen from the safe overnight, the fact that Stella knew the safe's combination and was seen the next day driving an expensive new car is evidence for the claim that she took it. It's not conclusive evidence—it wouldn't be enough to convict her in court—but it's relevant to the case, and it supports her guilt rather than her innocence. Aaron and I agree that if we appear to be material things, that's evidence for materialism. But we disagree about whether that *is* how we appear.

DOI: 10.4324/9781003032908-8

Does our ordinary experience give the impression that we're material, then, or that we're immaterial? Or is it neutral, telling us nothing either way? It seems natural to say that we appear to be material things within the physical world, not immaterial things in two-way communication with it. We seem to take up space, to be visible and tangible, and to have weight and temperature and a solid surface. As only material things can have these properties, we appear to be material things.

Aaron thinks this is too quick: it doesn't show that we appear to be *wholly* material (§4.2). The appearances may tell us that we have material parts, but they don't rule out our having an immaterial part as well. The appearances are neutral as between materialism and compound immaterialism: they don't distinguish between our being wholly material and our being only partly so. That's because our senses are blind to the existence or nonexistence of immaterial things. A thing composed of a physical organism and a soul would look and feel just the same as a physical organism. Our ordinary experience can't tell us that we either have a soul or lack one because it would be the same either way.

I myself said this in §1.6. I now wish I hadn't said it. I should have said that we appear to be wholly material. It's true that our experience would be the same either way. If some human beings were composed of a soul and a body and others were wholly material, you couldn't tell them apart simply on the basis of ordinary appearances—not even in your own case. But things can appear to be one way rather than another even when it would make no difference to our experience.

Not so long ago nearly everyone believed that the earth stood still and the heavenly bodies revolved around it. Nowadays we know that the earth turns on its axis while the sun and stars stand more or less still. Our experience would be the same either way: if there were a planet just like ours except that the heavenly bodies did revolve around it, you couldn't know, just by the way things looked and felt, which one you were on. Our senses can't tell the difference. Even so, the appearances are not neutral as between these two views. The earth *seems* to stand still: that's why this was the dominant view for thousands of years and was only overturned (by Copernicus, Galileo, and others) in the 17th century. We don't find cultures before this time evenly divided between Copernican and geocentric views. Given the appearances, the Copernican view is unquestionably the more surprising one: it's really quite astonishing to think that the ground beneath our feet is moving eastwards at 500 miles per hour. The Copernicans knew this very well, and went to a lot of trouble to explain why the appearances are misleading: how the earth's rotation causes the apparent motion of the stars, why it doesn't give us the sensation of movement we get when we ride on a carousel, and so on.[1]

I claim that our having a soul—whether we *are* souls or only have them as parts—would be surprising in the way that the earth's motion is surprising. Our ordinary experience gives the appearance that we're wholly rather than just partly material, just as it gives the appearance that the earth stands still rather than turning rapidly on its axis, even though our senses can't tell the difference. It's not just that we don't appear to have a soul: we appear not to have one.

How can something undetectable to the senses appear not to exist, as opposed to merely not appearing to exist but not appearing not to exist either? That's a hard question that I won't try to answer. But there are many examples of this phenomenon. Suppose you go to the theater and are startled to see Peter Pan flying above the stage. We know, of course, that he must be suspended by invisible wires, but it looks like he's flying: that's the point of the stunt. The appearances are not neutral as between his flying and his being suspended. He appears to be flying precisely because (if the trick is done well) he appears *not* to be suspended. There appear to be no wires holding him up. And this is so even though (from where we're sitting) our senses are blind to the wires. Or again: science has discovered that 100 trillion neutrinos pass through each of us every second. It's an amazing fact. It's not at all how things appear. It's not just that there don't seem to be such particles and there don't seem not to be either. The appearance is not neutral on the question: that's what makes the fact amazing. No one would be amazed to hear that there are no such particles. And this is so even though our senses can't detect them. Many things appear to be absent even though we couldn't detect them if they were there. And that's how it is with immaterial souls.

For this reason I think, contrary to what I said earlier, that we appear to be wholly material. But however that may be, it's even more evident that we appear to be at least partly so: to have hands and feet as parts, for example. Otherwise we'd be completely invisible, intangible, and weightless, and that's *not* how it seems. Someone innocent of philosophy would be just as surprised to be told that we're wholly immaterial as someone innocent of modern science would be to hear that the earth is spinning rapidly on its axis or that 100 trillion neutrinos pass through us every second. Even if our ordinary experience says nothing about whether we have or lack any immaterial parts, it seems to say that we have material ones.

Yet Aaron disputes even this. He says our ordinary experience gives no suggestion that we have material parts: for all it tells us we might be wholly material, wholly immaterial, or a mixture of both. None of these three views is any more surprising on the face of it than the others. This, he says, is because our experience would be the same in all three cases: again, if some human beings were wholly immaterial and others were only partly so, we couldn't tell which ones were which. But although that may be true, we've seen that it doesn't rule out our appearing one way rather than the other.

> Does our ordinary experience give the appearance that we have a soul, or that we don't? Aaron argues that experience is silent on this question, because our senses are blind to immaterial things. I argue that just as there appear to be no invisible particles passing through us, there appear to be no souls, even though our senses are blind to both. But even if this is wrong, our experience tells us that we're at least partly material.

5.2   Souls, Zombies, and Wotsits

I argued in §1.11 that if we were to make a perfect physical duplicate of you by arranging atoms, we'd expect him or her to have a mental life like yours. We'd expect it because of the strong correlation between physical and mental properties. We never find people with dramatic mental differences—one who's fully conscious and one who's unconscious, say—without a corresponding physical difference. I said that this is what we'd expect if our mental lives were physical activities in the body. If they were nonphysical activities in the soul, we'd expect the duplicate to have no mental life, because the machine doesn't create a soul.

Aaron accepts that the duplicate would at least *appear* to have a mental life—she would behave just as you do rather than being comatose—but offers two explanations of this that are consistent with immaterialism.

One is that the appearance would be false (§4.3). The duplicate could write insightful philosophy essays, keep a large circle of friends, and so on, so that no one could tell the two of you apart, even though she was never any more conscious than a stone. She could have what Aaron calls "faux mentality." Call this the *zombie explanation*.

Alternatively, the machine might duplicate the soul as well as the body (§4.4). Creating the right sort of physical organism might create an immaterial soul and attach the two (that is, enable them to interact in a special way). That one causes the other would be a law of nature, like the law saying that rubbing objects together creates heat. So the duplicate *would* have a mental life, but it would take place in a soul. Aaron says that's in fact what the immaterialist should expect, based on the observed correlation between the physical and the mental. Call this the *correlation-by-natural-law explanation* (it's a version of emergent dualism). Either story would account for the presumed fact that the duplicate would behave just as you do even if we had a soul.

He wants to infer from this that the thought experiment provides no evidence for materialism. This is not just because the result could be explained in a way that's consistent with immaterialism. It's not the mere *existence* of the zombie and correlation explanations that undermines the duplication argument. Every observed phenomenon can be explained in more than one way. Even the fact that cars without radiators overheat doesn't absolutely prove that they need one. There may be something else they need that's merely correlated with having a radiator: a nonphysical wotsit somehow supplied to all and only cars with radiators, say. The mere existence of this alternative explanation doesn't mean that what we observe is no evidence for the claim that cars need a radiator. Aaron's unstated assumption is that at least one of his proposed explanations is as good as the materialist's account.

Is that true? Take the zombie explanation first. If the duplicate acted just like you in every situation (as well as being physically no different), would she really be just as likely to be entirely unconscious as to have a mental life? If so, this would hold not just for human beings produced by our imaginary machine, but also for those produced in the usual way. If Stella, born of woman, spent months gathering information about the bank's security systems and then broke in and got away with a million dollars in cash, we'd be jumping to conclusions if we supposed that she had the slightest awareness of what she was doing: she could just as well have been unconscious from birth. But even if that's possible, it's not very likely. You can imagine how sympathetic the judge would be if Stella were to claim innocence on the grounds that she had never had any mental life. And if it would be reasonable to account for the duplicate's behavior by saying that she's a zombie, it would be equally reasonable to suppose that your closest friends are zombies.

That's certainly a fascinating hypothesis, but it's almost impossible to believe; and to be fair, Aaron never suggests that it's likely. He prefers the correlation explanation: that the duplicate's mental life would take place in an immaterial soul created by the process of arranging atoms in human form. And likewise, some stage in the physical development of an ordinary human being in the womb creates a soul. Arranging physical particles in a certain way produces a nonphysical entity not composed of particles or any other preexisting material.

Aaron finds this just as good, as an account of what would happen in the duplication experiment, as the materialist's account. If we made 100 organisms physically identical to you and every one of them behaved just as you do, the most we could conclude, he says, is that the organisms are either conscious like you are (as materialism has it), or are animated by immaterial souls created by the process of arranging atoms. (I leave aside the zombie explanation.) But we'd have no reason to prefer one of these accounts over the other.

Compare this with the following claim: if we manufactured 100 identical cars, half with radiators and half without, and all those with radiators ran well and the rest overheated, the most we could conclude is that either the radiators stop the cars from overheating, or else what prevents overheating is an immaterial wotsit brought into existence by the process of installing a radiator. (Leave aside other possible explanations.) But we'd have no reason to prefer one account over the other.

The "radiator theory" is clearly superior to the "wotsit theory" as an account of what happens in the automotive experiment. Why? Well, the wotsit theory is complicated and extravagant: it posits an immaterial entity exempt from any known laws of nature, whereas the radiator theory explains everything in terms of familiar physical objects. And it's ad hoc: wotsits are introduced in order to explain just one thing, namely how engines keep cool. There's no other reason to believe in them: they can't be observed, and they have no effects apart from their supposed cooling of engines by which we could confirm their existence. Radiators, by contrast, are observable and have many detectable effects.

Finally, the wotsit theory is deeply mysterious. We know nothing about wotsits apart from their claimed immateriality and cooling powers. We have no idea how the process of building a car could bring one into existence, or how they do their cooling. And there's no apparent way of finding out: being nonphysical, they're more or less impossible to investigate. Radiators, by contrast, are completely *un*mysterious: we know all about what properties they have in addition to their cooling powers (or at least the experts do), how they work, how they come into being, and so on. There may be mysteries about the matter making up radiators—about the physics of elementary particles—but there are no mysteries about radiators in particular.

So the wotsit theory is extravagant, ad hoc, and mysterious. The radiator theory has none of these defects. These are strong reasons for preferring it as an account of what happens in the automotive experiment.

Return now to the duplication experiment. Aaron's correlation account posits an immaterial entity exempt from the established laws of nature, whereas the materialist's account explains everything in terms of familiar physical objects. Aaron's account is just as extravagant as the wotsit theory, while the materialist's is just as unextravagant as the radiator theory.

Immaterial souls can't be observed or detected in any way apart from their supposed ability to produce thought. There may be other reasons to believe in their existence: we've discussed a number of arguments for immaterialism, though we've seen that they're inconclusive at best. As we'll see in §5.4, further observations *could* support their existence, but what we in fact observe is the opposite. The nervous system, by contrast, is observable and does many things in addition to producing our mental lives. So although Aaron's account may be less ad hoc than the wotsit theory, it's still inferior in this respect to the materialist's account.

What about mystery? Well, we know nothing about souls apart from their supposed immateriality and mental powers. We don't know what nonmental properties they have—whether they have features that stand to their mental powers as the other physical properties of radiators (shape, size, chemical properties, and so on) stand to their cooling powers. We have no idea how the process of arranging atoms into a physical organism could bring a soul into existence. And we know no more about how a soul could think than about how a wotsit could cool an engine. Souls are no less mysterious than wotsits.

I can't say that the materialist's explanation of what would happen in the duplication experiment is entirely free from mystery: our understanding of how the nervous system could produce our mental lives is badly incomplete. But the scientific research projects devoted to this, though in their early stages, have had considerable success.[2] By contrast, there is no serious research into how the soul could produce thought and consciousness.

For these reasons the materialist's account of the duplication experiment looks preferable to Aaron's (and I know of no better immaterialist proposals). I concede that it doesn't explain what happens as well as the radiator theory explains what happens in the automotive experiment. The radiator theory is a scientific triumph, and no one can yet say that about materialism. But Aaron's account is little better than the wotsit theory. So although the duplication experiment may not support materialism to the same degree that the automotive experiment supports the radiator theory, it does support it.

> Aaron accepts that a physical duplicate of you created by arranging atoms would have a mental life like yours, but proposes that her mental life would take place in a soul created by this process. But although this explanation is consistent with immaterialism, it's extravagant, ad hoc, and mysterious. The materialist's explanation, by contrast—that our mental lives are physical activities—is not extravagant or ad hoc, and is less mysterious.

5.3   Materialism and Property Dualism

Aaron makes the surprising claim that the materialist's account of the duplication experiment is no less extravagant and mysterious than his own (§4.4). (I'll set aside the charge that his account is ad hoc.) Why? Because materialists, like immaterialists, should accept that mental *properties* are nonphysical. Being conscious, feeling afraid, and being depressed are examples of mental properties; weighing ten kilograms, conducting electricity, and floating on water are physical properties. The nature and arrangement of neurons in your brain is a physical property of you (or of your body). The claim is that mental properties are not arrangements of neurons, or physical properties or conditions of any other sort. They're entirely nonphysical, in that they don't obey the laws of physics and their occurrence is not settled by the physical facts. Fear may be *caused by* a certain neural property, just as it's caused more indirectly by disapproving aunts and rabid dogs, but that's the only connection between them. This view is called *property dualism*. (*Substance* dualism adds to it the claim that nothing can have both mental and physical properties, so that thinking things are entirely nonphysical.) Immaterialism entails property dualism, but Aaron thinks materialists should accept it too: even if we're material things, our mental properties are distinct from any of our physical properties.

Think of the duplicating machine again. It takes atoms of the same kinds and numbers as yours and arranges them just as yours are now. The physical laws then ensure that the resulting being is physically identical to you. But Aaron says this is not enough to make her *mentally* identical to you: she could still have the psychology of Genghis Khan or even no mental life at all.

Again, he accepts that if we actually did the experiment, the duplicate *would* be mentally like you; but this, he says, is only because there are laws of nature connecting physical properties with mental ones. And these laws are contingent. They're not like the mathematical law that for every prime number there's a larger one. They don't *have* to hold: that's what makes it possible for the duplicate to lack any mental life. Compare: rubbing sticks together creates heat, but this may not be absolutely necessary. There might be no impossibility in the idea of rubbing sticks without producing heat: it just happens to be ruled out by a contingent physical law. The laws connecting physical and mental properties, Aaron says, are contingent in the same way. And they're not physical laws like those connecting friction and heat. So the physical properties of things and the physical laws governing them are not enough to give us anything mental: in this sense the mental "floats free" from the physical.

That's what immaterialists say. Aaron claims that materialists should say the same: even if you're made entirely of matter, a physical duplicate of you could have different mental properties from yours or even none at all, given the same physical laws. If the duplicate *would* have your mental properties, that's only due to contingent, nonphysical laws connecting physical properties with mental ones.

Immaterialists say in addition that there are nonphysical laws connecting physical and nonphysical *objects*: bodies and souls. But both views—immaterialism and materialism combined with property dualism—require nonphysical laws connecting the physical with the mental, and Aaron says this makes them "substantially the same"

(p. 157). If immaterialism is wild and extravagant, then so is materialism, because it too requires a sort of dualism of the mental and the physical.

Now I don't accept property dualism. Why does Aaron think I should? He gives two reasons. First, no one knows how a thing could think by engaging in certain physical activities. But that's not a very compelling reason to suppose that it couldn't do so: it may just be a limitation on our part. And as we saw in §1.9, no one knows how a thing could think in any other way either. His second reason is that we can see, on reflection, that nothing *could* think simply by engaging in physical activities: it's possible for a perfect physical duplicate of you to lack any mental life. But can we really see this? We can of course imagine renting a high-quality duplicating machine from a local business, persuading you to step inside, finding in the "out" box a comatose being who never wakes up, and being assured by colleagues from the medical school that this being is nevertheless physically identical to you. But that hardly shows that this is possible, because we can just as easily imagine discovering the largest prime number, even though there can be no such number. I'm not saying that the duplicate *would* have a mental life. (I did say this in §1.11, but I'm not relying on that claim now.) I'm not arguing *against* property dualism. My point is only that Aaron's argument *for* it is unconvincing.

(It's unconvincing for a second reason as well. Even if the duplication experiment really could have the imagined result, that would establish property dualism only if it's possible *given the same physical laws*. Otherwise the possibility of a physical duplicate of you with no mental life would no more show that the mental was nonphysical than the possibility of rubbing sticks without producing heat would show that friction was nonphysical. If a physical duplicate of you could be completely unconscious, then the laws connecting physical and mental phenomena must be contingent. But this would support property dualism only if those laws were also nonphysical, and we've been given no reason to accept that.)

But set all this aside. Suppose materialists accept property dualism. Would that leave their view with no advantage over immaterialism? I said that immaterialism was complicated and extravagant in that it posits entities exempt from physical laws. It says, in effect, that there are two separate worlds: the physical world of space, matter, and radiation, subject to physical forces such as gravity and electromagnetism but completely devoid of mentality, and the mental world of souls having no physical properties. The mental world and its interaction with the physical are governed by nonphysical laws.

By contrast, the combination of materialism and property dualism posits *properties* exempt from physical laws. It posits just one world, but with two aspects. You and I have both a physical aspect consisting of our mass, shape, anatomy, chemical makeup, and so on, and a mental aspect that does not consist of physical properties. The mental aspect and its connection to the physical aspect are governed by nonphysical laws. (Materialists needn't deny that there is a nonphysical world in addition to the one we inhabit: they could accept the existence of gods or angels or numbers. They deny only that we ourselves belong to such a world.)

By any standard, a theory attributing nonphysical properties to material things is less complicated, other things being equal, than one positing entities having *only* nonphysical properties. One world with two aspects is simpler than two worlds. That said, both theories are extravagant compared to materialism *without* property dualism, and the difference between them may appear insignificant—much as, to someone who has only ever traveled on foot, riding in a car might seem little different from flying.

How do the views compare when it comes to mystery? I said that immaterialism was mysterious because we know nothing about what nonmental properties souls have, how they produce thinking, or how arranging atoms could bring them into being; and there seems to be no way of finding out. Nor does anyone know why it should be impossible for material things to think. Materialism with property dualism has none of those mysteries. Its most puzzling implication is that physical activity and physical laws are not enough to yield anything mental: a physical duplicate of you could be completely unconscious even given the same physical laws. No one knows why that should be. But immaterialism has this mystery too.

So I think materialists have no compelling reason to accept property dualism; and even if they do accept it, their view is considerably simpler and less mysterious than immaterialism.

Aaron claims that even materialists should accept that our mental properties are nonphysical: property dualism. Both materialism and immaterialism must posit nonphysical laws connecting the physical with the mental. This, he says, makes materialism just as extravagant and mysterious as immaterialism. I've argued against both these claims.

5.4   Is Immaterialism Unfalsifiable?

We would expect a physical duplicate of you to have a mental life like yours. Severe mental defects are always correlated with physical abnormalities. Small amounts of alcohol in the blood—less than one part in a thousand—dramatically alter our mental activities, and the drugs used in general anesthesia stop them completely. In short, mental properties are profoundly sensitive to the physical condition of the nervous system. Aaron says this is no reason, or at least no very good reason, to suppose that mental activity is a sort of physical activity occurring in the body: it could just as easily be a nonphysical activity in the soul. If that's right, there could *never* be good evidence against our having a soul. If anything *would* tell against it, it would be just what we actually observe. He appears to regard immaterialism as unfalsifiable.

That's a troubling claim. There could certainly be evidence *for* our having a soul. It could turn out that physical duplicates of you were invariably comatose. There might be no systematic correlation between mental defects and physical abnormalities, so that people who can't form memories or recognize faces, or even those with severe dementia, are physically identical to people with normal mental abilities. Head injuries, no matter how severe, might never cause unconsciousness, but only prevent us from interacting with the body. There might be no chemical substance capable of stopping our mental activity, and alcohol might have no effect on it. Any of this would be powerful evidence against the claim that mental activity takes place in the nervous system. It would be a materialist's nightmare.

Not that materialists would have to take this lying down. They could try to explain it in a way that's consistent with their view, just as Aaron tries to explain what we actually observe in a way that's consistent with immaterialism (the zombie and correlation explanations of §5.2). If head injuries never caused unconsciousness, that could be because stopping your brain activities creates an immaterial soul with your mental properties, just as making a physical duplicate of you does on Aaron's view. This newly created soul would be conscious but unable to move or perceive anything until your brain recovers sufficiently. At that point it would vanish and its memories would be copied to your brain, giving you the appearance of remembering what you were thinking while you were physically unresponsive. (In that case there would be souls, but most of the time we wouldn't have one, and no soul would ever be a part of you or me.)

What could account for the imagined fact that a physical duplicate of you would have no mental life? Materialists could say that a thing's having a mental life at a certain time consists only partly in its current physical properties, and partly in its history. Being conscious might amount to having a brain that's in the right condition *because of* a certain sort of growth and development. It might be like the property of being chronically ill: whether you have it at a given time depends partly on how you were at earlier times. In that case a human being produced in adult form by the machine, lacking any history of growth and development, could not, at that time, have a mental life—just as, however ill it might be when it's freshly made, it could not then be *chronically* ill.

But these proposals are impossible to take seriously. Even if the imagined observations would not conclusively disprove materialism, they'd certainly tell against it. They're the opposite of what we'd expect if we were material things. They're exactly what we'd expect if we were *im*material things. But then our *not* observing them—the actual case—would go against that expectation and would therefore be an indication that we're material. Given that the materialist's nightmare would be evidence for immaterialism, the opposite must be evidence against it.

Let me explain this in more detail. Evidence for a hypothesis or claim is something we'd expect to find if the hypothesis is true, raising its probability. More precisely, evidence is something that's more likely to occur if the hypothesis is true than if it's false. But then it must be more likely *not* to occur if the hypothesis is false than if it's true. Its not occurring is evidence against the hypothesis, reducing its probability.

Take the claim that intelligent beings from outer space often visit the earth. If this were true, we'd expect to see signs of them: unidentifiable flying objects, local radio signals of no known human origin, strange footprints, and so on. Not that we'd *necessarily* see these things: the visitors might take care to avoid detection. But we'd be a lot more likely to see them if we really are being visited than if we're not. So seeing them would be a reason to suppose that we're being visited: it would raise the probability of the hypothesis. And of course they're *not* things we'd expect to observe if we had no alien visitors. In that case we'd expect to see the opposite: no signs of visitation. Our not seeing the signs would support the claim that we're not being visited. It would reduce the probability of the space-alien hypothesis.

The precise details are complicated. The occurrence of the signs would support the claim that we're being visited to a higher degree than their absence would support the opposite claim. Suppose the likelihood of our seeing the signs is 60% if we're being visited and 5% if we're not. The first figure is only 60% because the aliens might avoid detection, a chance which I've estimated at 40%. (Hiding from human beings probably wouldn't be much of a challenge for beings capable of insterstellar travel.) And the second figure is greater than zero because there's a chance—I've guessed 5%—that pranksters are fooling us into thinking we're being visited even though we're not.

Given that observing signs of alien visitation is 60% likely if we're being visited and only 5% likely if we're not, observing them would be strong evidence for our being visited. Again, there would still be a chance that it's a hoax, but if we had no other relevant information—if we considered both hypotheses equally likely to start out with—then seeing the signs should lead us to consider the space-alien hypothesis twelve times more likely to be true than false: 60% compared to 5%.

In that case, the probability of our *not* observing the signs would be 40% if we're being visited and 95% if we're not—40% being the chance that the aliens are hiding given that they're here, and 95% being the chance that we're not being fooled by pranksters given that the aliens are not here. Of course, we either observe the signs or we don't: there's no third possibility. So if the probability of seeing them is 60% if we're being visited, the probability of not seeing them in that case must be 40% (100 minus 60). Likewise, if the probability of our seeing the signs if we're not being visited is 5%, the probability of our not seeing them in that case must be 95%. The probability of our seeing no signs of alien visitation, then, would be 40% if we're being visited and 95% if we're not. So if we failed to see the signs and had no other relevant information, we ought to consider the space-alien hypothesis more than twice as likely to be false than true: 95% compared with 40%. That wouldn't show conclusively that we're not being visited—there would still be a chance that the aliens are hiding—but it would be significant.

So if certain observations would be evidence of alien visitation, our not seeing such things would have to be evidence, even if it's weaker evidence, against our being visited. The space-alien hypothesis can't be unfalsifiable.

Return now to the case at hand. Imagine again that perfect physical duplicates of you are always comatose, that there's no correlation between mental defects and physical abnormalities, that head injuries never cause unconsciousness, and so on: the materialist's nightmare. That would support immaterialism. How strong would that support be? The usual view is that these things are just what we'd expect if we had souls: their probability, given immaterialism, would be high. (That's what I said in §1.11.) Aaron disagrees: he thinks that if we had souls we'd be just as likely to observe what we actually do as to observe the materialist's nightmare, and the immaterialist shouldn't be surprised either way. That's because of his high opinion of the correlation-by-natural-law explanation (§5.2). In that case immaterialism would give the nightmare a likelihood of only 50%. But even if that's right, the nightmare would be extremely *un*likely—1%, say—if we were entirely material. (The low figure reflects how hard it would be for a materialist to explain these phenomena.) That would make the nightmare strong evidence for immaterialism: if we had no other relevant information, we ought to consider it 50 times more likely than materialism.

But then the likelihood of our *not* observing the nightmare would be 50% if we have souls and 99% if we don't have them. The nightmare has a far higher chance of occurring—nearly twice as high—if we have souls than if we don't. So in the absence of any other information, our not observing the nightmare should lead us to consider materialism nearly twice as likely as immaterialism. And that's the actual situation. These numbers are of course only crude estimates, and the true figures may differ. And we do have other information about the likelihood of materialism and immaterialism: that's what the rest of this book is about. But the point remains that because the materialist's nightmare would support immaterialism, what we actually observe tells against it.

Aaron says that the presumed result of the duplication experiment and the dependence of the mental on the physical are not good evidence for materialism. This implies that there could never be good evidence against immaterialism. But immaterialism could not be unfalsifiable in this way. If physical duplicates of you would be unconscious and the mental did not depend on the physical, that would be evidence *for* immaterialism. And in that case the absence of such evidence must tell against it.

Notes

1   Kuhn (1957) is a fascinating study of this topic.
2   See e.g. Ramachandran and Blakeslee (1999), Humphries (2021).

Chapter 6

Materialism Is Metaphysically Messy or Morally Absurd

Aaron Segal

Contents

6.1 Laying Out the Materialist Strategies

In my opening statement, I argued that the material world is metaphysically inhospitable to us, that *its* nature is deeply mismatched with *our* nature. Eric lays out two general strategies for dealing with the alleged mismatch.

One strategy grants my contention about the nature of the material world but denies my contention about our nature. We can learn to live with some surprises about the material world. Call this the 'Learn to Live with It' strategy. The second strategy grants my contention about our nature, but denies my contention about the nature of the material world. If it succeeds, it cuts my argument off at the pass. Call this the 'Cut it Off at the Pass' strategy.

A materialist can mix and match strategies, of course. She might adopt the Learn to Live with It strategy to deal with the Fuzziness Argument, and the Cut it Off at the Pass strategy to deal with the Flux Argument, or vice versa. So I'll have to counter *both* strategies regarding *both* arguments.

My reply will be structured by strategy: I will first respond to the Learn to Live with It strategy, taking its application to each argument

DOI: 10.4324/9781003032908-9

in turn. Then I'll respond to the Cut it Off at the Pass strategy. Here I can take the two arguments in one fell swoop, because Eric thinks there's a single mistaken picture of the material world that lies behind both of them. Finally, I'll address an entirely different strategy that Eric pulls out at the end: the claim that the immaterialist is hoisted with his own petard.

6.2   Learn to Get along with Others

Suppose you go along with the Argument from Fuzziness and accept what Eric terms 'the neat-and-tidy-picture': where your body is now, there are millions of massively overlapping human animals, all or none of them thinking. It's quite natural to then go along with the argument's last step: there being millions of overlapping thinking animals near you has absurd moral consequences, and so is to be rejected. Thus, none of the animals is thinking, and there's nothing left for you to plausibly be but an immaterial thing.

Not so fast with that last step, says Eric. Stop being so pedantic. Yes, strictly and pedantically speaking, there *are* millions of overlapping thinking animals there, just as there are millions of overlapping tables in front of me, and millions of overlapping chairs underneath me. To use Eric's helpful coinage, crowded materialism is true. But for all practical purposes, we count all of the human people as one, all of the tables as one, and all of the chairs as one. If we need to know how many chairs we can fit at the table, or how many people we can seat on those chairs, the strict and pedantic truth is irrelevant and misleading. Strictly speaking there might be many more human people in this room than there are chairs, for example, because the average surface area of a human animal is bigger than the average surface area of a chair. But that has no bearing on whether someone's going to be left without a place to sit. What matters is the *loose and ordinary* truth. Loosely and ordinarily speaking, the room contains just two human beings, two chairs, and a single table large enough to seat both of them. (A translation of 'there are two chairs in the room' into strict and pedantic language might go something like this: there are at least two non-overlapping chairs in the room, and any chair in the room massively overlaps exactly one of those two chairs.)

What goes for all practical purposes, Eric continues, goes for moral purposes as well. What matters for all moral purposes are *the loose and ordinary truths* about the number of people and things. At the very least, I've given no argument to think otherwise.

Eric's right that I've given no argument to think otherwise. That's because I didn't think I *needed* an argument. Whenever it makes sense to count in the loose way, rather than in the strict way, there's always some reason. When we're trying to figure out whether there are enough seats for everyone, there's a reason it makes sense to count in the loose way. The reason is that having enough seats isn't *really* a matter of how *many* seats and people there are; it's a matter of how the seats and people are collectively distributed in space. More generally, I think, whenever it makes sense to count Xs in the loose way, that's because for those purposes it doesn't really matter how *many* Xs there are; what really matters for those purposes is something else. Like how much space they take up, or how much they weigh. Otherwise, why *wouldn't* the strictly correct answer about how many there are be the one that's relevant?

When it comes to morality—and to the specific moral purposes I relied on—I just assumed that it really *does* matter how many human people there are in the situations I described. After all, it's not as though their size or weight could really be what matters instead. That was part of the *point* I was taking to be obvious. Absent anything else that could matter morally instead, the number of people must really matter—otherwise, nothing in those situations would matter morally—and so the strict way of counting is the right way.

In a nutshell, no argument is usually needed to justify counting in the strict way. On the contrary, one should always count in the strict way, unless there's some reason to think that the count doesn't really matter. And I didn't see any reason to think that the count doesn't really matter for the moral purposes under discussion.

But in addition to pointing out that I gave no positive argument for counting strictly, Eric also provides a suggestion for something *else* that matters morally, something *other* than the number of people in the situation. Eric suggests that when we're morally evaluating my causing suffering or happiness in others, the only thing that *really* matters is how *much* suffering or happiness I cause, not how *many* other people I cause to suffer or be happy. And since all of the massively overlapping people share the very same nervous system, the amount of suffering (or happiness) they collectively experience isn't multiplied or even increased by their being so many. You cause no more suffering by breaking the neck of millions of overlapping people than you do by breaking the neck of exactly one; you alleviate no more suffering by donating a kidney to billions of overlapping people than you do by donating to millions. All the overlapping people share *the very same* aches and pains and discomforts and joys and reliefs. So loose counting is called for, not strict counting.

This reply raises difficult issues, both moral and metaphysical. On the moral side: it's far from trivial that it doesn't really matter how many other people I cause to suffer or be happy. When you cause billions to suffer rather than one, even if you haven't thereby caused more suffering, you've still harmed more people, violated the rights of more people, and thwarted the interests of more people. It's not obvious, to put it mildly, that this makes no moral difference.[1]

On the metaphysical side: it's far from trivial that the overlapping people share the very same aches and pains—'very same' in the sense that there is literally just one pain there. They are, after all, distinct subjects. We might plausibly think that distinct subjects automatically give us distinct pains. On top of that, it's far from trivial that *if* they do in fact share the very same pain, then the *amount* of suffering they collectively experience is the same as it would be if just one of them had that pain. On the one hand, there is something intuitive about the idea that figuring out how much suffering there is requires nothing more than identifying the various instances of suffering, and determining each one's intensity. On the other hand, there's *also* something intuitive about the idea that a distinction between people—between suffer*ers*—can all by itself increase the total amount of suffering. If you and I share the same pain, there are still two inner lives filled at that moment with pain, even if the same pain is filling both of them. We're two people after all. And it seems like that should be relevant when calculating the total amount of suffering in the world.

So I don't know what to say about the moral or metaphysical issues raised by Eric's suggestion. But the suggestion is in any case inadequate. Let's just concede that increasing the number of subjects, while keeping the number of episodes of suffering (happiness) constant, doesn't itself increase the amount of suffering (happiness); and that *when we're morally evaluating my causing suffering or happiness in others*, the number of other people whom I cause to suffer or be happy doesn't really matter. But notice the italicized condition. What happens when we're morally evaluating something *else*, besides causing suffering or happiness? Or when we're trying to determine *if* I'm causing suffering or happiness *in others* to begin with? What I've just conceded says nothing about *that*. And the deliberations of the bungee jumper and kidney donor call for just those kinds of evaluation.

First of all: each one involves the risk of death, not just painful injury. If crowded materialism is true, then each involves the risk of mass *killing*. That raises its own moral issues. On the face of it, the *number* of dead people certainly matters in morally evaluating any course of action that eventuated in those deaths. Indeed, what would be the alternative? That it's the *amount* of death, rather than the number of dead? What does 'the amount of death' even mean?

Second of all: if crowded materialism is true, then in deciding to bungee jump or donate a kidney I risk causing suffering to *others*. If I'm the only one there, then my decision affects *no one but myself*. That all by itself makes a massive moral difference, even if the exact number of others I might cause to suffer is immaterial. That is: even Eric should concede that the difference between 1 and 2 matters morally if the person acting is number 1, because that's the difference between affecting only oneself and also affecting another!

Hopefully it should now be clear why I don't think it's worse to lose a billion overlapping watches than to lose just one—and so why we count watches in the loose way—even while I do think crowded materialism has absurd moral implications. Watches have no rights or interests, no inner lives, and none has to deliberate about what to do. We human beings do.

> Crowded materialism has absurd moral implications. Those implications could be avoided if there were some good reason to *always* count overlapping people in the loose and ordinary way. But there is no such reason. When it comes to morality, the number of people often really matters.

6.3   Learn to Live in the Moment

Suppose you go along with the Argument from Flux and accept that nothing can change its parts. Given facts about metabolic turnover, this means that Goofy, the human body currently typing on my laptop, won't last for very long—at least not in humanoid form. And his humanoid form is a very recent feature of his. For the longest time he was spherically shaped and spread throughout the atmosphere, a state he will soon enough occupy again. To be sure, there have been many other human bodies, each of whom had similar histories (sphere-shaped, then briefly humanoid, then sphere-shaped), and all of whom relate to Goofy in a special way. These are Goofy's '**temporal counterparts**'. Goofy and his temporal counterparts—at least in their stints as human bodies—are links in a chain, each one giving way to and directly influencing the next link, and each one highly similar to the ones immediately before and after it. Nonetheless, they're distinct things. It's quite natural to then go along with the argument's last step: *I* don't have any such bizarre history and future as do Goofy and his temporal counterparts—I exist as a human being for much longer than that. Thus, I am not identical with any of the human bodies, and there's nothing left for me to plausibly be but an immaterial thing.

Not so fast with that last step, says Eric. Stop being so pedantic. Yes, strictly and pedantically speaking, my history and future *are* bizarre and non-humanoid. And yes, I *am* just one of an untold number of distinct human people each successively playing the Aaron-role. To use Eric's helpful coinage, Heraclitean materialism is true. But in the loose and ordinary way of speaking, I have a normal human history and future, and there's just one human person who plays the Aaron-role from birth to death. Because Goofy and his temporal counterparts are so closely related, and all play the Aaron-role, we ordinarily just *identify* all of them with each other. That is, loosely speaking we count them all as one. And the loose count is what matters for all intents and purposes.

I find this hard to believe. The loose count might be what matters for *some* purposes. But I don't understand why it would be what matters for all the important purposes, let alone for *all* intents and purposes. The special relationship I'd have with my temporal counterparts would perhaps explain and justify an especially intense concern for their well-being, maybe even one that approaches the intensity of the concern I have for my *own* well-being (my so-called egocentric concern). After all, I temporarily assumed the plans and hopes of my earlier counterparts, and tried to realize them as best as I could; and my later counterparts will in turn assume roughly the same plans and hopes, and their realization will be in the hands of those later counterparts. We're all very much together in this life we're collectively building. So I can see how counting us all as one would make sense when addressing such questions as: Should I exercise? Should I quit smoking? Should I regret the childhood mischief that landed me in prison? Even if, strictly speaking, exercise and quitting smoking won't help *me*, it'll help people I care about very much, as much as I care about my children and grandchildren. And even though, strictly speaking, it wasn't *me* who committed that childhood mischief, I'm so much a product of his deeds that I can see his mischief as a reflection of me.

That's all well and good. But the thing is that it's *also* true that my temporal counterparts and I are *not entirely* in this together. We will all go our very separate ways. I will need to face the world and what becomes of me, all alone. And I'll be a shell of my former self. Literally. So why don't I care? Why don't I get terribly depressed or nervous about the fact that very soon I'm going to exist as nothing but a gigantic sphere? Indeed, why *shouldn't* I? The special relationship I have with my temporal counterparts explains why I *do* have an intense concern for them. But it does nothing to explain why I *don't* also have an intense concern for myself, the thing that strictly speaking is identical with me, and which won't be humanoid for long. Regarding such questions as—Should I devote my remaining moments to looking into whether a gigantic spherical shell of atoms can feel anything? Should I look into self-annihilation so I don't have to worry about becoming a gigantic spherical shell?—the strict and pedantic way of speaking sure seems relevant. And supposing, as our hypothetical materialist is, that strictly speaking each of us *will* become a gigantic spherical shell, the answer to those questions would seem to be yes. But no one in their right mind answers these questions in the affirmative. Heraclitean materialism has absurd practical implications, and so we shouldn't accept it.

> Heraclitean materialism has absurd practical implications. Those implications could be avoided if there were some good reason to *always* identify with one's temporal counterparts. But there is no such reason. When it comes to certain practical judgments, the distinction between a person and his temporal counterparts really matters.

6.4   Rough-and-Messy Materialism

A materialist would do well to avoid both crowded materialism and Heraclitean materialism. Eric's second strategy is intended to do just that. According to this strategy, there's just one human being where I am right now, and that human being will persist in humanoid form—by way of exchanging parts with its environment—for another fourscore (if all goes well). The material world would be rather hospitable to us, if that were true.

Of course, I provided *arguments* to show that these claims about the material world *aren't* true. But Eric thinks these arguments fail, because they proceed from a mistaken starting point. I'm making a very general mistake about the material world, Eric contends, which then leads me down a number of other mistaken paths. Very briefly, the mistake is in thinking that the material world is neat-and-tidy. In reality, it's rough-and-messy.

These are just images. But when Eric speaks of the material world being neat-and-tidy, he has a couple of specific claims in mind, claims that he thinks are both false and essential to my arguments. I will focus on just one of the claims he identifies: that when collections of atoms compose something further, they compose something *precise*, something whose atomic parts are definitely all and only the atoms in that collection. Eric is certainly right that this assumption does play an essential role in the Argument from Fuzziness.

Unconditional and Unrestricted Composition?

I should note that this assumption plays no role in the Argument from Flux. But Eric identifies another claim that he sees at work in both the Arguments from Fuzziness and Flux, the Atomic Composition Principle. That principle says that for *any* atoms whatsoever, there is an object composed (precisely) of them. If the principle is true, then there are all manner of bizarre objects, like an object composed of my left shoe and your laptop. Eric sees the principle at work in my assumptions that there *are* all those human beings that massively overlap (Goofy$_1$, Goofy$_2$, etc.), and that there *is* such a thing as Goof.

But I don't think my arguments need anything so strong as that unconditional and unrestricted principle. What they need is that *if* Goofy exists, then so do some other things that are very much like Goofy (Goofy$_1$, Goofy$_2$, etc.), and so does something shaped just like Goofy himself will soon enough be shaped. Notice the if-then structure; for all my argument assumes, there is no such thing as Goofy at all! And notice the restricted nature of how it generalizes; just to things that are also humanoid, in one piece, and perfectly useful, not to bizarre things such as the sum of my left shoe and your laptop.

But to be clear, the Argument from Fuzziness doesn't just *assume* it to be the case that if materialism is true, then I am one of a horde of perfectly precise human animals, and leave it at that. It *argues* for it. I spent a great deal of time responding to a potential materialist reply that says that I am, instead, a vague object, i.e. an object such that it is indeterminate what its precise parts and boundaries are (§2.12 and §2.13). My response was multi-pronged. I will review two of those prongs, and add a third one.

The first prong of my response was that the very idea of a vague object makes little sense. It requires there to be vagueness in the world, not just in how we represent the world. And, as Eric acknowledges (§3.5), it's difficult to see how that could possibly be. If there can't *be* any vague objects, then *all* macroscopic material objects—if there are any—have neat-and-tidy boundaries.

The second prong of my response was that even if the idea of a vague object makes sense, it won't help the materialist to claim that I (aka Goofy) am such an object. The reason is that even if I am a vague object, there'd still *be* all the other precise objects, $Goofy_1$, $Goofy_2$, etc. And consciousness, I argued, trickles down to all of these other precise objects. So even if the materialist claims that I'm a vague object that does nothing to help her avoid the horde of conscious beings where I am.

But here I underestimated just how far a materialist might go in the rough-and-messy direction. Eric doesn't just propose that you and I are vague objects; or even just that you and I and all the familiar macroscopic objects we speak of are vague objects. If I understand Eric correctly, he proposes to *do away entirely* with precise macroscopic material objects. The *only* macroscopic material objects there are, on this proposal, are vague objects. This is a rather thoroughgoing version of the rough-and-messy view. It makes the macroscopic world *perfectly* messy. And it's one that I summarily dismissed in my opening statement, based on the thought that it would be pretty surprising if only the metaphysically peculiar objects existed, and not the more metaphysically tractable ones.

I still find that surprising, but I take it the element of surprise won't move Eric very much. So here's an argument, first, that a rough-and-messy materialist can't do away *entirely* with the precise human animals. Even if he wants to say that it's *not definitely* the case that $Goofy_1$ exists (it's not definitely the case that the $Goofy_1$-atoms compose something), and *not definitely* the case that $Goofy_2$ exists (it's not definitely the case that the $Goofy_2$-atoms compose something), and so on, he *can't* reasonably maintain the stronger position that it's *definitely not* the case that Goofy$_1$ exists, or that it's *definitely not* the case that Goofy$_2$ exists, and so on. Regarding each collection of Goofy$_n$-atoms, the rough-and-messy materialist will have to agree that it's at least indeterminate whether there is something precise composed of just the atoms in that collection.

Why suppose this? Consider a world much like ours, but in which material objects *aren't* fuzzy. Pepper material doesn't taper off gradually. Instead, there's a surface at the edge of every pepper, inside of which pepper material abounds, and beyond which, in its immediate environs, is completely empty space. And likewise for human animals. Eric would agree, I take it, that in a world like *that* there *are* precise macroscopic material objects, such as precise peppers and precise human animals (at least if there are peppers and human animals in our world). It's not as though precise macroscopic objects are *impossible*.

Now suppose that God decides to make that world much like ours, by turning all the material objects into fuzzy things. He does this by lightly sprinkling matter at the edges (adding what we might call 'adjacent atoms') so that now pepper material *does* taper off gradually, as does human animal material, and so on. He doesn't touch the matter inside the original surface (what we can call 'original atoms'). Question: Are there still precise peppers and human animals and what nots, each one made of some collection of original atoms? I should think so. What would now *prevent* those original atoms from continuing to compose precise things? Don't say it's the fact that these atoms are now parts of larger, vague objects—vague objects that have the adjacent atoms as parts. Or, at least don't say that as if it's *definitely* true. It's not definitely true, because the adjacent atoms are not definitely parts of the vague object. And so the original atoms *don't definitely fail* to compose precise objects; it's at the very least indeterminate whether they do.

But note that the unfolding divine drama was purely for illustrative purposes. The depiction doesn't need God, or any sprinkling at all, for the basic point to stand. Each collection of Goofy$_n$-atoms (the Goofy$_1$-atoms, the Goofy$_2$-atoms, etc.) *could* have been surrounded by empty space; and *would* have composed a precise human animal; and so still *should* compose a precise human animal—or at least it *shouldn't definitely fail* to compose a precise human animal—even if there's a bizarro vague human animal in the vicinity. For each such collection, it's at least indeterminate whether it composes a precise human animal (Goofy$_1$, Goofy$_2$, etc.). In a word: a rough-and-messy materialist can't reasonably make the macroscopic world *perfectly* messy.

But once a rough-and-messy materialist concedes at least some imperfection in her messiness, then she confronts an unenviable choice between two options. Option 1: maintain that although for each collection of Goofy$_n$-atoms it's indeterminate whether it composes some precise thing, it's *not* indeterminate whether *more than one* of the collections does; rather, it's definitely the case that *at most one* of the collections composes something. But this sort of definitive and singular resolution would be peculiar. Each collection of Goofy$_n$-atoms is 'on the fence' about composing something. What would be responsible for coordinating the collections, so that if one of them composes something, none of the other millions of collections goes ahead and does so? Whatever it is, it's mysterious. Option 2: agree that since for each collection of Goofy$_n$-atoms it's indeterminate whether it composes some precise thing, it's *also* indeterminate whether *more than one* of the collections does. It's not definitely true that there's at most one, or two, or two hundred precise human organisms where Goofy is. There might well be millions. But for the reasons I detailed in my original argument, it's definitely true that any of them that exists is conscious. So there might well be millions of conscious beings. It's not the case that there *definitely isn't* a horde of conscious beings where I am, feeling what I'm feeling, right now. And even though this isn't quite as strong as the conclusion that there *definitely is* a horde of conscious beings where I am right now, it's nearly as absurd. And it too has moral and practical implications that no one in their right mind accepts.

Unlike in the non-metaphorical case, a little metaphysical tidiness has a tendency to spread, generating still further tidiness. A rough-and-messy materialist can't so easily contain the tidiness. Once she acknowledges, as she should, that the macroscopic world isn't perfectly messy, she'll have a hard time keeping it as messy as she needs to in order to avoid disaster.

There's a third prong to my response, on top of what I argued in my opening statement. Even if I grant the materialist the extreme version of the rough-and-messy picture—even if I grant that it's definitely the case that *every* macroscopic object is vague—I don't think she's really out of the woods. The problem is that *there'd be a profusion of vague objects, just as there'd be a profusion of precise ones* (if there were any).

Let's look in the general area where Goofy is. We've already noted that there's no 'bright line' surrounding the human material. There's no sharp 'cut-off surface' such that everything inside it is definitely human material, and everything beyond it is definitely not. That's what the fuzziness of the material world consists in. But the situation is actually quite a bit worse than that. There's no 'bright line' surrounding the indeterminate human material either. Even *that* boundary—the boundary between the indeterminate and the definitely not—is itself fuzzy. And it doesn't stop there, of course. It's as though everywhere we try to draw a boundary, our line inevitably has some thickness. And each of the edges of that line has some thickness. And so on, and so forth. This rather vexing phenomenon—even more vexing than the already vexing phenomenon of vagueness—is known as **higher-order vagueness**. But vexing or not, it makes trouble for a materialist who seeks refuge in messiness.

Goofy is supposed to be a vague object. But *which* vague object? Suppose I had lots of time on my hands, and I could go one-by-one through every atom there is, and about each atom ask the rough-and-messy materialist: is it a part of Goofy? Of course she's permitted to use the word 'definitely' (and the word 'not', and 'indeterminate' as shorthand for 'not definitely and not definitely not'), and to use it (in each answer) as many times as she wishes. So she can say things like: "that atom is not definitely definitely part of Goofy, but it's also not definitely not definitely part of Goofy; in other words it's indeterminate whether it's definitely part of Goofy". My only requirement is that she answers me each time with maximal specificity. Of course I have no interest in testing this particular materialist's knowledge, so I will allow her to consult an omniscient oracle if there are any answers she doesn't know. After finishing with this interrogation, I'll have a *parthood profile* of Goofy, a precise accounting of which mess Goofy is.

But then my question is: why is there *just this macroscopic mess* where I'm sitting and no others? Choose an arbitrary atom that's 10 miles to my right. It's absolutely positively not part of Goofy. That is, it's definitely, definitely…(fill in as many 'definitely's as you please) not part of Goofy. But of course there are also atoms, such as those deep inside Goofy's brain, for which that's not the case. Pick an arbitrary one of those atoms. If we 'journey' from the atom 10 miles to my right toward the atom we've picked inside Goofy's brain, there's a *transition*. At some point we'll encounter an atom, the *first* such atom, regarding which it's not absolutely positively not a part of Goofy. Call it 'Righty'. Righty is an atom at the outermost outskirts of Goofy's right side, but still having some parthood connection to Goofy. We can of course do the same thing 'journeying' toward Goofy's left side, this time starting from a faraway atom to Goofy's left. At some point in *that* 'journey' we'll encounter an atom, the first such atom, regarding which he wouldn't give the 'absolutely positively answer'. Call the atom we encountered *right before* that atom, the last atom on our journey that is 'absolutely positively' not part of Goofy, 'Lefty'. Lefty is on the outermost outskirts of Goofy's left side, but has *no* parthood connection whatsoever to Goofy.

But that's Goofy. And *we* know that as a matter of fact there's no sudden and important dropoff just beyond Righty, or just inside Lefty. Wouldn't it stand to reason then that there'd be some *other* vague human animal, call it 'Goofy*', who is just like Goofy in his parthood profile with the sole exceptions that Righty has no parthood connection whatsoever to Goofy*, while Lefty does (just barely) have some parthood connection to Goofy*? And if Goofy is conscious—as he had better well be, according to materialism!—then doesn't it stand to reason that Goofy* is also conscious? What lies behind these assumptions is exactly the same conviction that lay behind the parallel assumptions (about the precise human animals, Goofy$_1$, Goofy$_2$, etc.) in the original argument.

Of course, once this is granted, then there are going to be many more than just two conscious human animals where I am. There'll be a vast number of them. And thankfully this isn't my problem. The same way I'd have no problem with there being a vast number of precise human animals where Goofy$_1$ is, I'd have no problem with there being a vast number of vague human animals where Goofy is (if I didn't have a problem with there being vague objects, period): none of them would be conscious anyway.

So a materialist, who seeks refuge from the Argument from Fuzziness in vague objects, even if she adopts the radical view that the *only* macroscopic objects are vague, is going to be disappointed. It'll just move the horde of conscious beings from the population of precise human animals to the population of vague ones. Hardly an advance.

> Eric suggests I've mistakenly assumed that Goofy is a precise object. But it's not clear that there's any coherent alternative. And even if Goofy is a vague object, that won't definitely do away with *other*, precise thinking animals, overlapping Goofy. And even if *all* macroscopic objects are vague, there'll still be a

horde of thinking animals overlapping Goofy: they'll just all be vague objects, instead of precise ones.

6.5   Is Immaterialism in the Same Boat?

I've replied to the Learn to Live with It and Cut it Off at the Pass strategies. But Eric has one more card to play. It's the card that says immaterialism is in the same boat as materialism. Suppose you grant me that the material world is metaphysically inhospitable to us. You might still stick to materialism and this for two reasons.

First reason: even if the immaterial world is more hospitable to *us*, locating us in the immaterial world does nothing to make the material world more hospitable to *its* conscious denizens. So immaterialism (as I've characterized it and argued for it) effectively leaves us with all of the same problems as materialism: we still have hordes of massively overlapping and short-lived conscious human organisms—even if, according to immaterialism, none of them is one of *us*. We're left with these hordes, Eric contends, because I've given no reason or argument to believe that material things can't think. And absent such an argument, we should think that at least some of them do (the ones with highly developed nervous systems, for example). As Eric says, "My being immaterial would not make the great horde of material thinkers go away, or make its members any less conscious or intelligent".

Second reason: the fact that the material world is inhospitable to us is a reason to accept immaterialism only if the *immaterial* world is *more* hospitable to us. (Compare: the fact that the North Pole is inhospitable to us is no reason to move to the South Pole if the latter is equally inhospitable!) And Eric contends that I've given no argument for thinking that the immaterial world is indeed more hospitable to us than the material world.

This all seems wrong to me. The first reason seems to me to get the dialectical situation exactly backward. As I see things, the only grounds I have to begin with to believe that there are thinking material objects is that I'm a thinker, in conjunction with whatever grounds there are to believe that I'm material. If those latter grounds were good and undefeated, then it'd be reasonable for me to believe in at least one material thinker (i.e. myself). And then it would make sense to generalize from there, first to other human beings, and then presumably to other animals. But the entire *point* of everything I've argued so far is that there *are* no good grounds to think that I'm material, and that there are in fact decisive grounds to think I'm *not* material. Given that that's the situation, I have no reason at all to believe that there are any thinking material objects. So then of course I have no reason to believe that there are hordes of them and so no troubles in general involving the material inhospitality to its conscious denizens—because I have no reason to think it *has* any conscious denizens.

You might find it hard to understand my view of the dialectical situation. You might think it's pretty obvious that even setting aside any materialist view about *me*, I still have good grounds to maintain that some actual material things think. I strongly suspect this difference between us is due to a recurring disagreement, a disagreement about what thinking *is*. If I could get on board with, say, **functionalism**, then I would see the dialectical situation the same way (on functionalism, see §4.6). I would see that the very fact that human animals, for example, can perform complicated computations and process lots of information is enough for them to be thinking. And then I'd also see that locating me in the immaterial world does nothing to make the horde of material thinkers in my chair go away. But as I've said, I can't get on board with any such view. Thinking, *genuine* thinking, isn't just a matter of playing a certain causal role. Thus, I have no a priori grounds to believe that any material object as capable of performing computations and processing information as a human animal does in fact think. My only grounds would be the a posteriori ones: I experience my *own* genuine mental life, and I conjoin that with whatever good reasons there are supposed to be for thinking that I'm a material object. But there are no such good reasons.

To be sure, none of what I've just said does anything to *explain* why material things don't think, let alone why they *can't* think. But as I've previously noted (§4.7), I myself believe that it is possible for material things to think, so I certainly wouldn't want to explain why it's impossible. And I don't have an explanation for why material things don't *actually* think, even though they *could*. But I don't see why I owe an explanation of that fact, any more than I'd think Eric owes us an explanation of why electrons don't think, even though, at least in my view, *they* could.

In reply to Eric's second reason, let me start with a rather obvious point. I *have* given an argument—indeed, I've given two!—that the immaterial world is more hospitable to us than the material world. The Arguments from Fuzziness and Flux weren't directly for that claim, but they indirectly support it. What they each directly support is that the nature of the material world is deeply mismatched with our nature—or at least with what we assume our nature to be. As I said in §2.17, we could be radically mistaken about the number of conscious beings in our chairs, about what considerations are practically and ethically relevant, and about our lifespans or shape. But those are merely skeptical possibilities, to be taken no more seriously than the idea that there is no external world, or that there are no other minds. Assuming we *aren't* radically mistaken, then the material world is inhospitable to us, in the strong sense that we just *can't* inhabit it. This in turn supports the claim that the immaterial world *isn't* mismatched. It does so because we are, after all, 'somewhere', and if we're not part of the material world–because we can't be–then we must be part of the immaterial world. But then the immaterial world must not be mismatched with our nature.

I take it this sort of answer won't satisfy Eric, because what he's really asking for is a *direct* argument for the conclusion that the immaterial world is more hospitable to us than the material world. What he wants is an argument that *doesn't* go by way of first showing that the material world is inhospitable. Rather, it's presumably supposed to go by way of reflection on the nature of immateriality itself, and the argument is supposed to show that its nature makes it a suitable arena for things like us.

Now, if this is what Eric expects, I don't think I'm going to provide anything that's *fully* satisfactory. I do, however, think I can provide something that's at least *partially* satisfactory. At least regarding those ways that are relevant to the Arguments from Fuzziness and Flux—those aspects of the material world that make it demonstrably inhospitable to us—we have reason to be optimistic that the immaterial world fares better than the material world.

There are a number of very specific features that the material world has without which fuzziness wouldn't be possible. Matter comes in tiny bits (particles, or waves, if those are different); these bits are located in a shared space (they're at some distance from each other); they can be grouped into a small number of basic kinds (such as *electron*, *up-quark*, etc.); a bit's basic kind determines how the bit moves in space over time and what changes it causes in other things; and, as it happens, the distribution in space of these bits is such that those large collections of them that 'act as one' massively overlap other such collections that differ by just a few bits that anyways belong to the same kind, and so equally well 'act as one'—indeed, that are therefore guaranteed to act in the very same way as the original collection.

It's that last fact on the list that constitutes the problematic fuzziness. But it's made *possible* by the previous facts in the list. If matter didn't come in little bits; or if it did, but different bits didn't occupy a shared space; or, if they did, but instead of them belonging to just a small number of basic kinds, each of them was one-of-a-kind; or if there were just a small number of basic kinds, but they didn't determine how a thing moves in space or what is causes; if any of these things were true, the phenomenon of problematic fuzziness—at least as we know it—couldn't even get off the ground.

An Illustration

To illustrate, suppose every bit of matter was one-of-a-kind. Then we'd have no reason at all to think that exchanging one bit of matter on Goofy's left side for another on his right side would make no difference for whether the new set of bits would compose something, let alone something that's a human animal, let alone still more something that's a thinking human animal. What allowed us to assume that each collection of $Goofy_n$-atoms composes a thinking human animal if any of them does is the interchangeability of different bits of matter that belong to the same kind.

And there's good reason to believe that at least *one* of these things must be true regarding the immaterial world. Any things that in all of those respects were just like material things, would *be* material things. Or, at least I know of no good way of drawing the distinction between the material and the immaterial that would still put things like that on the immaterial side of the divide. As I argued in §2.3, anything whose movements are subject to some completely general law is automatically material. So if the immaterial world were also 'made of' bits that belonged to a small number of basic kinds, and those kinds determined how the bits moved and what they caused—which would mean they are subject to some completely general law— then it wouldn't be the *immaterial* world after all. You might disagree with the way I've drawn the line between the material and the immaterial. Perhaps you think it's simply the line between the spatial and the non-spatial. But then immaterial things wouldn't be located in a shared space, since they wouldn't be located in a space at all. And so you too would agree with my bottom line: that if the immaterial world were like the material world in *all* the respects that make fuzziness possible, then it wouldn't be the immaterial world after all. I challenge you to find a plausible way of drawing the line that doesn't have that consequence.

The same is true regarding flux. Indeed, *the very same features* of the material world that make fuzziness possible are also features without which the phenomenon of flux, at least as we know it, would be extraordinarily unlikely, if not downright impossible. The phenomenon of flux consists in the fact that as it happens, given the ways that the basic kinds of material bits lawfully move in space over time, those large collections of them that 'act as one' are regularly and reliably exchanging bits with the nearby environment. But if matter wasn't made of bits, or if it was, but different bits didn't occupy a shared space, then the phenomenon of flux—at least as we know it—couldn't even get off the ground. And if they did occupy a shared space, but instead of them belonging to just a small number of basic kinds, each of them was one-of-a-kind, or if there were just a small number of basic kinds, but they didn't determine how a thing moves in space, then the phenomenon of flux—at least as we know it—would be extraordinarily unlikely. It might be *possible* for the parts of a thing to get destroyed, or to fly off on their own, but there'd be no reason to expect that to happen and certainly no reason to expect that it would be happening all the time. And so the immaterial world, which must be unlike the material world in at least one of these ways (if it's to be immaterial at all), is not at all likely to be the site of flux as we know it, if it's even so much as possible.[2]

So, I can go quite a ways toward satisfying Eric's demand for a direct argument that the immaterial world is more hospitable to us than the material world. But, I don't see why I have to. It's not at all clear to me what's wrong with the *indirect* arguments I gave. They're perfectly familiar instances of reasoning by *process of elimination*. If we know that Judah's murderer was either a Green or a Blue; and we know that Judah was murdered in New Jersey on New Year's Eve; and then after some investigation we discover that the Greens were all on a team-building mission in the Cayman Islands that night, then we can reasonably conclude that the murderer was a Blue. And we can do that even if we know nothing else about the whereabouts of the Blues. We don't have to know on *independent grounds* that one of the Blues was in New Jersey on New Year's Eve. We can just deduce it from the fact that one of them was the murderer, and the murder took place in New Jersey on New Year's Eve.

Likewise, if I know that I am either material or immaterial; and I know that I am the only conscious being in my chair, and that I have been in existence on this Earth for at least 40 years, all the while remaining fairly localized in space; and then after some investigation I discover that no material thing fits that bill, then I can reasonably conclude that I am immaterial. And I can do that even if I know nothing else about the suitability of immaterial things. I don't have to know on independent grounds that some immaterial thing is better suited to be me. I can just deduce it from the fact that one of them *is* me.

> Eric offers two reasons that immaterialism is no better off than materialism. First reason: moving *me* to the immaterial world does nothing to get rid of the millions of thinking human animals in my chair. But if I'm immaterial, then I've got no good grounds to think there *are* any thinking human animals that need to be gotten rid of. Second reason: we've got no argument that the immaterial world is any more hospitable to us than the material world. But we do have such arguments, both direct and indirect.

Notes

1   These facts might make a moral difference even given consequentialism. See Yetter Chappell (2015).
2   Here's another precondition for the phenomena of fuzziness and flux: that some things are parts of other things. Some philosophers have suggested that no immaterial thing could have parts. (As a matter of fact, that was the dominant view among medieval philosophers.) According to them, the immaterial world consists entirely in mereological simples. If they're right, that's yet another reason that the immaterial world couldn't be the site of fuzziness or flux.

Glossary

Abstract object   An object with no causal powers (or no spatio-temporal location): e.g. a number, a property, or a proposition. (§4.5)

Amputation paradox   The puzzle of how a thing can get smaller by losing a part. (§2.16, 3.8)

Animalism   The thesis that human people are animals, more precisely physical organisms. (§4.5)

Arbitrary undetached part   A part of something that is attached to other parts of it, but whose boundary with them is arbitrary and not marked by any physical difference: e.g. your northern half, or all of me but my left pinky. (§3.6, 3.10)

The atomic composition principle   The thesis that for any atoms (or things generally), there is an object such that each of those atoms (or other things) is definitely a part of it (at a given time) and every other atom is definitely not a part of it (at that time). In other words, any things whatever compose a precise object. (§3.3)

Behaviorism (or analytic behaviorism)   The thesis that psychological language can be translated without loss of meaning into physical language. To have a mental property (e.g. being in pain) is to be disposed to behave in certain ways (e.g. wincing, screaming, or taking painkillers) in certain circumstances. The mental is not something that goes on within us: it consists of nothing more than our bodily movements (or dispositions to make such movements). (§4.6)

Body   A person's body is a material thing, usually a physical organism, that she can normally move at will and by means of which she can perceive physical objects and events. (§1.3)

Border-sensitive feature   A property, the having of which is not just a matter of its bearer's function and shape, but also a matter of what's going on at its border. (Every border-sensitive feature is an extrinsic property.) (§2.10)

Complete conception   Knowledge of all the essential properties of something. (§2.7)

Compose   Some things, the *x*s (or more loosely, the collection of the *x*s), compose something *y* if and only if each of the *x*s is a part of *y* and every part of *y* shares a part with one or more of the *x*s and no two of the *x*s share a part.. E.g. a Lego house is made up or composed of Lego bricks. Each brick is a part of the house. And every part of the house is either a brick or else something that shares a part with one or more of its bricks: the roof, say, or an individual molecule. (§1.4, 2.9)

Composite object   A thing having parts, e.g. a tree or a human being. (§3.6)

Compound immaterialism   The thesis that a human person is composed of a material thing (such as a physical organism) and a soul, so that each of us is partly material and partly immaterial. (A version of immaterialism.) (§1.4)

Conceivable   A proposition is conceivable if we can imagine or picture it being true. (§2.6)

Concrete object   An object with causal powers and a location (at least in time), e.g. a tree or a soul (if there are such things). (§4.5)

Consciousness isn't vague   The claim that everything is either definitely conscious or definitely not conscious; there are no borderline cases of consciousness. (§2.13)

Contingent   A proposition is contingent if it can have different truth values in different circumstances: if it's true but could have been false (contingently true) or false but could have been true (contingently false); see necessary. (§4.6)

Cooperative dualism   The thesis that neither the soul nor the body thinks; rather, they cooperate to produce thinking. They think together, like two people singing a duet. (§1.15)

Crowded materialism   Materialism combined with the thesis that what we call a single person is really a vast number of them, differing from one another by only a single atom. (§3.4, 3.5)

De re possibility   A property to do with how a particular thing could have been, e.g. the property of possibly doing better in school. (§2.7)

Disposition   A property characterizing the way a thing would behave in certain circumstances. E.g. fragility: a fragile thing is one that's likely to break if handled roughly. Also called a tendency or propensity. (§2.3)

Dualism   See Immaterialism, Substance dualism.

Electric dualism   The thesis that the soul cannot function without the help of the body, much as an electric bulb can't light up without a power source. The reason general anesthesia makes you unconscious, on this view, is that it prevents the body from enabling the soul to function. (§1.14)

Emergent dualism   The thesis that a physical organism produces a soul when it's in the right physical condition. (§1.12)

Ensouled organism   A thing composed of an organism's atoms together with its soul. Materialists deny that there are any ensouled organisms. (§1.3)

Entailment   One proposition entails another just if it's impossible for the first to be true while the second is false. This is sometimes put by saying that the second proposition *follows from* or *is a logical consequence of* the first.

Essential property   A property is essential to something if it's not possible for that thing to exist without having the property. (§2.6)

Evidence   Information bearing on the truth or falsity of a proposition.

Extrinsic property   A property that a thing has or lacks depending on how it relates to something else (something other than its own parts), e.g. being an uncle or being 50 miles north of a burning barn. Perfect duplicates can differ in their extrinsic properties. (See intrinsic property.) (§2.10)

Faux mentality   The property of being functionally just like someone who's thinking—i.e. sharing with that being all features that can be characterized by their typical causes and effects—but without having any mental life oneself. (Faux mentality is impossible if either analytic behaviorism or functionalism is true, since according to those views anything that's functionally just like someone who's thinking is ipso facto thinking.) (§4.3)

Finger complement   The part of you made up of all your parts except those in your finger: an example of an arbitrary undetached part. The existence of finger complements is disputed. (§3.8)

Functionalism   The thesis that mental properties are characterized by their typical causes and effects, where those causes and effects can include other mental properties. E.g. to be in pain is to be in a state that's typically caused by tissue damage and tends to cause wincing, a desire for relief, and the intention to avoid it in future. (§4.6)

Global materialism   The thesis that everything is made of matter (as opposed to *materialism*, the narrower claim that human people are made entirely of matter). (§1.4)

Heraclitean materialism   Materialism combined with the claim that nothing can have different parts at different times. It implies that what looks like a single persisting person is really a series of different people (who are temporal counterparts of each other). (§3.9)

Higher-order vagueness   A term exhibits higher-order vagueness when it has borderline borderline cases, i.e. when the line between the borderline and the definite (or the definitely not) is itself vague. For example, some people are rich, some are not rich, and some are borderline cases. There is higher-order vagueness if some people are on the borderline between being rich and being borderline—if the boundary between the clear cases and the borderline cases is itself not sharp. (See vagueness.) (§6.4)

Idealism   The thesis that the world consists only of souls and their mental activities. Material things consist entirely of nonphysical sensations: a stone, for example, is nothing more than our visual and tactile sensations of it, or our dispositions to have such sensations. (§1.4). Or perhaps more precisely, every property of a thing (including physical properties like mass or charge) is settled by its mental properties: necessarily, any two things that are alike in all mental respects are alike in every respect. The general thought is that the world is fundamentally mental and the physical is derivative. (§4.8)

Idealist immaterialism   The conjunction of immaterialism (a thesis about human beings) and idealism (a thesis about the primacy of the mental). (§4.8)

Identity (numerical identity)   For this thing and that one to be identical is for them to be one and the same—to be one thing rather than two. (§2.6) This contrasts with qualitative senses of identity. For things to be physically identical, for example, is for them to share all the same physical properties, even though they may be numerically distinct (nonidentical).

Immaterial object (or immaterial thing)   A thing that is not a material object.

Immaterialism The thesis that a human person is not made entirely of matter, but has an immaterial part (a soul) that enables her to think. (The person might be that part, as pure immaterialism says.) Sometimes called Cartesian or substance dualism, but we use those terms in a narrower sense. (§1.4)

Intrinsic property A property that a thing has or lacks entirely by virtue of how it is in itself, not how other things are: e.g. being cubical or being conscious. Exact duplicates can't differ in their intrinsic properties. (See extrinsic property.) (§2.10)

Intrinsicality of consciousness The claim that the property of being conscious is intrinsic. (§2.10)

Law of nature A principle governing the behavior of natural objects, e.g. the laws governing gravity, electricity, chemical reactions, and genetics stated in science textbooks. (§1.10)

Leibniz's law The principle that if this thing and that one are identical—if they're one thing rather than two—then whatever is true of one is true of the other as well. (§2.6)

Material object (or material thing) An object made of matter—of physical particles like quarks and electrons. For some attempts at a more precise definition, see §2.3.

Materialism The thesis that human people are made entirely of matter. That is, that they are material things. (§1.1)

Mental property A psychological property such as being conscious, feeling hungry, believing that it's raining, remembering what day it is, preferring Bach to Beethoven, or being a yummy chocolatey experience. More generally, it's a property that can be had only by a thinker or a thought. (§4.4)

Monism The thesis that all things belong to a single kind, for example that all things are material (global materialism) or that all things are immaterial (idealism). (§1.3) Alternatively, the thesis that there is just one thing and all appearances of plurality are an illusion. (§4.7)

The neat-and-tidy picture The view that any things whatever, no matter what their nature or arrangement, compose a precise object and there is no ontic vagueness. (§3.4)

Necessary A proposition is necessary if it's not contingent: if it's true and could not have been false (necessarily true) or false and could not have been true (necessarily false).

Necessity of identity The principle that if things are identical—if they're one thing rather than two—then they're necessarily identical. What are in fact a thing and itself could not have been a thing and another thing. (§2.6)

Ontic vagueness   Vagueness that is due neither to our ignorance nor to the imprecision of our language or thought, but to the nature of the thing we're speaking or thinking of. Also known as "vagueness in the world." (§2.12, 3.6)

Panpsychism   The thesis that the mental pervades the whole of reality: everything, including water and air, has mental properties. (§4.7)

Physicalism   The thesis that all properties are physical properties. More precisely, settling a thing's physical properties fixes all its properties: it's necessary that any two things alike in all physical respects are alike in all respects. (§4.8)

Physicalist materialism   The combination of materialism (a thesis about human beings) with physicalism (a thesis about the primacy of the physical). (§4.8)

Physical organism   The thing composed of the material parts of an organism (as opposed to an ensouled organism, which would also includes the organism's soul). (§1.3)

Physical property   This term is notoriously hard to define. Intuitively, a physical property is one studied in physics: mass, energy, force, or temperature, for example. Or more broadly, one fixed by the properties of things studied in physics together with the physical laws: this will include such properties as having a beard or wearing sandals. Alternatively, it's a property that can be had only by a thing that's at least partly material. (See §2.3 for further discussion.)

Possible   A proposition is possible if it could have been true, i.e. if it's not necessarily false. The proposition that there are no elephants is possible: there didn't have to be elephants. But the proposition that there are elephants is also possible, since every true proposition is ipso facto possible.

Precise object   An object is precise just if anything whatever is either definitely a part of the object or definitely not a part of it. (As opposed to a vague object.) (§2.12)

Property   Something that describes or characterizes something (or purports to): e.g. being red, being conscious, being a dog, or not being divisible by ten. Synonyms: feature, quality, trait, attribute, characteristic, respect.

Property dualism   The thesis that there are mental properties and physical properties, but no property is both mental and physical. More precisely, settling all the physical properties of things does not fix their mental properties: two things could be physically the same yet mentally different. And conversely, settling all the mental properties of things does not fix their physical properties: two things could be mentally the same yet physically different. (§4.4)

Proposition   A statement, thesis, claim, or belief, which can be true or false.

Psycho-physical law   A law of nature connecting mental properties with physical properties, e.g. that nerve stimulation of a certain sort causes pain or that fear increases muscle tension and sweating. (§4.4)

Pure immaterialism   The thesis that human people are wholly immaterial, having no material parts. In other words, a person is a soul. (A version of immaterialism.) (§1.4)

The rough-and-messy picture   The view that composition is restricted: not all things compose something bigger. Further, not all vagueness is due to thought and language: there is ontic vagueness. (§3.6)

Soul   An immaterial thinking thing. (§1.2)

Substance   Something that is not a property or state or activity, but rather has properties, is in states (sitting, for example), and engages in activities (like running or thinking). (§1.4)

Substance dualism   The thesis that there are thinking things, there are material things, and nothing is both. It follows that we, who think, are at least partly immaterial. Substance dualism entails immaterialism but not vice versa. Also known as Cartesian dualism. (§1.4)

Temporal counterpart   The temporal-counterpart relation replaces being the same person in Heraclitean materialism. If you can remember being a certain child and have inherited her physical or psychological properties in a certain way—if there is a certain sort of physical or psychological continuity connecting you—then you and she are temporal counterparts. On other views you are your own temporal counterpart and no one else's, so that x and y are temporal counterparts just when x is y. (§3.9)

Thinking   Any mental property or activity, e.g. wondering what's on TV, finding something funny, solving a crossword, or feeling nauseous. (§1.2) A thinking thing is anything having mental properties.

Transitivity of identity   The principle that if $x = y$ (that is, if x and y are one thing and not two) and $y = z$, then $x = z$. (§2.16)

Unrestricted composition   The principle that any things whatever always compose or make up something bigger. More precisely, for any things, the xs, there is a thing y such that each of the xs is a part of y and every part of y shares a part with one or more of the xs. The atomic composition principle adds to this the claim that all things having parts are precise objects: nothing has any borderline parts. (§3.6)

Vague identity   A case where it's indeterminate whether this thing and that one are one or two: they're not definitely one and the same, but not definitely one thing and another thing either. (§2.12)

Vague object   An object is vague if there is something that is neither definitely a part of it nor definitely not a part of it. (As opposed to a precise object.) (§2.12)

Vagueness   A term exhibits vagueness when it admits of borderline cases. A general term F (such as "bald", "tall", or "smart") is vague when it can be correct to say "Such-and-such is not definitely F but not definitely not F either". A singular term A (such as "the Sahara Desert" or "Mt. Everest") is vague when it can be correct to say "Such-and-such is not definitely part of A, but not definitely not part of it either" (e.g., "This grain of sand is not definitely a part of the Sahara desert, but not definitely not a part of it either"). Note that a vague singular term such as "the Sahara" need not refer to a vague object: it may instead refer ambiguously to many precise objects that are all equally good candidates for being the Sahara.

Valid   An argument is valid when it's impossible for its premises to be true and its conclusion false—that is, when it's necessary that if its premises are all true, its conclusion is also true. In other words, a valid argument is one whose premises together entail its conclusion. An argument is formally valid when it's valid by virtue of its form: e.g. P; if P then Q; therefore Q.

Wholly immaterial   An object is wholly immaterial when none of its parts is a material object. (§2.1)

Wholly material   An object is wholly material when all its parts are material objects. (§2.1)

Further Readings

Suggested Readings (Eric T. Olson)

Here are some introductions to the debate between materialism and immaterialism suited for beginners, listed in roughly increasing order of difficulty: Richard Taylor, *Metaphysics* (1992), ch. 2–4; Keith Campbell, *Body and Mind* (1984), ch. 1–3; Peter van Inwagen, *Metaphysics* (2014), ch. 10, 11; E. J. Lowe, *An Introduction to the Philosophy of Mind* (2000), ch. 2; David Braddon-Mitchell and Frank Jackson, *Philosophy of Mind and Cognition* (2007), ch. 1; Peter Smith and O. R. Jones, *The Philosophy of Mind* (1986), ch. 1–5; Jaegwon Kim, *Philosophy of Mind* (2018), ch. 2. These authors are all convinced materialists. There are books defending immaterialism, some of which are cited in the main text, but none, apart from the one you have in your hands, that I can recommend to the novice.

John Perry's *A Dialogue on Personal Identity and Immortality* (1978) is an eminently readable discussion of the soul and life after death.

My own book *What Are We?* (2007) discusses all the main accounts of our metaphysical nature, including immaterialism, several versions of materialism, and even the view that we don't really exist at all. Beginners will find it rather hard.

Phantoms in the Brain (Ramachandran and Blakeslee 1998) and *The Spike* (Humphries 2021) are accessible treatments of what science currently knows (and doesn't know) about the physical basis of the mental. Oliver Sacks' *The Man Who Mistook His Wife for a Hat* (1987) covers some of the same ground as *Phantoms*; it's beautifully written and very entertaining. These books give a good sense of why few brain scientists are immaterialists.

In §2.12, Aaron argues against the possibility of vague identity on the grounds that it violates Leibniz's Law. §18 of Peter van Inwagen's *Material Beings* (1990) is the best response to this argument that I know of, though the topic is very difficult.

Suggested Readings Aaron Segal

The most historically influential philosophical developments of immaterialism are Plato's *Phaedo* and Descartes' *Meditations*.

There are a number of recent scholarly collections devoted in whole or in part to challenges to materialism, including Kevin Corcoran (ed.) *Soul, Body, and Survival* (2001); Peter van Inwagen & Dean Zimmerman (eds.) *Persons: Human and Divine* (2007); Robert C. Koons & George Bealer (eds.) *The Waning of Materialism* (2010); and Jonathan Loose, et al. (eds.) *The Blackwell Companion to Substance Dualism* (2018). A very nice collection geared toward a general audience is Mark C. Baker & Stewart Goetz (eds.), *The Soul Hypothesis* (2011).

There is a large literature on how to define "material/physical object" (§2.3). Daniel Stoljar's *Physicalism* (2010) is a comprehensive and very readable overview of that and related issues.

As for Cartesian arguments (§2.6), Saul Kripke's seminal and accessible *Naming and Necessity* (1980) lent new life to arguments from conceivability. Richard Swinburne develops the Cartesian line of argument in greater detail than any other contemporary philosopher, and *Are We Bodies or Souls?* (2019) is his most recent defense. For advanced treatments of conceivability and possibility (§2.7), see Tamar Gendler & John Hawthorne (eds.), *Conceivability and Possibility* (2002).

On the Argument from Fuzziness (§2.9), see Peter Unger's "The Problem of the Many" (1980) and "The Mental Problems of the Many" (2004), and Dean Zimmerman's "From Property Dualism to Substance Dualism" (2010). While my development of the argument differs in important respects from both Unger's and Zimmerman's, their papers are essential reading on the topic.

For very careful and comprehensive treatments of the possibility of ontic vagueness and related issues (§2.12), see J. Robert G. Williams, "Ontic vagueness and metaphysical indeterminacy" (2008) and Elizabeth Barnes "Arguments against Metaphysical Indeterminacy and Vagueness" (2010). On whether consciousness can be vague (§2.13), see Jonathan Simon, "Vagueness and Zombies: Why 'phenomenally conscious' Has No Borderline Cases" (2017), and Michael Tye, *Vagueness and the Evolution of Consciousness* (2021).

For a somewhat different argument from flux (§2.15), see Roderick Chisholm, "Is There a Mind-Body Problem?" (1978) and Dean Zimmerman, "Material People" (2003). The argument that nothing can gain or lose parts (§2.16) has an ancient pedigree. See A.A. Long and D.N. Sedley, *The Hellenistic philosophers, Volume 1* (1987), 28A. Both Peter van Inwagen, "The Doctrine Of Arbitrary Undetached Parts" (1981), and Eric Olson, "The paradox of increase" (2006), discuss the argument's possible implications for materialism and lay out a number of responses to the argument, including a few important ones that Eric and I don't directly address in this volume.

On the nature of mentality in general (§1.5, §4.4, §4.6), a lively introduction is the debate between Amy Kind and Daniel Stoljar (2023). For defenses of idealism in particular (§4.8), see Tyron Goldschmidt & Kenneth L. Pearce (eds.), *Idealism: New Essay in Metaphysics* (2017). But if you haven't yet read George Berkeley's classic, *Three Dialogues Between Hylas and Philonous*, first read that.

For a wonderful and accessible discussion of loose counting (§6.2), see David Lewis, "Many, But Almost One" (1999). But Lewis does not address the moral problems that arise from there being, strictly speaking, so many thinkers in your chair. Derek Parfit's "Personal Identity" (1971) is an influential defense of the view that strict identity over time is not really what matters (§6.3).

Bibliography

Eric T. Olson's Chapters:

Adams, Robert (2007). Idealism Vindicated. In Peter van Inwagen and Dean Zimmerman (eds.), *Persons: Human and Divine*. Oxford: Oxford University Press. pp. 35–54.

Baker, Lynne Rudder (1995). Need a Christian be a Mind-Body Dualist? *Faith and Philosophy* 12:489–502.

Baker, Lynne Rudder (2005). Death and the Afterlife. In William J. Wainwright (ed.), *Oxford Handbook for the Philosophy of Religion*. Oxford: Oxford University Press. pp. 366–391.

Barnes, Jonathan (1982). *Aristotle*, Oxford: Oxford University Press.

Bennett, Jonathan (2001). *Learning from Six Philosophers*, vol. 1. Oxford: Oxford University Press.

Bloom, Paul (2005). *Descartes' Baby: How Child Development Explains What Makes Us Human*. London: Random House.

Braddon-Mitchell, David and Frank Jackson (2007). *Philosophy of Mind and Cognition: An Introduction*, 2nd ed. Oxford: Blackwell.

Campbell, Keith (1984). *Body and Mind*, 2nd ed. Notre Dame: University of Notre Dame Press.

Chisholm, Roderick (1976). *Person and Object*. La Salle, IL: Open Court.

Churchland, Paul (1988). *Matter and Consciousness*, rev. ed. Cambridge, MA: MIT Press.

Dennett, Daniel C. (1991). *Consciousness Explained*. Boston: Little, Brown.

Descartes, René (1984 [1641]). *Meditations on First Philosophy*, trans. John Cottingham. In John Cottingham, Robert Stoothoff, and Dugald Murdoch (eds.), *The Philosophical Writings of Descartes*, vol. 2. Cambridge: Cambridge University Press. pp. 3–62.

Descartes, René (1985 [1637]). *Discourse on the Method*, trans. Robert Stoothoff. In John Cottingham, Robert Stoothoff, and Dugald Murdoch (eds.), *The Philosophical Writings of Descartes*, vol. 1. Cambridge: Cambridge University Press. pp. 111–151.

Foster, John (2001). A Brief Defense of the Cartesian View. In Kevin Corcoran (ed.), *Soul, Body, and Survival*. Ithaca, NY: Cornell University Press. pp. 15–29.

Goswick, Dana Lynne (2013). Change and Identity Through Time. In Heather Dyke and Adrian Bardon (eds.), *A Companion to the Philosophy of Time*. Chichester: Wiley. pp. 365–386.

Hart, W. D. (1988). *The Engines of the Soul*. Cambridge: Cambridge University Press.

Hasker, William (1999). *The Emergent Self*. Ithaca, NY: Cornell University Press.

Hasker, William (2011). Souls Beastly and Human. In Mark C. Baker and Stewart Goetz (eds.), *The Soul Hypothesis*. New York: Continuum. pp. 202–217.

Hatfield, Gary (2003). *Descartes and the Meditations*. London: Routledge.

Hudson, Hud (2007). I Am Not An Animal! In Peter van Inwagen and Dean Zimmerman (eds.), *Persons: Human and Divine*. Oxford: Oxford University Press. pp. 216–234.

Humphries, Mark (2021). *The Spike: An Epic Journey Through the Brain in 2.1 Seconds*. Princeton, NJ: Princeton University Press.

Kim, Jaegwon (2018). *Philosophy of Mind*, 3rd ed. New York: Routledge.

Kuhn, Thomas (1957). *The Copernican Revolution: Planetary Astronomy in the Development of Western Thought*. Cambridge, MA: Harvard University Press.

Leibniz, Gottfried Wilhelm (1981). *New Essays on Human Understanding*, trans. and ed. Peter Remnant and Jonathan Bennett. Cambridge: Cambridge University Press.

Lewis, David (1986). *On the Plurality of Worlds*. Oxford: Blackwell.

Lowe, E. Jonathan (2000). *An Introduction to the Philosophy of Mind*. Cambridge: Cambridge University Press.

McGinn, Colin (1997). *The Character of Mind: An Introduction to the Philosophy of Mind*, 2nd ed. Oxford: Oxford University Press.

Merricks, Trenton (1999). The Resurrection of the Body and the Life Everlasting. In Michael J. Murray (ed.), *Reason for the Hope Within*. Grand Rapids, MI: Eerdmans. pp. 261–286.

Merricks, Trenton (2001). How to Live Forever Without Saving Your Soul. In Kevin Corcoran (ed.), *Soul, Body, and Survival*. Ithaca, NY: Cornell University Press. pp. 183–200.

Merricks, Trenton (2007). The Word Made Flesh: Dualism, Physicalism, and the Incarnation. In Peter van Inwagen and Dean Zimmerman (eds.), *Persons: Human and Divine*. Oxford: Oxford University Press. pp. 281–300. (Reprinted in J. Loose et al. (eds.), *The Blackwell Companion to Substance Dualism*. Oxford: Wiley. 2018.)

Olson, Eric T. (2006). The Paradox of Increase. *Monist* 89: 390–417. (Reprinted in Peter van Inwagen and Dean Zimmerman (eds.), *Metaphysics: The Big Questions*, 2nd ed. Oxford: Blackwell, 2008.)

Olson, Eric T. (2007). *What Are We? A Study in Personal Ontology*. New York: Oxford University Press.

Olson, Eric T. (2017). Ben's Body Reads the *Guardian*. *Chinese Semiotic Studies* 13 (4):367–380.

Olson, Eric T. (2021). The Dualist Project and the Remote-Control Objection. *Roczniki Filozoficzne (Annals of Philosophy)* 69:89–101.

Perry, John (1978). *A Dialogue on Personal Identity and Immortality*. Indianapolis: Hackett.

Plantinga, Alvin (2006). Against Materialism. *Faith and Philosophy* 23:3–32. (An almost identical essay is published as Materialism and Christian Belief, in Peter van Inwagen and Dean Zimmerman (eds.), *Persons: Human and Divine*. Oxford: Oxford University Press. pp. 99–141.)

Popper, Karl and John Eccles (1977). *The Self and its Brain: An Argument for Interactionism*. London: Routledge.

Prelutsky, Jack (2000). *It's Raining Pigs and Noodles*. New York: Greenwillow Books.

Pross, Addy (2012). *What Is Life? How Chemistry Becomes Biology*. New York: Oxford University Press.

Ramachandran, V. S. and Sandra Blakeslee (1999). *Phantoms in the Brain: Probing the Mysteries of the Human Mind*. New York: William Morrow.

Sacks, Oliver (1984). *A Leg to Stand On*. New York: Harper & Row.

Sacks, Oliver (1987). *The Man Who Mistook His Wife for a Hat*. New York: Harper & Row.

Shields, Christopher and Robert Pasnau (2016). *The Philosophy of Aquinas*. Oxford: Oxford University Press.

Sider, Theodore (2001). *Four-Dimensionalism: An Ontology of Persistence and Time*. Oxford: Oxford University Press.

Smith, Peter, and O. R. Jones (1986). *The Philosophy of Mind: An Introduction*. Cambridge: Cambridge University Press.

Swinburne, Richard (1984). Personal Identity: The Dualist Theory. In Sydney Shoemaker and Richard Swinburne (eds.), *Personal Identity*. Oxford: Blackwell. pp. 3–66.

Swinburne, Richard (1997). *The Evolution of the Soul*, rev. ed. Oxford: Oxford University Press.

Swinburne, Richard (2019). *Are We Bodies or Souls?* Oxford: Oxford University Press.

Taylor, Richard (1992). *Metaphysics*, 4th ed. Englewood Cliffs, NJ: Prentice Hall.

Unger, Peter (2006). *All the Power in the World*. Oxford: Oxford University Press.

van Inwagen, Peter (1978). The Possibility of Resurrection. *International Journal for Philosophy of Religion* 9: 114–121. Reprinted in Paul Edwards (ed.), *Immortality*, Amherst, NY: Prometheus Books. pp. 242–246.

van Inwagen, Peter (1984). The Doctrine of Arbitrary Undetached Parts. *Pacific Philosophical Quarterly* 62:123–137. (Reprinted in van Inwagen, *Ontology, Identity, and Modality: Essays in Metaphysics*. Cambridge: Cambridge University Press 2001.)

van Inwagen, Peter (1990). *Material Beings*. Ithaca, NY: Cornell University Press.

van Inwagen, Peter (1995). Dualism and Materialism: Athens and Jerusalem? *Faith and Philosophy* 12:475–488.

van Inwagen, Peter (2007). A Materialist Ontology of the Human Person. In Peter van Inwagen and Dean Zimmerman (eds.), *Persons: Human and Divine*. Oxford: Oxford University Press. pp. 199–215.

van Inwagen, Peter (2014). *Metaphysics*, 4th ed. Boulder, CO: Westview.

Zimmerman, Dean (2011). From Experience to Experiencer. In Mark C. Baker and Stewart Goetz (eds.), *The Soul Hypothesis*. New York: Continuum. pp. 168–196.

Aaron Segal's Chapters:

Adams, Robert Merrihew (1994). *Leibniz: Determinist, Theist, Idealist*. Oxford: Oxford University Press.

Adams, Robert Merrihew (2007). Idealism Vindicated. In Peter van Inwagen & Dean Zimmerman (eds.), *Persons: Human and Divine*. Oxford University Press. pp. 35–54.

Antony, Michael V. (2008). Are Our Concepts CONSCIOUS STATE and CONSCIOUS CREATURE Vague? *Erkenntnis* 68 (2):239–263.

Bailey, Andrew M. and Joshua Rasmussen (2016). How Valuable Could a Material Object Be? *Journal of the American Philosophical Association* 2 (2):332–343.

Bailey, Andrew M. (2020a). Material Through and Through. *Philosophical Studies* 177 (8):2431–2450.

Bailey, Andrew M. (2020b). Magical Thinking. *Faith and Philosophy* 37 (2):181–201.

Bailey, Andrew M. (2021). *Monotheism and Human Nature*. Cambridge: Cambridge University Press.

Baker, Lynne Rudder (2007). Persons and the Metaphysics of Resurrection. *Religious Studies* 43 (3):333–348.

Bayle, Pierre (1710). An Historical and Critical Dictionary: By Monsieur Bayle. Translated Into English, with Many Additions and Corrections, Made by the Author Himself, That Are Not in the French Editions. C. Harper.

Berkeley, George (1979/1734a). *Three Dialogues between Hylas and Philonous, In Opposition to Sceptics and Atheists*, ed. Robert M. Adams. Indianapolis: Hackett.

Berkeley, George (1982/1734b). *A Treatise Concerning the Principles of Human Knowledge*, ed. Kenneth P. Winkler. Indianapolis: Hackett.

Block, Ned (1978). Troubles with Functionalism. *Minnesota Studies in the Philosophy of Science* 9:261–325.

Chalmers, David J. (1996). *The Conscious Mind: In Search of a Fundamental Theory*. New York: Oxford University Press.

Chappell, Richard Yetter (2015). Value Receptacles. *Noûs* 49 (2):322–332.

Chisholm, Roderick M. (1978). Is There a Mind-Body Problem? *Philosophic Exchange* 2:25–34.

Churchland, Paul M. (2006). Eliminative Materialism [Selection from *Matter and Consciousness*]. In Maureen Eckert (ed.), *Theories of Mind: An Introductory Reader*. Lanham, MD: Rowman & Littlefield. p. 115.

Clark, Andy and David J. Chalmers (1998). The extended mind. *Analysis* 58 (1):7–19.

Cooper, John (1989). *Body, Soul, and Life Everlasting: Biblical Anthropology and the Monism-Dualism Debate*. Grand Rapids, MI: Wm. B. Eerdmans Publishing.

Cover, J. A. and John O'Leary-Hawthorne (1996). Free agency and materialism. In Daniel Howard-Snyder and J. Scott Jordan (eds.), *Faith, Freedom, and Rationality*. Lanham, MD: Rowman & Littlefield. pp. 47–72.

Della Rocca, Michael (2008). *Spinoza*. New York: Routledge.

Descartes, Rene (1996/1641). *Descartes: Meditations on First Philosophy: With Selections From the Objections and Replies*, trans. and ed. John Cottingham. Cambridge: Cambridge University Press. (Page references to 1996 edition.)

Evans, Gareth (1978). Can There Be Vague Objects? *Analysis* 38 (13): 208. Reprinted in Keefe and Smith (eds.) *Vagueness: A Reader*. Cambridge, MA: MIT Press, 1997.

Fischer, John Martin and Benjamin Mitchell-Yellin (2016). *Near-Death Experiences: Understanding Visions of the Afterlife*. Oxford: Oxford University Press.

Foster, John A. (1982). *The Case for Idealism*. London: Routledge.

Goldschmidt, Tyron and Samuel Lebens (2020). Divine Contractions: Theism Gives Birth to Idealism. *Religious Studies* 56 (4):509–524.

Goldschmidt, Tyron and Kenneth L. Pearce (eds.) (2017). *Idealism: New Essays in Metaphysics*. Oxford: Oxford University Press.

Halvorson, Hans (2011). The Measure of All Things: Quantum Mechanics and the Soul. In Mark C. Baker and Stewart Goetz (eds.), *The Soul Hypothesis: Investigations Into the Existence of the Soul*. New York: Continuum Press. p. 138.

Harrison, Gerald K. (2016). A Moral Argument for Substance Dualism. *Journal of the American Philosophical Association* 1:21–35.

Hasker, William (1999). *The Emergent Self*. Ithaca, NY: Cornell University Press.

Hawthorne, John (2004). Why Humeans Are Out of Their Minds. *Noûs* 38 (2):351–358.

Hawthorne, John (2007). Cartesian Dualism. In Peter van Inwagen and D. Zimmerman (eds.), *Persons Human and Divine*. Oxford: Oxford University Press.

Hudson, Hud (2001). *A Materialist Metaphysics of the Human Person*. Ithaca, NY: Cornell University Press.

Jackson, Frank (1982). Epiphenomenal Qualia. *Philosophical Quarterly* 32: 127–136.

Jackson, Frank (1994). Armchair Metaphysics. In John O'Leary-Hawthorne and Michaelis Michael (eds.), *Philosophy in Mind*. Amsterdam: Kluwer Academic Publishers. pp. 23–42.

Kind, Amy and Daniel Stoljar (2023). *What is Consciousness? A Debate*. New York: Routledge.

Lebens, Samuel (2015). God and His Imaginary Friends: A Hassidic Metaphysics. *Religious Studies* 51 (2):183–204.

Lebens, Samuel (2017). Hassidic Idealism: Kurt Vonnegut and the Creator of the Universe. In Tyron Goldschmidt and Kenneth L. Pearce (eds.), *Idealism: New Essays in Metaphysics*. Oxford: Oxford University Press. pp. 158–177.

Leibniz, Gottfried Wilhelm (1967/1686). *The Leibniz-Arnauld Correspondence*, ed. and trans. H. T. Mason. Manchester: Manchester University Press.

Leibniz, Gottfried Wilhelm (1991/1714). *The Monadology*, in *Discourse on Metaphysics and Other Essays*, trans. Daniel Garber and Roger Ariew. Indianapolis, IN: Hackett Publishing Company.

Levin, Janet (2018). Functionalism. The Stanford Encyclopedia of Philosophy (Winter 2021 Edition), ed. Edward N. Zalta, URL = <https://plato.stanford.edu/archives/win2021/entries/functionalism/>.

Lewis, David K. (1986). *On the Plurality of Worlds*. Oxford: Wiley-Blackwell.

Lewis, David K. (1988). Vague Identity: Evans Misunderstood. *Analysis* 48 (3):128.

Lewis, David K. (2009). Ramseyan Humility. In David Braddon-Mitchell and Robert Nola (eds.), *Conceptual Analysis and Philosophical Naturalism*. Cambridge, MA: MIT Press. pp. 203–222.

Long, Anthony A. and David N. Sedley (1987). *The Hellenistic Philosophers, Volume 1: Translations of the Principal Sources, with Philosophical Commentary*. Cambridge: Cambridge University Press.

Lycan, William G. (2009). Giving Dualism Its Due. *Australasian Journal of Philosophy* 87 (4):551–563.

Lycan, William G. (2013). Is Property Dualism Better Off Than Substance Dualism? *Philosophical Studies: An International Journal for Philosophy in the Analytic Tradition* 164 (2):533–542.

Malcolm, Norman (1968). The Conceivability of Mechanism. *Philosophical Review* 77:45–72.

Merricks, Trenton (1998). Against the Doctrine of Microphysical Supervenience. *Mind* 107 (425):59–71.

Merricks, Trenton (2007). The Word Made Flesh: Dualism, Physicalism, and the Incarnation. In Peter van Inwagen and Dean Zimmerman (eds.), *Persons: Human and Divine*. Oxford: Oxford University Press. pp. 281–301.

Ney, Alyssa (2008). Defining Physicalism. *Philosophy Compass* 3 (5):1033–1048.

Olson, Eric T. (1997). *The Human Animal: Personal Identity Without Psychology*. New York: Oxford University Press.

Olson, Eric T. (2006). The Paradox of Increase. *The Monist* 89 (3):390–417.

Papineau, David (2002). *Thinking About Consciousness*. Oxford: Oxford University Press.

Plantinga, Alvin (2006). Against Materialism. *Faith and Philosophy* 23 (1):3–32.

Plantinga, Alvin (2007). Materialism and Christian Belief. In Peter van Inwagen and Dean Zimmerman (eds.), *Persons: Human and Divine*. Oxford: Oxford University Press. pp. 99–141.

Putnam, Hilary (1967). The Nature of Mental States, reprinted in *Mind, Language, and Reality*. Cambridge: Cambridge University Press, 429–440.

Robinson, Howard (1982). *Matter and Sense*. Cambridge: Cambridge University Press.

Robinson, Howard (2016). *From the Knowledge Argument to Mental Substance*. Cambridge: Cambridge University Press.

Russell, Bertrand (1927). *The Analysis of Matter*. London: Routledge.

Ryle, Gilbert (1949). *The Concept of Mind*. London: Hutchinson.

Schneider, Susan (2012). Why Property Dualists Must Reject Substance Physicalism. *Philosophical Studies* 157 (1):61–76.

Segal, Aaron (2013). Hume-Inspired Metaphysics. https://curate.nd.edu/show/k930bv75n1q

Segal, Aaron (2014). Causal Essentialism and Mereological Monism. *Philosophical Studies* 169 (2):227–255.

Segal, Aaron (2016). A Puzzle About Points. *Philosophical Perspectives* 30 (1):349–365.

Segal, Aaron and Tyron Goldschmidt (2017). The Necessity of Idealism. In Tyron Goldschmidt and Kenneth L. Pearce (eds.), *Idealism: New Essay in Metaphysics*. Oxford: Oxford University Press. pp. 34–49.

Shoemaker, Sydney (1980). Causality and Properties. In Peter van Inwagen (ed.), *Time and Cause*. Dordrecht: D. Reidel. pp. 109–135.

Sider, Theodore (2003). Maximality and Microphysical Supervenience. *Philosophy and Phenomenological Research* 66 (1):139–149.

Simon, Jonathan A. (2017a). Vagueness and Zombies: Why 'Phenomenally Conscious' Has No Borderline Cases. *Philosophical Studies* 174 (8):2105–2123.

Simon, Jonathan A. (2017b). The Hard Problem of the Many. *Philosophical Perspectives* 31 (1):449–468.

Skow, Bradford (2007). Are Shapes Intrinsic? *Philosophical Studies* 133 (1):111–130.

Stapleford, Scott and Alexander Wentzell (2019). Was Berkeley an Extracranialist? *Philosophical Forum* 50 (2):225–238.

Steiner, Richard C. (2015). Disembodied Souls: The Nefesh in Israel and Kindred Spirits in the Ancient near East, with an Appendix on the Katumuwa Inscription. Atlanta: SBL Press. Society of Biblical Literature ancient Near East monographs: 11.

Swinburne, Richard (1997). *The Evolution of the Soul*, rev. edn. Oxford: Clarendon Press.

Swinburne, Richard (2007). From Mental/Physical Identity to Substance Dualism. In Peter van Inwagen and Dean Zimmerman (eds.), *Persons: Human and Divine*. Oxford: Clarendon Press.

Swinburne, Richard (2013). *Mind, Brain, and Free Will*. Oxford: Oxford University Press.

Swinburne, Richard (2019). *Are We Bodies or Souls?* Oxford: Oxford University Press.

Taliaferro, Charles (1994). *Consciousness and the Mind of God*. Cambridge: Cambridge University Press.

Taurek, John (1977). Should the Numbers Count? *Philosophy and Public Affairs* 6 (4):293–316.

Tye, Michael (1990). Vague Objects. *Mind* 99:535.

Tye, Michael (2021). *Vagueness and the Evolution of Consciousness: Through the Looking Glass*. Oxford: Oxford University Press.

Unger, Peter (2004). The Mental Problems of the Many. In Dean Zimmerman (ed.), *Oxford Studies in Metaphysics, Vol. 1*. Oxford: Clarendon Press. pp. 195–222.

van Inwagen, Peter (1978). The Possibility of Resurrection. *International Journal for Philosophy of Religion* 9 (2):114–121.

van Inwagen, Peter (1980). Philosophers and the Words 'Human Body'. In van Inwagen (ed.), *Time and Cause*. Dordrecht, D. Reidel, pp. 283–299.

van Inwagen, Peter (1981). The Doctrine of Arbitrary Undetached Parts. *Pacific Philosophical Quarterly* 62 (2):123–137.

van Inwagen, Peter (1990). *Material Beings*. Ithaca, NY: Cornell University Press.

Wiggins, David (1968). On Being in the Same Place at the Same Time. *Philosophical Review* 77 (1):90–95.

Williamson, Timothy (2013). *Modal Logic as Metaphysics*. Oxford: Oxford University Press.

Wilson, Jessica (2006). On Characterizing the Physical. *Philosophical Studies* 131 (1):61–99.

Wilson, Jessica M. (2013). A Determinable-Based Account of Metaphysical Indeterminacy. *Inquiry: An Interdisciplinary Journal of Philosophy* 56 (4):359–385.

Yablo, Stephen (1990). The Real Distinction between Mind and Body. *Canadian Journal of Philosophy* 16:149–201.

Zimmerman, Dean (1991). Two Cartesian Arguments for the Simplicity of the Soul. *American Philosophical Quarterly* 28 (3):127–137.

Zimmerman, Dean (1999). The Compatibility of Materialism and Survival: The "Falling Elevator" Model. *Faith and Philosophy* 16 (2):194–212.

Zimmerman, Dean (2003). Material People. In Michael Loux and Dean W. Zimmerman (eds.), *Oxford Handbook of Metaphysics*. Oxford: Oxford University Press. pp. 491–526.

Zimmerman, Dean (2004). Christians Should Affirm Mind-Body Dualism. In Michael L. Peterson and Raymond J. VanArragon (eds.), *Contemporary Debates in Philosophy of Religion*. Oxford: Blackwell. pp. 315–326.

Zimmerman, Dean (2010). I—Dean Zimmerman: From Property Dualism to Substance Dualism. *Aristotelian Society Supplementary Volume* 84 (1):119–150.

Index

9780367333645